FILM FORUM

Film Forum

**Thirty-Five Top Filmmakers
Discuss Their Craft**

Ellen Oumano

St. Martin's Press/New York

Author's Note:

Many of the release dates for films listed in the filmographies are original European release dates, and may not necessarily correspond with American release dates for the same title.

Library of Congress Cataloging in Publication Data
Oumano, Ellen.
  Film forum.

  1. Moving-pictures—Production and direction.
2. Moving-picture producers and director—Interviews.
I. Title.
PN1995.9.P709 1985   791.43'023   84–23710
ISBN 0-312-28932-4

First Edition

10 9 8 7 6 5 4 3 2 1

For my son, Eric Roth

Contents

Acknowledgments

I wish to thank the following people for their invaluable help: Richard Altschuler; Dympra Bowles; Joy Gould Boyum; Joseph Calderone; Roger Cooper; the French Film Office, New York; Gaumont Films, Paris; Joan Herder; Dr. Paul Krooks; the Media Ecology Program at New York University; Reid Rosefelt of Reid Rosefelt Publicity; Barbet Schroeder; Ted Solotaroff; Dan Talbot and Suzanne Fedak of New Yorker Films; the Telluride Film Festival; my interpreter-translators, Deborah Young and Pat Kirk; my transcribers, Elaine Goodman, Shirley Sulat, and Elena Radutzky-Stockwell; and my editor, Bob Miller. I am especially grateful to Tom Allen for his generous asistance and to Geri Thoma and Elaine Markson of the Elaine Markson Agency for their support and perseverance.

Most of all, I wish to thank the real authors of this book, the filmmakers who gave their time and insights.

Foreword

One of Ellen Oumano's favorite quotes and a recurrent theme of this book is the famous Jean Renoir adage: "Everybody has his reasons." Renoir himself is not a subject herein, but he is surely the gray eminence hovering over its pages. Here, in one volume, are the true contemporary mavericks of the Atlantic Community, the Thoreau troops of the cinema who have not bothered to keep pace with their companions because they have marched to a different drummer.

And, oh, have their rhythms been dazzling! These are the stubborn people, the filmmakers who inherently and naturally take auteurism as a given, not an academic term. They refuse to let the commercial mainstream standardize all film product with a formulaic imprimatur. They communicate to their fellow adults what they feel within themselves. And every time they turn on their cameras—some for as long as three decades—they have been revolutionizing the very grammar of film and the way we perceive ourselves and our world.

How dull film criticism might have been since the fifties without these passionate individualists on hand. With no wish to slight any of the thirty-five filmmakers by omission—I truly can embrace them all even when their forms and styles tartly challenge my own preferences—I have the warmest gratitude especially toward such as Godard, Rohmer, and Chabrol for both their bold and subtle reconstruction of the French narrative film; toward Altman, Scorsese, and Romero for assaulting the Hollywood monolith from crown to underbelly; toward Rouch, the Maysles, de Antonio, and Kopple for holding up a mirror to people and a world we might never have seen otherwise; toward Olmi for holding the center against the exciting political forays of Petri and against Wertmuller's and Bertolucci's vertiginous reshuffling of sides in the wars between men and women; toward the sensitive expatriates like Forman and Makavejev and Zanussi and Almendros for the spice with which they have blended clashing cultures; and, finally, toward Fassbinder (like Petri, a great spirit departed in sorrow who will never get to see these pages) for the morbidly cleansing light that he brought to resurrect a nation's dead film heritage.

We know these protean talents by their finished films. Now, thanks to a highly unorthodox interviewer—a maverick among mavericks, for Dr. Oumano is as academically serious as she is zestfully playful if one reads between the lines of her original profiles—we have a unique chance to peek beyond the façades and witness the nimble philosophies and exercises of technique at work. As for the inspiration of coalescing these interviews into collective forums about the filmmaking crafts, it's a good enough idea for the rest of us to steal. I am sure the book's construction will be a trendsetter in its own right.

—ANDREW SARRIS

Introduction

Most books on film aesthetics are written by theorists who are not filmmakers and are directed to an audience of fellow *cinéastes*, that is, to other critics and theorists; books on film technique are aimed exclusively at film students and focus primarily on the mechanical-technical aspects of film. Between those highly specialized writings and the newspaper and magazine reviews that give the reader little more than an idea of what film to see Saturday night, there is an information gap. This book attempts to fill that gap. The material offered here is aimed at the film student, as well as the lay film buff, and was drawn for this purpose from my interviews with filmmakers who spoke on key elements and issues in the filmmaking process.

In order to examine the ways filmmakers work and for what reasons, I identified what seemed to be the more crucial issues and questions about filmmaking and created an interview format, on the basis of which I interviewed thirty-five filmmakers working in a wide variety of styles, genre, budgets, and cultures. An exploration of how film techniques and structures have been used to create and express meaning for a variety of purposes, this book is written, in effect, by the makers of the films.

As well as being "written" by the filmmakers interviewed, the information offered here is grouped by topic. The responses to each topic are drawn entirely from the interviews, which were conducted with this symposium-type structure in mind, and the questions asked during the interviews have been edited out.

Because this book covers a wide territory of subjects—aesthetic, technical, political, cultural—the filmmakers who participated could be classified as *auteur* types, although "independent" might be a less controversial description. Since an *auteur* is defined here as having total control of the three broad phases of the filmmaking process—writing, shooting, and editing the film—it seemed important to speak with filmmakers who are involved in more aspects of making a film than just directing the shoot. Even Sidney Lumet, who considers the notion of a filmmaker being the sole author of a film to be absurd ("How much of an *auteur* are you if you're dependent whether or not the clouds are over the sun?"), has always worked in New York City, a continent's breadth away from the old-time Hollywood assembly line, where, traditionally, the director had restricted control over the process: someone else wrote the script, the producer usually controlled the casting and shooting, and editors would shape the raw footage into the finished film.

I began interviewing in 1978, at the Telluride International Film Festival, high in the San Juan range of the Colorado Rockies. Telluride's secluded beauty and unusual programming attracted many fine filmmakers, among them Nestor Almendros and Krzysztof Zanussi, who kindly granted the first interviews for this book. I later went to Rome, Paris, and Cannes, and interviewed many filmmakers in New York City. The interviews were taped, transcribed, and, in the case of some French, Italian, and one German filmmaker, translated. When the interview phase was completed, I read through the interviews, delineating those responses in each interview that seemed to speak to the same subject. I edited out my questions and constructed narratives out of these related responses, which sometimes were formed from as many as six or seven answers to my questions. All the filmmakers' comments on each subject were then grouped together. This method allowed me to retain from the original interviews only that material which seemed the most interesting. It is also a more directed and concise way of delivering information.

The transition from interview to symposium format necessitated removing the filmmakers' discussions from their original contexts. In order to restore the sense and intentions of their remarks, I used a variety of compensatory devices, sometimes working my questions into a filmmaker's opening words in order to establish precisely what had sparked his or her comments. Conventional editing included rewording awkward passages, smoothing transitions, adding brief explanatory phrases, and generally eliminating the inevitable distortions in meaning that occur when one moves from the spoken to the written form of a language. Some of the filmmakers edited the transcripts of their interviews themselves, which was the ideal situation, as they then had control over their style and content.

Since the elements of film are so intertwined that one question or point always relates to or provokes discussion of several others, some overlapping of subject matter from topic to topic is unavoidable. For example, a topic such as "The Process" inevitably includes points made under "Cinematography." The differences between the topics are not, therefore, clear-cut in their more superficial details, but they are distinguishable in the general thrust and focus of the discussions.

Within each topic, the filmmakers' comments are ordered to create a sense of interplay among shared and contrasting points of view. Though there are many differences of opinion, it is important to keep in mind that contraries are not necessarily contradictory. The point of view underlying this book, if indeed there is any, is that in film, context is everything. There are no rules, no prohibitions. In fact, the only real rule is, If it works, it's good. As Jean Renoir said, "Everyone has his reasons."

But a film is much more than even the sum of its parts and the way they relate to each other. A film lexicon assigning definitive meanings to particular techniques, styles, and genres is not possible, or even desirable. When we try to single out any one element, we find it hitched not only to everything else in the film, but to the culture, and to ourselves. It is true that "everyone has his reasons," but it is often the case that the filmmaker does not even know himself what those reasons are. Nor is it necessarily important that he should. Even with the clarity of hindsight, the choices that develop into a work of art can remain a mystery. For example, one may ask a director why he chose to shoot a particular scene from a certain angle and receive no more of an answer than that he *felt* it should be viewed in such a way. The elusive struggle between the filmmaker and his medium is a constant fascination for the filmmaker and the filmgoer. Film's defiance of precise analyses, its presentations of continually evolving complexes of elements, is also a probable reason for the largely uncodified, unstructured state of the art of film criticism (its best practitioners being brilliant intuitors such as André Bazin).

No one can control the film totally, neither in its making nor in its viewing, and that ever-present touch of improvisation is its most powerful seduction. In my interview with him, Bertolucci quoted Renoir: "You should always leave the door open on the set." And, in fact, reality always does creep in, whether or not that door is left open. One is never in total control. Unchecked reality can manifest itself in the flight of a fly through a totally fabricated set, or it can intrude in the form of a decision to cut a scene because the film is over budget.

Film is a generous form, accommodating a variety of intentions, uses, and styles. Ultimately, a film expresses the deep and profound relationship between the filmmaker, his subject, and his art form, the triangular base upon which all films are built. Great artists are, above all, great observers and listeners, freeing the world to reveal itself. They look at life with avid and open curiosity. One refrain that was echoed by virtually everyone interviewed was, "Of course, this is the way I work; anyone can do what he wishes." Filmmaking is a very individualistic process, reflecting the filmmaker's own biases, experience, and view of reality, yet it is a purposeful, intentional activity with infinite variety of choice. There are no rules but there are many reasons.

FILM FORUM

·1·

PROFILES

CHANTAL AKERMAN

I first met Chantal Akerman in Paris, at the home of an American army deserter whose cheerful unconcern for all matters political made for an uncomfortable mix with the leftist feminism of Akerman and her friends. A few days later, I spent over three hours in a Champs d'Elysées screening room, trapped in the vision of Akerman's relentless camera frame, witnessing the gradual collapse of Jeanne Diehlman's precarious double life as a bourgeois housewife and call girl. My French male companion was infuriated by what he misinterpreted as the film's man-hating point of view, but the film's power derives not from anger or hate. It is grounded on the trust this young filmmaker has in herself. She holds her camera still, allowing what would be ordinary, trivial actions under someone else's direction to play out into revelations of the truths that undermine the rigidly ordered life at 23 Quai du Commerce. Her style is suggestive, tense, and totally cinematic: those careful, steady frames force us into the details of Diehlman's life until we finally *see*.

It wasn't until another Parisian winter, four years later, that I had the opportunity to meet with Akerman again. By then, she had won for herself a large and rabidly appreciative audience both in Europe and the United States. The 1979 New Di-

1

rectors—New Films series at the Museum of Modern Art screened her fifth feature, *Les Rendez-vous D'Anna*, to sold out houses two times, and in Paris, where she had moved from Brussels, *Anna* was playing in a nearby Montparnasse theatre.

We drank tea and spoke, Akerman somewhat reluctantly, feeling, as many filmmakers do, that analysis is, by definition, a reduction of expression already in its essential cinematic terms. But the thoughts she did offer were carefully considered and characteristically concise.

Akerman began her career after only three months of film school. Her first experience was "with my own thirty-five millimeter movie. We were three: my cameraman, my assistant, and me—that's it. And I acted myself. I did all the sound afterwards." She was eighteen years old.

Filmography

1967 *Saute Ma Ville*
1970 *L'Enfant Aimé*
1973 *Hotel Monterey*
      La Chambre
      Yonkers Hanging Out 1973
1974 *Je Tu Il Elle*
1975 *Jeanne Diehlman, 23 Quai du Commerce,*
      1080 Bruxelles
1979 *Les Rendez-vous D'Anna*
1982 *All in a Night*
1983 *The Golden 80's*

NESTOR ALMENDROS

Nestor Almendros's reliance on what the world offers has resulted in some of the most sensitively photographed films in modern cinema. Previously best known as cinematographer for Eric Rohmer and François Truffaut, Almendros won just about every prize in 1978 for his work as director of photography on Terence Malick's *Days of Heaven*. During the 1978 fall season, he seemed omnipresent, photographing almost every major film with a New York location and winning the award again for *Kramer vs. Kramer*. Rarely has a director of photography received so much acclaim.

Because of his associations with Rohmer and Truffaut, Almendros's background surprises many. He was born in Barcelona, but was brought to Cuba when Franco came to power. He then left to study filmmaking in New York at City College. (Of his early films, only *Gente en la Playa* is still in distribution.) Almendros also began to write his first film articles while still a student in New York. He returned to Cuba when Castro overthrew the Batista government, but the joys of making party line films wore thin, and he soon left for France, where he taught in a small school and worked in television and on film shorts until beginning his association with Rohmer.

At the time of the interview, I asked him if he still had a desire to make his own films. "No, not anymore. I did in the past. What stopped me is that I had more success as a director of photography. I was both directing and photographing documentaries, and hoping I would eventually do feature films. Of these simultaneous careers, one went up and the other just shrank." However, his success has been so great that his old desire has been provoked. The 1984 New Directors–New Films series exhibited his first feature film, *Improper Conduct*.

Filmography

1964 *Nadja à Paris* (short; Eric Rohmer)
1965 *Six in Paris* (Douchet's and Rohmer's episodes)
1967 *La Collectionneuse* (Eric Rohmer)

1968　*The Wild Racers* (co-photo.)
1969　*My Night at Maud's* (Eric Rohmer)
　　　Gun Runner
　　　More (Barbet Schroeder)
1970　*The Wild Child* (François Truffaut)
　　　Bed and Board (François Truffaut)
1971　*Two English Girls* (François Truffaut)
1972　*Chloë in the Afternoon* (Eric Rohmer)
　　　The Valley (Barbet Schroeder)
1973　*General Idi Amin Dada* (Barbet Schroeder)
　　　La Gueule Ouverte (Maurice Pialat)
　　　Poil de Carotte
1974　*Cockfighter* (Monte Hellman)
　　　Mes Petites Amoureuses (Jean Eustache)
1975　*Maîtresse* (Barbet Schroeder)
　　　The Story of Adele H. (François Truffaut)
　　　The Marquise of O (Eric Rohmer)
1977　*The Man Who Loved Women* (François Truffaut)
　　　Des Journées Entières dans les Arbres
　　　　　(Marguerite Duras)
　　　Madame Rosa (Moshe Mizrahi)
1978　*The Green Room* (François Truffaut)
　　　Goin' South (Jack Nicholson)
　　　Perceval (Eric Rohmer)
　　　Days of Heaven (Terence Malick)
　　　Love on the Run (François Truffaut)
1979　*Kramer vs. Kramer* (Robert Benton)
　　　The Last Metro (François Truffaut)
　　　The Blue Lagoon (Randall Kleiser)
1982　*Still of the Night* (Robert Benton)
1983　*Sophie's Choice* (Alan Pakula)
　　　Pauline at the Beach (Eric Rohmer)
　　　Confidentially Yours (François Truffaut)
1984　*Places in the Heart* (Robert Benton)
　　　Improper Conduct

ROBERT ALTMAN

Robert Altman has taken us to places that at first glance may seem familiar but soon prove to be new, often disturbing, views on old territories. The stock war movie celebrating American valor became in *M*A*S*H* a dizzy absurdist mix of humor and horror. The outlaw couple on the run, traditionally an escapist fantasy, became in *Thieves Like Us* a pair of gawky half-grown kids, learning to make love, rob banks, and kill people with the same awkward naïveté. Even our hero of the Old West, Buffalo Bill, became in Altman's revisionist film an aging impotent in a flea-bitten Wild West show. Altman takes our most cherished myths about ourselves—our movie genres—and subverts them, dislocating us from stale beliefs, reminding us that, as he puts it, "Wait a minute, come on, that's not the way things really happened. I mean, horses got tired, they ran out of bullets. How many times did the gun barrel blow up on them and blow their hand off? How many times did they miss? And you start dealing first with the story and ask, 'What *really* could happen?'"

Robert Altman wants us to feel the people in his films; he wants to make pictures that move us: "Ultimately the real, efficient use of the medium, which is moving pictures, is to have an audience not understand what they've seen, but have an emotional response to it. The ideal response to a film would not be to be able to articulate what they have just seen, but to be able to say, 'It felt good.'"

Altman has written, directed, produced, distributed, and lost films. But he figures he's been "lucky, very, very lucky. I think I've been the most fortunate of all the people I know that are dealing in film. It's certainly not by intelligence. It's by luck and timing. But I'm at the point now where I'm not going to starve to death. I don't have any money amassed but I don't have any need for it. I can speak at colleges and pick up enough money and keep myself busy for a while. And I'm old enough where I don't really give a shit. I'll always try to keep making films. I'd almost rather be in this position. I think it helps keep you active. Anything that helps keep your arrogance at a tolerable level is important, and you've got to be in a little bit of jeopardy all the time."

Filmography

1957 *The Delinquents*
      The James Dean Story
1968 *Countdown*
1969 *That Cold Day in the Park*
1970 *M*A*S*H*
      Brewster McCloud
1971 *McCabe and Mrs. Miller*
1972 *Images*
1973 *The Long Goodbye*
1974 *Thieves Like Us*
      California Split
1975 *Nashville*
1976 *Buffalo Bill and the Indians*
      or Sitting Bull's History Lesson
1977 *3 Women*
1978 *A Wedding*
      Remember My Name
1979 *Quintet*
      A Perfect Couple
1980 *Health*
1981 *Popeye*
1983 *Come Back to the Five and Dime Jimmy Dean, Jimmy Dean*
      Streamers

EMILE DE ANTONIO

Emile de Antonio covered a lot of ground before turning to filmmaking in early middle age: "I left college. I knew I would enlist, but before, since I'd been talking like a communist, I got a job as a longshoreman in Baltimore. I enlisted and when I got out I got an M.A. in literature and taught and hung out in the San Remo. I knew Auden, other poets, musicians, all the painters. I lived that young man's scene and made a lot of money, horsing around. I moved my then third wife to Rockland County, which was then an exurb—woods all around me—and then I met John Cage, and he was the most important person in my life except my father. He and I argued all the time. He was broke and used to come over every night and get drunk with my wife and me. He was a Zen Buddhist and I was a Marxist Aristotelian, and we argued and argued and argued, but he made visible to me that it's possible to be afraid, after I had proved to myself that I was not.

"I was really afraid to expose myself and that's when I threw a novel I wrote when I was twenty out of an airplane. It was because of John that I got into film. John lectured at the time on collage, which is where *Point of Order* began. But I never related it to him until long after *Point of Order* was in existence. I got into film backwards. I thought it was a step backwards created by the ruling classes to keep the masses in line. It's no accident that the only companies who made huge amounts of money during the Depression were the film companies. I saw Kerouac's *Pull My Daisy* and Dan Drasin's *Sunday,* which was about that riot in Washington Square Park. I thought they should be seen, but nobody would take those films, so I had some money and decided to distribute. But I immediately wanted to make films, and then *Point of Order* happened.

"Dan Talbot and I began it together as producers and Dan said, 'There's only one person who can do this: Orson Welles.' What could I say? I wanted to make the film but what could I do? So, he sent Orson a cable which he didn't understand because we couldn't afford a ten-thousand-word cable which would've explained it. Welles said 'No.' Then we brought in

Irving Lerner, who had done four or five very good low-budget films—fiction. He was a terrific guy but it didn't work out. And the movie began by my saying to Dan, 'O.K., we've now had this and that guy and another one we fired. And you're running the New Yorker Theatre on your own. I'll match you to see who does it, but if I do it, you won't get to see it until it's finished.' So, we didn't match; he said, 'Go ahead.'

"So, I hired a couple of kids—I paid myself nothing—and paid them to do all the physical cutting, and that's how it started. But it's characteristic that nobody waits to let somebody begin, and that's why I always want young people to begin. A lot of young people come to see me and ask, 'What should I do?' And I always say, 'Start. Just start a film. If it's a disaster, you will have learned more than by working for someone else. You'll be that much more ahead. So that the next time you go out, if you have any gift, then you'll know what it's about.'

"I had absolutely no technical experience with film at that time. I've never regarded that as the place where film begins any more than writing begins with typing. I became interested in film late, very late, but when I started, it was like a mad university of staring at pictures and the way they were put together and how a shot was made, etcetera. I had disliked the flicks: I used to go when I was hung over or bored, not because I thought they were art or anything. I missed all of that stuff until I started getting interested in film.

"I think in many forms of art, a certain innocence in a sophisticated mind is a good combination. I knew a lot about the structure of painting, for instance, and about film I was relatively innocent, and I don't think that's a bad introduction. What really goes on in most film schools is that people learn so much about technique that they forget that writing a book or making a film really has more to do with belief, sensibility, concept, passion, wanting to express yourself, and not just operating machinery."

Filmography

1964   *Point of Order!*

1967 *Rush to Judgment*
1969 *In the Year of the Pig*
1970 *America Is Hard to See*
1971 *Milhouse: A White Comedy*
1973 *Painters Painting*
1977 *Underground*
1983 *In the King of Prussia*

BERNARDO BERTOLUCCI

Bernardo Bertolucci's films are grounded on series of dialectical oppositions that operate throughout them on many different levels. Though traceable to Marxist theory, as well as to Freudian and Reichian psychology, these contradictions, which are the sense and structure of his work, seem to express Bertolucci's interpretation of the essential conflicts of human experience.

He began as a poet, and published a book of poems, *In Search of Mystery*, at the age of twenty. Although he had made several short films as a teenager, his first serious work was as assistant director to Pasolini on *Accattone*. He then made his own film, *The Grim Reaper*, followed by *Before the Revolution, The Spider's Stratagem*, and the films that gave him international acclaim, *The Conformist* and *Last Tango in Paris*.

"From the day when I began to make movies, I stopped writing completely. In the beginning of my life as a *cinéaste*, there was a confusion in my mind between poetry and the movies. I think that the language of cinema is much more similar to the language of poetry because in cinema, music, and poetry, the importance of the rhythm is stronger than in novels. When I made my first movie, *The Grim Reaper*, I thought that there was the same freedom in using the images as in using the words of a poem. Now I think of cinema as a sort of ideal place where all the languages come together: sculpture, music, painting, poetry, and prose."

Filmography

1962   *The Grim Reaper*
1964   *Before the Revolution*
1967   *Love and Anger*
1968   *Partner*
1969   *The Spider's Strategem*
         The Conformist

1972 *Last Tango in Paris*
1977 *1900*
1979 *Luna*
1981 *Tragedy of a Ridiculous Man*

CLAUDE CHABROL

Claude Chabrol might be the most infectiously joyful person I have ever met. As a fellow filmmaker commented, "He loves to shoot. Shooting films is a drug for him, so he makes a film a year just to be able to shoot." He is a man happy with his habit. Laughing, gesturing with animation, speaking English with a thick French accent, his liveliness is surprising in a filmmaker who has been talking, writing, and making film for quite some time, and who is known as "the French Hitchcock" for his skill in depicting grisly murder, suspense, and the ambiguity of life.

He is less demanding, however, on his audience than he is on himself—in fact, he makes no demands on the audience at all. For some, this willingness to just entertain is misinterpreted as a reluctance to fulfill his promise as a star of the sixties' *nouvelle vague.*

But Chabrol has a Gallic, not Parisian, ease of spirit, with a self-confidence that immunizes him against petty and pedantic criticisms. At the 1978 New York Film Festival press conference for *Violette,* an angry French woman berated him for dressing Isabelle Huppert in the "wrong shoes." She then amended the criticism: it was the heels, specifically, which were in error for the period depicted. Chabrol laughed and apologized without a trace of condescension. She is, after all, a member of his audience, and he is obliged to satisfy: "For me the audience is always ready to be bored. They sit there, poor people. So, the lesson is the audience doesn't want to think, they just want to be interested. They deserve that, we should give them that, too. If they want to think, okay, but if not, they deserve to be entertained, it's okay. Why not? So, I always try to. I hate plots, but we must give them a plot. I think the plot really doesn't matter."

Filmography

1958   *Bitter Reunion*
1959   *The Cousins*
1960   *Web of Passion*

Les Bonnes Femmes
Les Godelureaux
1961 *Seven Deadly Sins*
      The Third Lover
1962 *Ophélia*
      Bluebeard
1963 *The World's Finest Swindles*
1964 *The Tiger Likes Fresh Blood*
1965 *Six in Paris*
      Marie-Chantal contre le Docteur Kha
      An Orchid for the Tiger
1966 *Demarcation Line*
1967 *The Champagne Murders*
      The Road to Corinth
1968 *The Bitches*
      The Unfaithful Wife
1969 *This Man Must Die*
      The Butcher
1970 *The Rupture*
      Just Before Nightfall
1971 *Ten Days' Wonder*
1972 *Docteur Popaul*
      Wedding in Blood
1973 *The Nada Gang*
      De Grey—Le Banc de Désolation
1974 *A Piece of Pleasure*
      Dirty Hands
      Histoires insolites
1975 *Initiation a la Mort*
      Folies Bourgeoises
      Les Magiciens
1976 *Alice or the Last Escapade*
1977 *Blood Relatives*
1978 *Violette*
1980 *Le Cheval d'Orgueil*
1982 *Les Fantômes du Chapelier*
1983 *Le Sang des Autres*

JACQUES DEMY

Like his countryman, Claude Chabrol, Jacques Demy is everybody's favorite. Charming, handsome, sensitive, and extremely gifted, with a buoyant view of life, for those who like to believe that talent gets its rewards, the story of Demy's career is painfully frustrating. This is a man who offers us little escapes into fairytale fantasies of brightly colored worlds peopled by pretty, singing people. His style is completely original, so much so that the men who control the purse strings have consistently failed to understand and support his efforts. Though he has had great success with more conventional efforts, Demy is most known for his movie musicals, scoring a huge triumph with *The Umbrellas of Cherbourg*. He has failed, however, in his attempts to get financing for other musicals, particularly one he wrote with Yves Montand: "He's a great performer, a fantastic singer. Montand was so enthusiastic that he said, 'I don't want to be paid. I'll put my salary into the production just to be part of it.' But we couldn't find anyone interested. 'The French don't like musicals.' That's what the distributors and producers said. And then comes *Saturday Night Fever* and *Grease* and they're smash hits."

After an enforced hiatus of five years, an account of which appears later in this book, Toho Films of Japan rescued this valuable career with an offer to do a film based on the popular Japanese comic strip, "The Rose of Versailles." The result is Demy's wonderful *Lady Oscar*.

Demy characteristically opens each film with an ins-out: "It's like a peephole, you look through it and then you go into it. It's another world. I've always considered movies as a sort of second life. There's the day-to-day life and then life in movies, where you can escape and fantasize and be what you want to be.

"I'm not a thinker. I like to give the feeling of entertainment, but entertainment has a pejorative side nowadays, because the world has so many problems. Lately, filmmakers have been really serious about their films, which I appreciate and understand, but it's not my way of living, my way of talking to people. For example, when I was a student with nothing, just a room in the Latin Quarter, and I didn't know anyone, I had some friends who would come to me not to be entertained, but to be cheered up. I don't know why—maybe it's my face, but I would have people around and I would cheer them up. I was always that sort of guy and I kept the same thinking about movies, that it's going to help someone. That is my attitude."

Born in Brittany, the setting of many of his films, Demy studied film in Paris at the National School of Photography and Cinema. Like the filmmakers now dominating the Hollywood scene, he was a knowledgeable technician before becoming a director. Unlike his peers in the *nouvelle vague*, his background was not literary nor did he write extensive film criticism. He worked for several years as an assistant to various filmmakers before making his first film, a short subject, in 1955. He dedicated his first feature film, the marvelous *Lola*, starring Anouk Aimée, to Ophuls. Not surprisingly, his favorite film of all time is *Singin' in the Rain*.

Filmography

1960 *Lola*
1961 *Seven Deadly Sins*
1962 *Bay of Angels*
1964 *The Umbrellas of Cherbourg*
1966 *The Young Ladies of Rochefort*
1969 *The Model Shop*
1970 *Donkey Skin*
1971 *The Pied Piper*
1973 *A Slightly Pregnant Man*
1978 *Lady Oscar*
1983 *Une Chambre en Ville*

R. W. FASSBINDER

R. W. Fassbinder was one of the most extraordinary talents in the world of film, as much for his prolificness as for the quality of his films. Not only did he write, direct, and act in his films, but in the beginning of his career he had to invent pseudonyms for the other crew positions so the credit roll would not be an endless repetition of "R. W. Fassbinder." By the age of thirty-six, he had made approximately forty films. He wondered at the time it took some filmmakers to complete their films, as well as what they did between films: "I always said, that if you are doing films like a worker, you work all year, except for five to six weeks vacation. Then you have to make more than one film a year; you make two or three."

Those two or three films a year usually dealt with people living outside the sanctions of society: homosexuals, transsexuals, older women, Moroccan guest workers—those socially disenfranchised individuals not entitled to love, sex, respect, and position. Their struggles with isolation and rejection are the stuff of soap opera, but Fassbinder said, "All our lives are soap operas."

Toward the end of his short life, Fassbinder's films evidenced a search for newer forms, for "a new kind of film, something which is exclusively film. So far, film has been an assemblage of other genres of art, but I think it will become one in itself. I want to try to make a kind of film which does not carry an idea or the idea of a story like a traditional novel or a traditional theater piece."

Because of his desire to remain open, to rid himself of prejudicial notions of what film should be, he was reluctant to discuss film analytically: "The less theoretical definitions I give, the more possibilities I have, or it is probably the *only* possibility I have to create a new film genre."

Filmography

1969   *Love Colder Than Death*
       Katzelmacher

Gods of the Plague
Why Does Herr R. Run Amok?
1970 *Rios Das Mortes*
Whity
Die Niklashauser Fahrt
The American Soldier
The Coffee Shop
Pioneers in Ingolstadt
Beware the Holy Whore
1971 *The Merchant of Four Seasons*
1972 *The Bitter Tears of Petra von Kant*
Wildwechsel
Eight Hours Are Not a Day
Fontane
1973 *Bremer Freiheit*
1974 *Effi Briest*
Welt Am Draht
Fear Eats the Soul
Nora Hellmer
Martha
Like a Bird on a Wire
Faustrecht der Freiheit
1975 *Mother Kusters Goes to Heaven*
Fear of Fear
Ich Will Doch Nur, Dass Ihr Micht Liebt
1976 *Satan's Brew*
Chinese Roulette
Bolwieser
1977 *Women in New York*
Despair
1978 *The Marriage of Maria Braun*
In a Year of Thirteen Moons
1979 *The Third Generation*
Berlin Alexanderplatz
1981 *Lola*
1982 *Veronica Voss*
Lili Marleen
1983 *Querelle*

MILOS FORMAN

Milos Forman seems as comfortable in his living room over-looking Central Park South as he must have been in the late sixties, when he was a newly arrived discovery from Czechoslavakia, barely able to speak English but faced never-theless with either making it here or nowhere, as he couldn't go back. No problem. Not only has he floated like cream to the top of the American film industry, but he's retained in his work the best the Slavic style has to offer. In all his films we get a sense of little worlds peopled by charming eccentrics whose pri-vate moments we are privileged to witness. The Lower East Side of New York, Central Park, a mental hospital in Seattle—all are reduced to small villages. In Forman's films we are spared for once the open spaces and hugeness of the American landscape; things are scaled down to human size. Forman gives us what he prizes himself in film: "the credibility of human behavior."

Forman is a pretty credible human as well. It's hard to main-tain the image of superstar director as I watch him sitting in his favorite chair, eating a plate of fish, pressing me repeatedly to have some—"Come on, I cooked it myself." It's easy, however, to see why he's been so successful. Adaptability and patience are the keynotes here. Forman knows it's the work that counts. *Hair* is a good example. Forman waited years—through the making of *Taking Off* and the Academy Award-winning *One Flew Over the Cuckoo's Nest*—since the off-Broadway production, as a matter of fact, in order to make this film.

He explains his unusual success this way: "If you look at who succeeded of the foreign filmmakers in the past two years, it's Roman Polanski and myself, so one reason, I think, is that part of the Slavic character is patience. We are more patient. I know a few French and German directors who come here, and if nothing happens after two or three months, they lose patience and go back. Or if the doors are open, they just jump and plunge into work in the same rhythm as they did at home where they know every corner, every stone, the sound of every word, the smell of every wind. But you can't just take this over;

you have to substitute this knowledge with some kind of effort to absorb it. For example, when I was making *Taking Off,* my English was still poor. In scenes where I encouraged improvisation, very often I didn't understand a word the actors were saying. And, of course, I didn't say that. I pretended I understood everything and I was in control of everything. And I did, because I learned, and that took me about a year of being here. I started to judge by the melody of the sentence. I could tell if it was right or wrong in spite of the fact that I didn't understand a word. You can really judge by the melody whether the line is fake or right. So, that's one reason: I think we are more patient.

"And the second reason, which is probably more important, is it's a different situation when you come here and you know any time you want, you can go back. You have your position back there and your work and your career and everything. That somehow makes you more susceptible to the pain through which you have to go when you are dealing, when you are working, when you are trying to do something. The moment we knew that our roads were closed behind us, which was the case of Roman and myself, we went through the pain: we knew the doors were closed behind us, so we just forced ourselves to go through the pain because we had no other choice."

Filmography

1962 *Competition*
1963 *If There Were No Music*
1964 *Black Peter*
1965 *A Blonde in Love*
1967 *The Fireman's Ball*
1971 *Taking Off*
1973 *Visions of Eight*
1975 *One Flew Over the Cuckoo's Nest*
1979 *Hair*
1981 *Ragtime*
1984 *Amadeus*

JEAN-LUC GODARD

It had been ten years since anyone really heard much from the "saint of cinema," the "motor who drives all other film-makers," the ideologue who had startled us with *Breathless* and continued to do so, to push our understanding of "What is cinema?" with every film he made. The closest I thought I would ever get to him was by proxy: in Rome I met a man who claimed to be part of a twice-weekly poker game somewhere in Africa, where it was rumored Godard spent half his time. I asked if they talked about film. "Never," my informant said. Another cul-de-sac. I gave up.

But during the summer of 1980 I happened to be in a small town in southern France where Godard appeared for two days to talk about his first commercial film since *La Chinoise*, the brilliantly funny *Everyman for Himself*. As always, his film is a lesson in cinema, a lecture that entertains with jokes whose premises take off from the conventions of cinematic technique, but moves, as well, with its descriptions of the vagaries of human passion and dispassion.

I approached Godard and his friends sitting at a café, and he agreed: "Sure, how about tomorrow at nine?"

In person, this kind and humorous man is very much the brilliant young professor uncomfortable with the adoration of his students. His manner is hesitant, bolstered by a shy smile, and his conversation, like his films, lacks the apparent continuity of ordinary talk. His ideas dart in and out, seemingly dropped, but then weaved into one another, their relatedness and logic apparent only later when one replays the interchange and takes time to reflect upon delicate patterns of thought that the average mind would not quickly unravel.

Godard, like all superior men, is untouched by claims to greatness made on his behalf by his admirers. He wants to do his work—that is all—to learn, to grow as much as possible.

"At the moment I am taking an inventory, sort of an applied theory touched by social movements, which pushes one to take inventory, to reconquer one's territory. I always have felt close to people like the Palestinians and the Vietnamese, the American Indians, and women who say, 'I have to conquer my territory,' but I feel close to them from a filmmaker's point of view. I do not know Palestinians or Vietnamese, and I don't care, but at the same time, I do care. I do care from where I am, which is almost my complete life. I think I exist more as a picture than a real object, and since I make movies, my life is to do that. People close to me have reproached me that film was more important than life. Food does not interest me but I am interested in filming food and it is important to me. Relations with me have to go through this; and, as there are things in life to go through which I put through this filmic process, I am a different representation of life. It is a life that does not exist. When Rimbaud said that life is 'somewhere else,' it is not just words. This 'somewhere else' is *also* real life. Movies as a means of communication are part of this also."

Filmography

1960   *Breathless*
1961   *A Woman Is a Woman*
1962   *Seven Deadly Sins*
       My Life to Live
1963   *The Little Soldier*
       Les Carabiniers
       Contempt
1964   *Band of Outsiders*
       A Married Woman
1965   *Alphaville*
       Pierrot Le Fou
1966   *Masculine-Feminine*
       Made in the U.S.A.
1967   *Weekend*
       Two or Three Things I Know About Her
       Far From Vietnam (co-directed)
       La Chinoise
1968   *Un Film comme les autres*
1969   *Love and Anger*
       Le Gai Savoir

One Plus One
British Sounds (co-directed)
Wind from the East
Pravda (co-directed)
Struggle in Italy (co-directed)
1970 *Till Victory* (co-directed)
Vladimir and Rosa (co-directed)
1972 *Letter to Jane* (co-directed)
Tous Va Bien
1973 *Moi Je*
1975 *Numero Deux*
1976 *La Communication* (for TV)
Comment ça va
1977 *Ici et Ailleurs*
1980 *Everyman for Himself*
1982 *Passion*
1984 *First Name: Carmen*

PERRY HENZEL

Perry Henzel is a total original, a delight. He's refined the unmistakable Jamaican mentality, at once astute and philo- sophical: "It doesn't matter how far you go in either direction as long as you're balanced. Physics will tell you that. Reality is surely beauty and ugliness, polarities, plus-minus, neutron-pro- ton, yin-yang. There's always two sides. That's why schizo- phrenia is healthy. The dangerous people in the world don't understand this, because they don't understand that once you come to terms with schizophrenia all you have to do to stay balanced is to realize that if you're going to be that crazy, you're going to have to be that sane. Creative speed comes when you are fully extended in both directions, so that your scope includes fantastic thoughts. Your thinking connects fac- tors which were previously perceived as far apart."

Not surprisingly, Henzel speeds around the globe with the same ease you or I travel our immediate neighborhood, his mind moving freely, snatching ideas from all over, drawing them into his wide-angled view of the world. He's also learned his lessons well at the marketplace, having made over four hundred commercials for his own company. He knows the power of the media: "There seems to be this incredible idea that you can't tell anybody everything. What's the problem? You can tell the whole world anything you want in twenty-four hours. If Muhammad Ali dropped dead now, with one phone call, by eight o'clock in the morning, there'd be damn few peo- ple in the world who wouldn't be aware of it. So, if what you have to say is of interest to people, technically you can really disseminate it so fast.

"Assume your eyes are the lens and that your mind is a re- corder. Then you have seen and heard what you have seen and heard, which is determined by the way you are. And what you see and hear depends on what you have been conditioned to see and hear by your past experiences. So, if your eyes are lenses and your head is a recorder, you are always making a movie. So, if you can afford six thousand dollars or ten thou- sand dollars a day, you can put it on celluloid and play it and edit it for other people, and that's all that it is."

Perry Henzel *is* the film industry of Jamaica. *The Harder They Come*, one of the most beloved and longest running of all cult favorites, brilliantly expresses the Jamaican cultural spirit: Africa listening to Miami radio.

Determined to show us what else he knows, Henzel operates a mini-studio, financing its projects at the lowest possible level, where he can maintain control of a film from the writing through to its selling: "I regard a property as something to which I can sell ten different rights to major markets worldwide: television rights, cable rights, disc rights, cassette rights, theater rights, and these rights can be on short terms—six months to two years. You don't have to be George Lucas to do it, but you need that control, and I think this type of situation will become more prevalant in the future."

Filmography

1976 *The Harder They Come*
1985 *No Place Like Home*

HENRY JAGLOM

Henry Jaglom is one of the few filmmakers willing to tackle what used to be the exclusive province of literary modernists: the collision of apparent order with private inner worlds wherein rational notions of time, space, and causality break down into chaos. Like his literary counterparts, Jaglom is not concerned with aspects of plot but with following the vagaries of a character's consciousness: "If we're really going to understand how people feel and what they experience, we have to break into this notion of time as a linear, sequential thing. I think that's the hardest thing for audiences to break because their whole habit is to want an illusion of time to have taken place. If we can create that for them, they're happy. But if you just escape into your dream, into the illusion of the moment, you plunge into the chaos of your existence."

In her laudatory review of Jaglom's first feature film, *A Safe Place*, Anaïs Nin called Jaglom a "magician of film" and quoted Antonin Artaud on the special gift of cinema: "the perfect medium to depict our dreams, fantasies, the surreal aspect of our existence." For Nin, "Jaglom is one of the few to have fulfilled the early promise of film."

Jaglom was a philosophy student at the University of Pennsylvania, then spent ten years studying acting at the Actors Studio before his first professional experience: cutting *Easy Rider*, the rule-breaking quintessential sixties acid film: "I spent eight weeks, Bob Rafelson and I. An incredible experience. Bert Schneider was really the man responsible, because it was all finally his decision, whose cuts to use and so on. But everybody connected with the film got a chance to direct their own movie."

Filmography

1970 *A Safe Place*
1976 *Tracks*
1979 *Sitting Ducks*
1983 *Can She Bake a Cherry Pie?*

BENOIT JACQUOT

Benoit Jacquot is a brilliant theoretician, a special, refined filmmaker, working in a style that could only be compared with that of Robert Bresson.

"My basic themes are romantic ones, and the film is removed from the real world to the extent that it is romantic. I work against naturalism. So-called 'living camera' filming, based on imitating real life, in fact, is quite opposed to truth. I try to create emotional effects in a stylized, contrived way. I'm interested in the fire under the ice."

In the minds of many, "contrived" connotes false and untruthful. Benoit Jacquot and other "anti-naturalists" remind us that it is time to rid ourselves of the dictates of Naturalism and perhaps to recall W. B. Yeats's equation of creativity with artifice. Making art is a system of contrivances that seeks to reveal meaning by shaping bits and pieces of our world into new forms. Artifice is, therefore, man's bid for immortality.

For Jacquot, the artifice of a film lies in a "process of fascination, and you must play on this in the most honest but forceful way possible. It assumes a rather firm moral position of the director, but, of course, that could be anywhere from despicable to sublime. But both are possible because film is an instrument of fascination from the start. What is interesting to me is to have the spectator become completely unglued, totally taken by the story that is unraveling before him, as though he was a person of the screen, so that he becomes a complete idiot. This can be done with violent cop stories or with films like those of the Japanese directors Ozu or Mizoguchi. That is, one can be captivated and fascinated by the slow contemplation of the Japanese, as well as by the violence in the Hollywood films of anguish. Both are cinema, the rest are not cinema for me."

Filmography

1975 *L'Assassin Musicien*
1977 *Les Enfants du Placard*
1983 *Les Ailes de la Colombe*

BARBARA KOPPLE

The "crawl" showing the money sources for Barbara Kopple's Academy Award-winning documentary, *Harlan County, U.S.A.,* is endless. She even financed part of it on her Master-Card. Her determination and political position are implacable: they are the raison d'être of her films and the basis for the collective process by which they are made: "We have a company called Cabin Creek Center. During the time, for instance, of *Harlan County,* a lot of the people who worked on the editing were students who were part of an Urban Corps (now part of CETA), which means that the city of New York pays their wages. I found that a lot of people who became the most committed and dedicated really started to learn. I really liked the process of bringing everybody up to the same level and everybody having the same kind of information and sharing in the whole division of labor."

Kopple came to New York in 1967 and got a job with the Maysles: "My job was doing everything that nobody else wanted to do, like reconstituting trims, getting coffee, whatever people wanted me to do. To me it was so exciting, I would have worked twenty-four hours a day reconstituting trims or splicing pieces of film together, because it was just opening up a whole new world. For me, film is one of the most powerful mediums in the world. Where do you get people to sit in a theater, you turn off the lights, and you have their total attention for two hours? So, it happened out of luck and timing, but once it happened, I just took it and ran. There was nothing I wasn't going to learn about film and I started at the very bottom, from sweeping floors to doing assistant editing, editing, sound, camera, producing, directing, whatever, and I just did it little by little, so that I understood every single aspect of it, including the fund raising. Because I had to do that all by myself, as well.

"The great thing about film for me is that no matter what you're doing, you're discovering the world, new worlds, new people, new ideas. That, to me, is terribly exciting, no matter how difficult it is: the steps always change and they always move forward, so you're not ever stuck in the same kind of humdrum. You're always moving forward, you're always learning and taking all those experiences with you that help create you as a person, individually. All that history is so important for you to develop, to be able to bring the film forward, to bring your ideas forward.

"It's what C. Wright Mills used to write about: all of our past experiences create who we are today, and without really understanding and analyzing them, it's very difficult to be able to proceed in an organized way, where you can take that all with you and make it grow as you go along."

Filmography

1971	*Winter Soldier*
1975	*Richard III*
1978	*Harlan County, U.S.A.*
1981	*The American Writer in Crisis*
	No Nukes
1982	*Keeping On*
1984	*Cutting Edge*
1985	*Joe Glory*

SIDNEY LUMET

"How much of an *auteur* are you if you're dependent on whether or not the clouds are over the sun?" This sort of comment is not the stuff from which movie myths are made; it simply reflects the experience and horse sense that gets movies made. Sidney Lumet's unpretentious attitude, his willingness to serve the subject rather than his ego, and his great expertise account for his large output of films and their consistently fine quality. He is not a myth, but that's okay with him: he's been able to stay in New York—that is, away from Hollywood—while making twenty-six films in twenty years. Besides, he knows he's good: "I think over the years I've done more innovative camera stuff than an awful lot of other directors. Nobody ever sees it and that's my highest compliment."

From his first, *12 Angry Men,* to unforgettable films like *The Hill, The Fugitive Kind, The Pawnbroker,* and *Network,* Lumet has consistently proved himself to be a supreme professional, working in a variety of styles but always capturing and moving the audience.

"Sorry to use a pretentious word about it—it's the attraction of art, which is that it takes on its own life, and every good and honest artist will tell you it's an accident when it happens. That doesn't mean there isn't a reason it happens to some of us more than it happens to others of us, and that's where the talent lies. But basically, all you're doing is getting that garden ready for *it* to happen. When it happens, it's accidental: you've put together the right combination of elements—the soil is right, the wind is right, the amount of rainfall is right. And, like everything else, it comes from knowledge and instinct. But when the really magical thing happens, oh boy, are you glad to see it because you know it happened accidentally."

The son of one of the major forces on the Yiddish stage, Lumet worked as a child actor on radio, later in the theater, and even made one appearance as a screen actor opposite Sylvia Sidney in the thirties. In 1947, after returning from five years in the army, Lumet, with forty other actors, founded one of the first off-Broadway theatrical groups. He attracted the attention of the new medium, television, and from 1950 until 1960, turned out two hundred and fifty shows for some of the leading series, such as "You Are There," "The Alcoa Hour," and "The Goodyear Playhouse." Since 1957, which marked his film debut with *12 Angry Men,* he has worked steadily in movies, interrupted only by occasional New York stage productions.

Filmography

1957	*12 Angry Men*
1958	*Stage Struck*
1959	*That Kind of Woman*
1960	*The Fugitive Kind*
1962	*A View from the Bridge*
	A Long Day's Journey Into Night
1964	*Fail Safe*
1965	*The Pawnbroker*
	The Hill
1966	*The Group*
1967	*The Deadly Affair*
1968	*Bye Bye Braverman*
	The Sea Gull
1969	*The Appointment*
1970	*Last of the Mobile Hot Shots (Blood Kin)*
1971	*The Anderson Tapes*
1972	*Child's Play*
1973	*The Offence*
	Serpico
1974	*Lovin' Molly*
	Murder on the Orient Express
1975	*Dog Day Afternoon*
1976	*Network*
1977	*Equus*
1978	*The Wiz*
1979	*Just Tell Me What You Want*

1981   *Prince of the City*
1982   *Deathtrap*
1983   *The Verdict*
1984   *Daniel*
         Garbo Talks

DUŠAN MAKAVEJEV

At Harvard, where he taught in 1977–78, they still speak of him in the reverent tones befitting Dušan Makavejev, martyred saint of cinema, fallen from industry grace with the release of his most controversial film, *Sweet Movie*. His films have violated some of society's most sacred taboos, and not without a certain defiance; but like his mentor, Wilhelm Reich, Makavejev is more sinned against than sinner. Describing the parallels between political and sexual freedom, between fascism of the individual body and that of the body politic, his films propose the releasing of our animal natures as a solution, a notion guaranteed to make a few puritans squirm in their seats. Makavejev's extraordinary movies are collages: constructed from oppositions and ironic juxtapositions on levels ranging from differing film stocks to contrasting image content to total disruption of ordinary narrative concepts, his films reach out to meet our dreams. His own personality is distinguished by a childlike curiosity about the ways of his fellow humans—a quality I observed over and over in the characters of the most interesting filmmakers. Makavejev and his films are of a piece, and in his case, there is a special integrity. He rejects the image of cult figure, however, as unreal and false, especially since the reality of his situation is that from the time *Sweet Movie* was released in 1974 until *Montenegro* in 1981, he was unable to finance a film project.

"After *Sweet Movie* it was as if I had burned all my bridges. I just lost the chance to talk to producers." Part of this was due to leaving his country, Yugoslavia, where he was firmly established and almost automatically financed. But another reason was that many producers and distributors didn't know how to handle his films, which they misunderstood as pornographic. But it is the political, social, and spiritual repression that Makavejev challenges that is the true pornography.

Makavejev made his first feature, *Man Is Not a Bird*, in 1965, after studying psychology and working in the student theater at Belgrade University. In 1971 his *W.R.: Mysteries of the Organism* won international acclaim and the Luis Buñuel Prize at the

Cannes Film Festival, as well as an official indictment from the Belgrade prosecutor on a criminal charge of derision of "the state, its agencies, and representatives."

Filmography

1965 *Man Is Not a Bird*
1967 *Love Affair: Or the Case of the Missing Switchboard Operator*
1968 *Innocence Unprotected*
1971 *W.R.: Mysteries of the Organism*
1974 *Sweet Movie*
1981 *Montenegro*

AL MAYSLES

Independent documentary filmmakers Albert and David Maysles rarely go to the movies. In fact, movies as they are known today have little in common with their work. Their ties are more to the arts of photography and the novel, and their inspiration derives more from family experiences. They choose their subjects in order to study them, but the original attraction is often unclear at the start. The Maysles follow the film, allowing the life in front of their camera and sound recorder to unfold and reveal itself. Only then do they know what they have and why they have it.

Both men were psychology students, but began their film careers separately. They soon became partners, however, in filmic explorations of human behavior, American values, and the artistic process. Strikingly different in personal style and even in interests, they complement rather than contradict one another. Al is the cameraman, David the soundman, or, as they describe it, the eyes and ears, respectively, of their films.

According to the Maysles the key to their kind of filmmaking is active listening. For if their subjects—who range from Marlon Brando and Truman Capote to a failed Bible salesman and the impoverished aunt and cousin of Jackie Onassis—didn't feel comfortable enough to let the Maysles into their lives, there would be no film. This is "direct cinema," catching life as it happens, trusting that it will. Like life, this style of filmmaking is a gamble. For the Maysles, if you can't show life as it really is, why bother.

"I think humanity has been dealt a terrible disservice by the usual technique of moviemaking," says Al Maysles. "One of the by-products is misunderstanding through films, through stars and the star system, to the point where some people will look at a film of ours and not accept the most obvious kinds of facts of life because they've been so trained to see make-believe on the screen. What we've done is film people who would otherwise never be seen, and it serves as quite a compliment to people.

"Movies historically have been like *People* magazine, featuring youth and celebrities. The way *People* is a degeneration of

Life magazine, so movies began almost from the start in that degenerated form."

Al sees film as most akin to photography in its ability to "catch things as they happen. . . . With the kind of objectivity I wanted, somehow I felt film would catch information faster, in a more lively way than still photography, than any other means. Of course, years later, fourteen years later, when we did *Gimme Shelter*, that same technique caught a killing and became the material that everyone referred to."

Filmography

1955 *Psychiatry in Russia*
1957 *Youth in Poland*
1960 *Primary*
1961 *Yanqui No!*
1963 *Showman*
1964 *What's Happening: The Beatles in the U.S.A.*
1965 *Meet Marlon Brando*
1966 *A Visit with Truman Capote*
1969 *Salesman (co-dir.)*
1970 *Gimme Shelter (co-dir.)*
1973 *Christo's Valley Curtain*
1975 *Grey Gardens (co-dir.)*
1976 *The Burks of Georgia*
1978 *Running Fence*
1980 *Muhammad and Larry*
1984 *Islands*

PHILIP MESSINA

An award-winning filmmaker who has been living in Hollywood since 1979, Philip F. Messina has been struggling to remain independent while working within the American film industry. He was co-author of the film *Brainstorm* and is currently writing a spy thriller for 20th Century-Fox. While his screenwriting provides an inroad to mainstream filmmaking, he has always remained an adamant believer in the low-budget, independently produced film. He was one of the founders of the Association of Independent Video and Filmmakers, a group dedicated to keeping that belief viable. He is presently trying to finance one of his scripts, which he will also direct. In addition to his feature work, he has produced, written, directed and/or photographed dozens of prize-winning dramatic, documentary, and educational films, as well as television commercials and rock videos. He is a New York University School of Film graduate whose experience in the business of filmmaking has been classic. Messina's description of Hollywood deal making is an accurate, fair account of what can happen to the much-praised, award-winning, hard-working, multi-talented film school graduate way out West.

Filmography

1968   *Going to Work in the Morning From Brooklyn*
1971   *Skezag*
1975   *Mamma*
1979   *Brainstorm* (co-writer)
1984   *Spy* (writer)

ERMANNO OLMI

Nothing much happens in an Olmi film, that is, if you require a roller coaster ride with all the requisite thrills and chills. Instead of a boldly defined series of actions moving the story along at a furious pace, Olmi shares with his audience small moments that gradually build into a powerful understanding of an experience. Using real people instead of actors, Olmi follows his subjects as they live in real time, gently shaping their lives into fiction with his authorial hand.

"Shooting freely with a hand-held camera, never choosing anything in advance, everything happens almost spontaneously. It doesn't happen by design, by planning. Why do I work this way? Because it is important that the operative-technical moment be enveloped in the many emotions that are in the air in the moment one lives the scene. There must always be a participation, a collision with the moment; this is what determines the choice of the image. Otherwise, it's like going up to a loved person and first thinking, 'When we meet, I'll touch her hand, then kiss her like this, then say this phrase. . . .'"

The Tree of Wooden Clogs, winner of the 1978 Golden Palm at Cannes, is an exquisite illustration of "operative-technical moments enveloped by the many emotions in the air." As magnificent as the flow, tone, and composition of Olmi's frames are, the film nevertheless breathes in rhythms of real life, of the peasants, animals, and the land it depicts. This film is not, however, of the "salt of the earth" genre. It genuinely records a culture without sentimentality, condescension, or didacticism. Olmi interacts with his subjects and his form, trying not only to understand them but also himself.

Filmography

1959 *Time Stood Still*
1961 *The Sound of Trumpets*
1963 *The Fiancés*
1964 *A Man Called John*
1968 *One Fine Day*

1969   *The Scavengers*
1971   *During the Summer*
1973   *The Circumstance*
1978   *The Tree of Wooden Clogs*
1982   *Cammina Cammina*

ELIO PETRI

Dedicated to studying controversial socio-political subjects, the late Elio Petri's film reports employ a realistic style pierced by surrealistic effects. He sought to "debanalize" physical reality in order to penetrate truths lying below the surface appearance. Because of his deeply political concerns, Petri defined film vis-à-vis its relationship to culture.

Like his countryman Ermanno Olmi, Petri came from the peasant class and was proud of it. He left school after World War II at the age of sixteen and became active in politics, discovering neo-realism, jazz, and Hemingway along the way. He worked for several years as a journalist on leftist publications, which led him to write his first screenplay, the result of an investigation into a controversial news story. He went on to collaborate on several more screenplays and, in 1961, made his first feature film, *The Murderer,* starring Marcello Mastroianni. Petri's commitment to political issues in the broadest definition of political, was apparent in this first effort, as well as in his subsequent films.

Filmography

1961 *The Murderer*
1962 *The Days are Numbered*
1963 *Il Maestro di Vigevano*
1965 *High Infidelity*
      The Tenth Victim
1967 *To Each His Own*
1968 *A Quiet Place in the Country*
1969 *Investigation of a Citizen Above Suspicion*
1971 *The Working Class Goes to Heaven*
1973 *La Proprietà non è più un Furto*
1976 *Todo Modo*
1978 *Mani Sporche*
1979 *Le Buone Notizie*

MICHAEL POWELL

Released during the tail end of the McCarthy years, *Peeping Tom* outraged critics with its heavily Freudian-cum-pre-snuff film account of an amateur photographer who kills his victims with a knife mounted in the leg of his tripod, thereby filming their actual deaths.

Michael Powell's wildly macabre sense of humor was always a bit much for the sensibilities of that time. He saw too well, took it all with humor, and gave it back to us in his deliciously shocking movies. *Peeping Tom* was the beginning of the end of a career marked by great achievement against formidable obstacles—that is, until Martin Scorsese brought him to light again, most noticeably at the 1979 New York Film Festival, where avid cinemaphiles crowded the two screenings of *Peeping Tom*, deluging Powell after with film buff type questions, which he gracefully managed to evade. "I don't get excited," he told me later during our interview. Dressed in black, the lean and energetic Powell delighted me with his wonderfully matter-of-fact views on film—a much-needed antidote to the discussions I'd been hearing on the mysteries of cinema. As it happened, the first film I ever saw was his *Red Shoes:* the image of the ballet slippers skipping across the screen in brilliant forties Technicolor is engraved forever in my mind. What a treat it was to listen to Powell recount his experiences, dating back to the days of silent films when he worked for the great Rex Ingram on the Riviera, when everyone who was anyone hung out on the set, and when the studio was so far away that he couldn't check on the company that took three days to film a dance-orgy sequence with the dancer Stowitts. ("Those poor girls," Powell recalled.)

Filmography

1931   *Two Crowded Hours*
       My Friend the King
       Rynox
       The Rasp

The Star Reporter
1932 *Hotel Splendide*
Born Lucky
C.O.D.
His Lordship
1933 *The Fire Raisers*
1934 *The Night of the Party*
Red Ensign
Something Always Happens
The Girl in the Crowd
1935 *Some Day*
Lazybones
Her Last Affair
The Love Test
The Price of a Song
The Phantom Light
1936 *The Brown Wallet*
Crown vs. Stevens
The Man Behind the Mask
1937 *The Edge of the World*
1938 *The Spy in Black*
1939 *The Lion Has Wings*
1940 *Contraband*
The Thief of Bagdad
1941 *49th Parallel*
1942 *One of Our Aircraft Is Missing*
1943 *The Life and Death of Colonel Blimp*
The Silver Fleet
The Volunteer
1944 *A Canterbury Tale*
1945 *I Know Where I'm Going*
1946 *A Matter of Life and Death*
1947 *Black Narcissus*
End of the River
1948 *The Red Shoes*
The Small Back Room
1950 *Gone to Earth*
The Elusive Pimpernel

1951   *The Tales of Hoffman*
1955   *Oh Rosalinda!*
1956   *The Battle of the River Platte*
1957   *Ill Met by Moonlight*
1958   *Honeymoon*
1960   *Peeping Tom*
1961   *The Queen's Guards*
1964   *Bluebeard's Castle*
1966   *They're a Weird Mob*
1967   *Sebastian*
1969   *Age of Consent*
1972   *The Boy Who Turned Yellow*
1974   *The Tempest*

MARK RAPPAPORT

Modernist comedies of manners, Mark Rappaport's films deal in isolation, missed cues, romantic intrigues, and our general inability to communicate to each other what we *think* we really mean. Rather than dwell on the tragedy of it all, Rappaport gives us wit and cinematic metaphors referring to music, literature, and painting, expanding the small worlds of his characters to the size of our universe. His characters function as straight men for his commentary. Usually involved with each other in baroque and funny combinations, they view themselves and each other with deadpan seriousness. Rappaport has achieved what could be a minor miracle: six full-length features budgeted somewhere around one hundred thousand dollars (often shot in his lower Manhattan loft). He has turned the restrictions of low-budget filmmaking in America into the artistic controls of a genre. Though his films are not often released theatrically in America, he enjoys great success in Europe. His fourth film, *The Scenic Route,* won the 1978 British Film Institute's award for "the most original and imaginative film." Previous winners include Bresson, Oshima, Rivette, Fassbinder, and Bertolucci.

Rappaport began his career as an editor for "Radley Metzger, who later became a soft-core porn-cult director, but that was before he was directing movies. He was buying French films and shooting inserts for them so there would be a hot version and a cool version. That was the first editing I did. Then I got so bored I went back to college. After I finished college, I went to graduate school, but after a week I quit and said, 'What am I going to do with my life?' Since I'd always been crazy about movies and I had no way of earning money and since I knew how to edit, I got a job as a film editor. Two years later I made my first film, *Mur Nineteen,* sixteen millimeter, twenty-three minutes. I think it's a very good, talented first film—very serious, *très* serious, deadly serious, the way only young people can be. But it's very interesting; I think there are things in that film that are in every film I've made subsequently. It's a very peculiar elliptical narrative; it's very truncated; it uses images in a very strange kind of loaded way that doesn't correspond to any kind of literal meaning, but creates its own meaning. I use photographs and people in the same situations—that is, you can't tell what's photographed and what's real, which is something I've done subsequently with a lot more precision and a lot more effect. It's a smart movie. I'd never disown it. It's very serious though—a lead knish."

Filmography

1973 *Casual Relations*
1975 *Mozart in Love*
1977 *Local Color*
1978 *The Scenic Route*
1979 *Imposters*
1984 *Chain Letters*

ERIC ROHMER

Although Eric Rohmer is known for his conservative Catholicism, his films are certainly not. Humorous, high-spirited, literate rather than literary, they explore the conflict between human sexuality and societal restrictions. As one critic commented to me, "He appreciates beautiful young girls as much as any of them, but he's the only one who feels any guilt." His priestliness, then, is a devilish agent of provocation, making only more delicious his protagonists' struggles with temptation.

The style of Rohmer's films, particularly those of the "moral tales" series, defies some cherished notions of what cinema is not: they include long-winded discussions, stationary framing of the camera, and as complex, intellectual, and subtle characterizations as can be found in any novel. Rohmer makes talking cinematic. His open willingness to pay attention, to refrain from judgmental commentary, is also profoundly cinematic, and directly in the tradition of Renoir. He is one of the few practitioners of a cinema of ideas that is also dramatic, visual, and moving. Rohmer has extended and deepened the province of film.

Rohmer was born in Nancy, France, August 4, 1920, under the name of either Maurice Scherer or Jean-Marie Maurice Scherer, but not even that is certain. He became interested in cinema in the late forties, along with his friends Truffaut, Godard, and Rivette. In 1951 he started his own film magazine, *La Gazette du Cinéma,* and then helped to found *Cahiers du Cinéma,* serving as editor-in-chief from 1957 to 1963, finally leaving the magazine when it drifted too far to the left. He made a series of short, educational films for French television before forming Les Films du Losange with Barbet Schroeder, the production company that would make his Six Moral Tales, films that deal "less with what people do than with what is going on in their minds while they're doing it." The first two, short subjects, are rarely seen; the third in the series, *My Night at Maud's,* became an instant international success.

Despite fame and his celebrated reclusiveness, he opens his door to almost anyone who seeks him out, particularly young filmmakers. Rohmer is a true gentleman, an aristocrat of the spirit, a democrat at heart.

Filmography

1950 *Journal d'un Scélérat* (short)
1951 *Présentation ou Charlotte et son Steak* (short)
1952 *Les Petites Filles Modèles* (co-directed; unfinished)
1954 *Bérénice* (short)
1956 *The Kreutzer Sonata* (short)
1958 *Véronique et son Cancre* (short)
1959 *The Sign of the Lion*
1962 *La Boulangère de Monceau* (short)
1963 *La Carrère de Suzanne* (medium-length)
1964 *Nadja à Paris* (short)
1965 *Six in Paris*
1967 *Une Étudiante d'Aujourd'hui* (short)
       La Collectionneuse
1968 *Fermière à Montfauçon*
1969 *My Night at Maud's*
1970 *Claire's Knee*
1972 *Chloë in the Afternoon*
1976 *The Marquise of O*
1978 *Perceval*
1980 *The Aviator's Wife*
1981 *Le Beau Mariage*
1982 *Pauline at the Beach*
1984 *Full Moon in Paris*

GEORGE ROMERO

Affable yet serious, George Romero puts one in mind of a friendly bear blinking in the sun after a long winter in his cave. Romero's cave is his editing room—that's where he's happiest, piecing together his films: "I have all the stuff and I'm in my little room and everybody's gone and I can have a lot of fun." When his big hit, *Dawn of the Dead,* opened in New York, *The Village Voice* printed a photograph of Romero hunched over his editing table, back to the camera. It's a comic and beautifully apt image: something in his back says, "This is all I've ever wanted to do. Making movies should be fun."

He makes it sound easy, yet this film buff has been shooting film almost since his first steps, managing to employ himself since leaving school by making documentaries, glossy commercials, and features for his own film companies, all of which have been based in Pittsburgh (about as far away as you can get from Hollywood, at least the Hollywood of our minds). The critical and financial success of *Dawn of the Dead* proves unequivocally that he and his partner-producer, Richard Rubinstein, known corporately as The Laurel Group, have beat the system so far. In fact, The Laurel Group will package a property for a major studio when Romero does the film version of *The Stand,* the apocalyptic best-seller written by another big bear, Stephen King. If they can get through that process and remain independent, they'll make a lot of people happy.

When *Night of the Living Dead* first terrified the countless viewers who came stoned and willing to those midnight shows at Ben Barenholtz's Elgin Theatre, we knew it worked, but we weren't sure why. I asked Romero about the film's roughness, which gave it so much reality: "Technically, it has a very documentary flavor. I wanted some of that stuff to look like UPI footage. I often tell people if they look at my commercial reel—all that stuff was done before *Night of the Living Dead*—you'll see all these beautiful commercials for Calgon and all this flashy commercial stuff. So, it's not that the look of *Night* wasn't intentional; it's not that we don't know how to make a film and so that's why it turned out the way it turned out. As far as the performances are concerned, there are a couple of people who really did a great job, and the rest of the people were the only people who were around Pittsburgh at the time who were half-way vocational, and we did have problems with them. And so we also played off it to a certain extent, too, for a nice melodramatic effect, which really worked. But the grainy texture, particularly the footage with the posse, was a deliberate UPI, almost like foreign correspondent footage. I like that for *Night* because we were a lot angrier then—it was 1968—we were pissed off. So, it's very different. Yet it still has that *Tales From the Crypt* kind of comic-book edge to it which makes it fun, so you can goof on it even though the imagery triggers a consciousness which is more automatic than *Dawn of the Dead*. That film is *Sergeant Pepper's Lonely Hearts Club Band*—it's out there somewhere else, it's almost a Peter Max strip.

"But I'd also like to do a movie that's straight ahead without this multi-layered social comment kind of thing. I'd like to do an action film where all the energies go into that veneer, something like *Tarzan of the Apes*. But I think those days may be gone forever, because to try to make a deal like that, they'd tell you that you can't do *Tarzan of the Apes* without forty million bucks."

Filmography

1968	*Night of the Living Dead*
1972	*The Affair*
	Jack's Wife
1973	*The Crazies*
1977	*Martin*
1978	*Dawn of the Dead*
1982	*Knightriders*
1983	*Creepshow*
1985	*Day of the Dead*

JEAN ROUCH

Ethnographic documentarian, revered father of Direct Cinema, pioneer in the development and use of the 16mm Eclair camera, major influence on the style of the sixties, New Wave filmmaking, Jean Rouch sat on the steps of the Musée du Cinéma in the Cinémathèque Française at the Palais du Chaillot surrounded by relics from cinema's brief history: a costume from *Potemkin,* Marilyn Monroe's flapper dress from *Some Like It Hot.* We were far from his beloved Africa, the major subject of his numerous films. Rouch has remained faithful to his film aesthetic, working alone with light-weight equipment on three or four short 16mm studies at once, giving of his energy, knowledge, and time to film groups all over the world, always completely alive and full of incredible enthusiasm, so much so that his words seemed unable to contain his energy as we talked:

"Documentary filmmakers, even fiction filmmakers, sometimes have to be at the same time the director and the cameraman. For me it's impossible to have a staff of people. And, as I go further along, I have to be alone when I'm making a film. For example, I'm going to Africa. I am alone. My staff is myself with a single sound camera. My tape recorder is from the country where I'm working. I train the people in the village just to use the sound recorder. Then when I'm making a film, I move with the camera. I'm somebody else, I'm no longer Jean Rouch. I'm in a kind of what I call 'cine-trance'; it's like a position dance and I'm just moving around the people. When you see a man making a film in this way, it's really a kind of dance. At this time, with this mechanical eye and this electronic ear, I am really in a trance, a cine-trance. And that's for me the way to approach the truth.

"But the editor's role is very important, and then the second point, when the film is edited, you ask some very good friends to see the film, and a very good friend is somebody who'll say, 'No, it's a mess.' That's a good friend. Not someone who always says, 'Oh, Jean, it's wonderful.' That's not a good friend. There were many good friends at the beginning of the *nouvelle vague* in France. We were a kind of college, and all the people like Truffaut and Godard were at the Cinémathèque, in this place, devouring films, three or four films a day, just sitting in front of the screen. Then, when we started to make films, we shared the experiment, shared the screen, and we spoke very frankly because we were interested in making films and not in the star system or the business system. But, unfortunately, that was the old time and only Godard is still making experimental films." That is, only Godard and Rouch.

Filmography

1947 *Au Pays des Mages noirs*
1949 *Hombroi*
     Les Magiciens noirs
     La Circoncision
1951 *Cimetière dans la Falise*
     Bataille sur le Grand Fleuve
     Yenendi, Les Hommes qui font la Pluie
     Les Gens du Mil
1953 *Les Maîtres Fous*
     Mammy Water
     Jaguar
1955 *Les Fils de l'Eau*
1957 *Moro Naba*
     Moi un Noir
1959 *La Pyramide humaine*
1960 *Hampi*
1961 *Chronique d'un Été*
1962 *Rose et Landry*
     Abidjan—Port de la Pêche
     Urbanisme Africain
     Pêcheurs du Niger
1963 *Monsieur Albert, Prophète*
     Le Mil
     La Punition
     Les Cocotiers
1964 *Batteries Dogon, Éléments pour une Étude des Rhythmes*

Les Veuves de Quinze Ans
The Adolescents
1965 The Lion Hunters
Six in Paris
1968 Un Lion Nommé L'Américain
1969 Sigui 1969—La Caverne de Bongo
Le Signe
1970 Petit à Petit
1971 Sigui 1971—La Dune d'Ideyli
Architectes Ayorou
1972 L'Enterrement du Hogon
Sigui 1972—Les Pagnes de Iame
1973 Tanda Singui
V.V. Voyou
Boukoki
1974 Pan Kuso Kar
La 504 et Les Foudroyeurs
Cocorico! Monsieur Poulet
1975 Hommage à Marcel Mauss
Taro Okamoto
Initiation
Souna Kouma
Faran Maka Fonda
1976 Yenendi Simiri
Babatou Les 3 Conseils
Chantons Sous l'occupacion
1977 Isphahan
Makwayela
Médecins et Médecins
Badye, Griot du Niger
1978 Margaret Mead, A Portrait by a Friend
1979 Funerailles à Bongo
Ganjibi
Sidokuma
1984 Dionysos

WERNER SCHROETER

I was told that he is a "genius," that wherever on this globe he should go, devotees await him, eager to smooth his passage. As we sipped champagne served by a member of the New York contingent of devotees one sunny September morning, I, too, was enthralled by his graceful blend of European aristocrat and streetwise hustler. But it wasn't until a good six months later that I saw my first Werner Schroeter film, *Regno di Napoli*, at the 1979 New Directors–New Films series at the Museum of Modern Art and really understood his ability to inspire awe and slavishness. An ambitious film, *Regno* manages to trace the history of a community in Naples from 1944 to 1976 in a style that combines the realism of documentary with the emotionalism of opera. It is a seduction carried out on a grand scale.

Schroeter's overriding concern is for the socio-political state of the world, so much so, in fact, that his style has undergone a major change: from highly experimental to a more accessible, narrative-based structure: "I don't believe anymore in the importance of that kind of artistic experiment, not if you don't have an audience to see it. After the sixties, the audience for that kind of cinema became really very limited. So, for me, it is avant-garde to have a message or meaning or analysis in cinema rather than to try to transport the ideas of new meanings of aesthetic expressions or forms. For example, *Regno di Napoli* is a straight story of a family in Naples, and I transported into my story a lot of political and social facts people don't know about Italy. It's very important that people recognize why life has become so bad, why we are so unhappy nowadays, and rightly so. There is no doubt about it. You shouldn't be happy today considering the state of mind and of politics. So I think my movies should become more direct politically. I always regarded my films as political, but political on the artistic level, as the statement of someone who does not believe in that kind of commercialized cinema, cliché cinema. So I used the form artistically in a political way. And now it becomes more or less evident that I prefer to use the more conventional cinematographic techniques and transport a more unconventional meaning."

Filmography

1968   *Neurasia*
       Argila
1969   *Eika Katapppa*
       Nicaragua
1970   *Bomberpilot*
       Anglia
       Salome
1971   *MacBeth*
       Hit Parade
       Der Tod der Maria Malibran
1972   *Willow Springs*
1973   *Der Schwarze Engel*
1976   *Flocons d'Or*
1977   *Regno de Napoli*
1983   *Dress Rehearsal*

MARTIN SCORSESE

The nineteenth century, that age of grand passions and commitment, lives on in the person of Martin Scorsese. Scorsese cares with a burning intensity. His concerns range from the fading color stock manufactured by Eastman Kodak to reviving the careers of older filmmakers, such as the great Michael Powell, to making films that are as perfect as our imperfect condition will allow. One is most impressed, I think, by how much Martin Scorsese loves film. It is clearly the obsession of his life.

Martin Scorsese may be America's best filmmaker. His films reflect an intellectual expansiveness, a depth of feeling, and an insistence on working out every minute detail that is unrivaled among his peers. Where he distinguishes himself most, however, is in his determination to bring the reins of production as close to home as possible. Disgusted with the "dinosaurs" of filmmaking—giant equipment, huge soundstages, bloated salaries—Scorsese cut most of *Raging Bull* in his spare bedroom, working at a steady but furious pace, usually at night, taking only little snatches of sleep during the day. And the results were well worth it. *Raging Bull* is an exquisitely wrought gem whose intricate facets of sound and image exonerate Scorsese from any accusations of monomania.

But if in some ways he seems a man out of time, with a style and spirit belonging to another age, his surroundings epitomize the fantasies of every child of the twentieth-century global village. It seemed to me that his apartment abounded with every artifact of the electronic era: tape recorders, amplifiers, monitors, editing equipment, pieces of film, books, and, of course, film posters. We had to conduct the interview in his bedroom, he on the left side of the bed, myself at the foot, piles of papers serving as our bundling board.

Filmography

1970　*Who's That Knocking at My Door?*
1972　*Boxcar Bertha*

1973   *Mean Streets*
1974   *Alice Doesn't Live Here Anymore*
1976   *Taxi Driver*
1977   *New York, New York*
1978   *The Last Waltz*
1979   *Raging Bull*
1980   *Italian-American*
          An American Boy
1982   *King of Comedy*

JOAN M. SILVER AND RAPHAEL D. SILVER

In terms of energy and accomplishment, Joan Micklin Silver and Raphael D. Silver disprove the time-honored equation, one plus one equals two. Since 1973, when Raphael Silver formed Midwest Film Productions, Inc., in order to produce and distribute *Hester Street* (written and directed by Joan Silver), they have demonstrated the force of ten. In 1976 they brought out their second film, *Between the Lines,* again produced by Raphael and directed by Joan, and in 1979 they switched roles with the ease of practiced trapeze artists, Joan Silver producing and Raphael Silver directing *On the Yard.*

Scaled down to the modest proportions of real life, all their films share an honesty and authenticity toward their subjects that distinguishes them from the usual larger-than-life Hollywood products. For example, *On the Yard* was shot entirely at the Rockview State Correctional Facility near State College, Pennsylvania, with many inmates performing as extras and featured players, as well as serving on the crew. Raphael Silver explains: "I don't think you could really convey the authenticity and the realism of prison by taking an empty prison and filling it full of actors and extras. One of the interesting things about the movie is the reality of using a mass of inmates and individual convicts for certain scenes. I was very determined in *On the Yard* not to go for some big sprawling macho kind of dramatic, old-fashioned prison film. I wanted to explore the effects of that kind of world of tension and of potential violence on the lives of some people who were caught up in it. And so, the small character of the film in terms of the scope is very intentional. I think audiences will respond to any film where they find reality and believability. How extensively they respond is a different question."

Raphael Silver seems to provide the business expertise for his and Joan's efforts, having been president of Midwestern Land Development Corp., a company specializing in urban redevelopment, commercial building, and the manufacture of modular housing. Joan Silver, however, spent a good part of her childhood in movie theaters, wrote for the theater, and had a successful career making educational films: "I grew up on movies—they were by far the most popular form of entertainment of my era. I think I have an attachment to them that was formed then which never diminished—it's only increased. I think the best training I had was actually in going to a lot of films, especially my first move to New York. I lived in the basement of the Museum of Modern Art. I had a very good friend at the time who has since died very sadly. He was making a documentary for David Wolper and the plane crashed. Dennis and I were at exactly the same stage in our careers and we were both working, writing scenarios for an educational film company. And we went to MOMA all the time, and we sat there, whispering to each other about what was happening in the films."

Filmography

1975 *Hester Street*
1976 *Bernice Bobs Her Hair*
   Between the Lines
1978 *On the Yard* (R. Silver directing)
1979 *Head Over Heels* (First released as *Chilly Scenes of Winter*)

JEAN-MARIE STRAUB

During the 1970 New York Film Festival press screening of Jean-Marie Straub's *Othon*, half the audience walked out; Roger Greenspun considered this to be the festival's "highest tribute," an evaluation with which Straub himself concurs.

Our interview took place late one evening at the Cinémathèque Française at the Palais du Chaillot after a screening of Straub and Danièle Huillet's *Fortini/Cani*, also deserted by one third of its audience: "I think a film should be made so that people can leave the room. Films that pretend to be made for the masses are really made to keep them in their place, to violate them, or to fascinate them. Consequently, those films are made in such a way that they don't give the people the liberty to get up and leave. Our films are made so that people can leave if they want." Danièle Huillet qualified her husband's response: "We are not happy when people leave the room during our films, but it is clearly a risk, for those who leave might have been moved if they had seen more."

More than any other filmmaker with political concerns, it is Straub who really makes clear the deep and profound connection between the form of a film and the process by which it is made, and its ideology. As a Marxist, Straub does not attempt to "fascinate," to capture the audience either affectively or even intellectually: "I don't think a film should impose at all the ideas of the director. He should propose ideas that people can accept or refuse. He shouldn't impose them, no matter what they are. Even if he wants people to participate in his ideas, he must present them in radically different ways than commercial films. If he used those same selling methods to sell his so-called beautiful and good ideas, it's an absurd contradiction, because those methods only hit you on the head, and even if you are hit on the head with the best intentions, it still hurts.

"If I show you an audio-visual object which deafens you or blinds you under the pretext of convincing you of a beautiful and good idea, I can't even convey the idea to you because it must be perceived by the senses I have just diminished. So, I will succeed only in making you more unconscious. And the society in which we live is such that the totalitarian dream of the bourgeoisie—who invented the television, a monster more totalitarian than the cinema—is that each national TV station fascinate and chain twenty million people for a broadcast, not even knowing what they are talking about. In a world where such a totalitarian dream exists, it's worth more to make films for the minorities, for as Lenin said, 'The minority of today will be the majority of tomorrow.' If we do anything else, we are only serving the totalitarian dream of the bourgeoisie, which is the most monstrous class humanity has ever produced, much more monstrous than the aristocracy of olden times or the gods of antiquity invented by man in the days of the pharoahs."

The uncompromising morality that informs all of the Straubs' films implies that every element, every micro frame, is a commitment, a revelation of self in the world. Commercial success is of such minor concern to them that when their distributor, Dan Talbot of New Yorker Films, called Rome to tell the Straubs that one of their films had actually broken even, their only concern was for the print—wasn't it damaged from all that use?

Filmography

1963 *Machorka-Muff* (short)
1965 *Not Reconciled*
1967 *The Bridegroom, The Comedian, and the Pimp*
1968 *The Chronicle of Magdalena Bach.*
1970 *Othon*
1973 *History Lessons*
1975 *Moses and Aaron*
1976 *Fortini/Cani*
1979 *Dalla Nube alla Resistenza*
1982 *En Rachachant*
1984 *Class Relations*

ANDRÉ TECHINE

"For me, it is the architecture of the labyrinth that is evoked in film, where the spectator looks for the exit." *Barocco,* André Techine's fantastic thriller, is aptly titled. It is an architectural maze, a highly embellished convoluted piece of music. For Techine, this is pure cinema, a mix of the real with the surreal. "I don't see myself as avant-garde. I'm not for a totally experimental cinema. I'm talking about my own work here only. I don't want to generalize at all, but I am for a cinema that tells a story, because I like to be told stories, and it is this pleasure that I'd like to communicate. They can be troubling, bizarre, off-beat stories, like I did, or tried to do in *Barocco.* To tell a story doesn't mean it should be banal or boring—no, it can be fantastic, total fiction. That's why I don't feel close to the French naturalist tradition because I like stories that are like dreams.

"When I discovered movies as a child, what I liked about them was they made me dream. And I still like those kinds of films. What I like to do in the story I'm telling, or the film I'm making, is to create a movement in the characters of coming and going, where they are at times very close to the audience, very identifiable, and then also very distant, almost mythic and legendary. You can go from totally identifying with a character to being plugged into a myth. I find this, for example, in Humphrey Bogart and Lauren Bacall. What was very rich in the fiction they portrayed was this double movement—they went from being identifiable with the spectator to becoming total legends or mythic characters. It doesn't work for me if they are purely legendary—too artificial. Nor does it work if it is pure and simple identification, purely naturalistic; that doesn't interest me. I like a kind of movement here, and I think it should never stop. It's really like that in life, I think."

Critic-turned-filmmaker, Techine has not altered his aesthetic sense of film in a bow to commercial considerations. Film theory and practice are of a piece: "There are two periods in my life: first was when I didn't have the means to make films, but I had, of course, the desire to talk about film, so I talked about it by writing for *Cahiers du Cinéma*. Then, after, when I did have the means to make films, I continued to talk about making films in making them, but for me there was no difference."

Filmography

1969 *Paulina s'en va*
1974 *French Provincial*
1976 *Barocco*
1979 *The Brontë Sisters*
1982 *Hôtel des Ameriques*

LINA WERTMULLER

Rings on her fingers (at least two per digit), harlequin glasses on her nose, follower of "Thanatos and Eros," wife of Enrico Job, an elegantly handsome avant-garde artist and production designer in theater and film (most notably hers), Lina Wertmuller exceeds all description. I visited the Wertmuller–Job home by the Spanish Steps in Rome three times, always dazzled by the prisms of mirrors and skylights, the life-size sculpture, the countless objets d'art, the huge tomes chronicling the history of the noble Wertmuller family. I would show Lina my day's shopping: my red boots, which were "sexy," my brown satin men's pajamas—also "sexy." My interpeter, Deborah Young, had a "sexy" voice. In short, Wertmuller was more alive, warm, curious, dynamic, and appreciative than anyone else imaginable, and she was great fun.

Multi-layered, near-chaotic constructions of sex and politics, Wertmuller's films, like their maker, burst with life, their appearance of disorder underlaid with a very deliberate structure through which she explores man's innate attraction to anarchy and its expression in a variety of forms: "As in life, we can change the rules of the game, but we need rules for everything. I'm always saying this because we, with all our passion, follow freedom in this country, and especially me. My flag is man and his disorder, but I don't want to be misunderstood: without rules you can't play. From love to social struggle, from cinema to theater. Even when you box, when you play poker, without rules it isn't amusing, you can't play.

"In fact, there should be more rules in film. Really, it should be the conquering of a type of serenity, an interior calm. It should be a faraway light that illuminates the area of a circle.

"Ideologies are always very dangerous. Many people have been lost in them. What's important is enlightenment, light. The eighteenth century was the greatest century because it had the light, the intelligence. But this doesn't mean you shouldn't keep mystery in mind. Mystery is very important now. There is the mystery of Eros, of Thanatos, of so many things, so many wonderful mysteries near our human nature. It's a very important zone. It's not easy to go around like the Messiah: 'Let's be policemen, let's do good work.'"

Wertmuller began her work as a writer and director in the theater. It wasn't until 1963, when she served as Fellini's assistant director on *8½*, that she began her film career. What did she learn from him? "Nothing! I only learned Fellini! He's wonderful, but there's nothing to learn from him; he's 'out of the pentagram.' You learn from him to respect yourself, your ideas, that's all. But in a technical way—nothing. I'm very different from Fellini though I love him; he's the light of my life. Living an adventure like a film with him is one of the most beautiful things that can happen in life because he's really crazy; he's cinema. I love him, but it's not possible to work like him. I worked with him on *8½* and no one understood what was going on, what the picture was about, what we were going to shoot tomorrow, nothing. We all had to try to understand to work; it was a kind of escape for him and everyone who worked on it. It was wonderful. You can't work *with* him on a film because only he knows what is happening."

Above all, Wertmuller sees art as a means to communicate: "It's important to communicate. I love people very much and I like to speak to them. I think the movies are a social possibility of speaking. If you work only for your aristocratic, political, cultural friends, it's dangerous. You can begin to think aristocratically. Fellini, too, is now a little aristocratic, but he's only beginning to be that way. Antonioni has always been like that. Yes, it means I want to have a large audience. But it's not totally true that I am 'commercial,' because you can have more people if you're 'sweeter' than me, more amusing. Unfortunately, I'm not; my life would be easier. Life would be easier for Warner Bros.! No. I'm sorry, I'm not as commercial as people think."

Filmography

1963   *The Lizards*
1965   *Let's Talk About Men*
1966   *Rita the Mosquito* (musical numbers only)

1967 *Don't Sting the Mosquito*
1972 *The Seduction of Mimi*
1973 *Love and Anarchy*
1974 *All Screwed Up*
   Swept Away
1976 *Seven Beauties*
1978 *The End of the World in Our Usual Bed in a Night Full of
   Rain*
1979 *Blood Feud*
1981 *Si Sospettano Moventi Politici*

BILLY WILLIAMS

Tall, azure-eyed, with prematurely silvered hair and a soft English accent, Billy Williams could have assumed Leslie Howard's mantle as the quintessential English gentleman. But he was born on the other side of the lens, inheriting instead the camera of his cinematographer father, Billie Williams: "I watched my father—he did all kinds of films, from newsreels to documentary to instructionals to features. And I started with him, essentially as an apprentice."

At the age of twenty-five, Williams became a free-lance documentary cameraman. His first assignment was *The Rivers of Time*, filmed in Iraq. (Eighteen years later he went back to many of the same sites in order to prepare for the shooting of the breathtaking opening sequence of Billy Friedkin's *The Exorcist*.) In the fifties, he began shooting commercials, some with new directors such as Ken Russell, John Schlesinger, and Ted Kotcheff—all of whom he later worked with on feature films. "I think commercials teach one shorthand. I don't enjoy shooting commercials anymore, but I did spend a long time doing them, and they do teach you this visual shorthand—how to say it, how to sell a story in fifteen, thirty seconds. It does sharpen you up and I think audiences are sharpened up to accept that quicker visual presentation. I think audiences are picking things up more quickly now because they're so exposed to television, so exposed to the visuals."

Williams views each film as presenting "another opportunity, something new, another look at life, and I think when you're exploring a new subject you're going to shoot, you try and think in terms of something you haven't done before, or improving on what you have done, rather than repeating yourself. It's not always possible, but I think one should always be reaching out a little bit further. And I think, with the equipment we have today, that it's possible. We are able to explore things with a much greater depth. Even an amateur can pick up an eight-millimeter camera with a zoom lens and have a lot of fun and suddenly see things differently. That's elementary, that's the first way you find out what you can do with a lens."

Though Williams hasn't "worked with a great director in recent years, not someone I take my hat off to," he has not been moved sufficiently to make his own films—at least not yet. "I think I would like to be a director at times, and I feel it most, I suppose, when I don't think the director is directing as well as I think he should be. It does happen that one is really disappointed in the way a shot is handled by the director, and it has happened a lot to me recently. I've been really disappointed in the way a director has put a scene together or the way he's handled the actors by the emphasis he gives to certain things, and those are the times I think I would like to be a director, when I think I could do it better. But when I think about directors like John Schlesinger—I think he's the best director I've worked with—then, I don't think I want to be a director, because I think working with Schlesinger—he gets so much more out of a scene than I can see. That's why it's so exciting to work with someone like that. But, unfortunately, there aren't many of that calibre."

Filmography

1966   *Just Like a Woman* (Robert Fuest)
1967   *Billion Dollar Brain* (Ken Russell)
1968   *The Magus* (Guy Green)
1969   *Women in Love* (Ken Russell)
1970   *Two Gentlemen Sharing* (Ted Kotcheff)
      Tam Lin (Roddy McDowell)
1971   *Sunday Bloody Sunday* (John Schlesinger)
1972   *Pope Joan* (Michael Anderson)
      X Y & Zee (Brian Hutton)
1973   *Night Watch* (Brian Hutton)
      Kid Blue (James Frawley)
      The Devil's Advocate (Guy Greene)
      Glass Menagerie (Anthony Harvey)
      The Excorcist (William Friedkin)
1975   *The Wind and the Lion* (John Milius)
1976   *Voyage of the Damned* (Stuart Rosenberg)
1978   *Eagle's Wing* (Anthony Harvey)

Boardwalk (Steven Verona)
Saturn 3 (Stanley Donen)
1979 *Going in Style* (Martin Brest)
The Silent Partner (Daryl Duke)
1982 *On Golden Pond* (Mark Rydell)
1983 *Monsignor* (Frank Perry)
Gandhi (Richard Attenborough)

YVES YERSIN

Few films provoke audiences to applaud in the middle of their screenings, but *Les Petites Fugues,* a sleeper at the 1979 Cannes Film Festival, was interrupted several times by such applause. This film of exquisite beauty and sentiment tells of the "little escapes" made by a sixty-six-year-old worker in Switzerland, on a motor bike financed by his retirement pension, into the unknown world outside his farm.

Les Petites Fugues was the first feature film by Yves Yersin, whose previous work had consisted solely of ethnographic documentaries. Yersin has the documentarian's eye for small details that evoke an experience and describe a culture. Having abandoned documentary for fiction, *Les Petites Fugues* offered Yersin the opportunity to use a "given situation and project onto it all that we are. This permits us to mix different kinds of information and reshape them without any sociological or ethnographical considerations."

He is considering yet another career shift, however: "I presently find myself very attracted to the theater and by more abstract films because I find myself tied up to reality in fiction film. Before I made this fiction film, I made many ethnographic documentary films. During the last ten years in which I made these films, I tried to find images which were faithful to reality. But what I'm saying is, I did not give an image of reality; I tried to find images which were faithful to reality. I'm discovering that fiction can be truer than documentary. I also do television and film political documentary to make it more readable. I think it's more interesting, culturally, to give my subjective vision, my perception of what reality is, rather than to try to film a reality which doesn't exist—an objective reality."

Filmography

1965 *Le Panier à Viande*
1966 *Les Cloches de Vache*
1967 *Le Licou*

Chaines et Clous
Valvieja
Le Tennerie de la Sarraz
Angele
1968 *Celui Qui Dit Non*
Le Huilier
1969 *Les Boites à Vacherin*
Les Sangles à Vacherin
Une Fromagerie du Jura
Le Cordonnier Ambulant du Loetschental
La Chapelière du Loetschental
Le Four en Pierre Olaire
1972 *La Passementerie*
1973 *Les Derniers Passementiers*
1976 *Le Reveil de L'Ordre*
Le Prix d'un Divorce
1979 *Les Petites Fugues*

KRZYSZTOF ZANUSSI

It's not hard to imagine Krzysztof Zanussi in his earlier professions: physics and philosophy. He has the air of a gentleman professor who spends most of his time musing about the mysteries of the quark. But intellectualism for its own sake, unennobled by the humanizing influence of art, does not suffice: "Before I was making films I was somehow disappointed, and had this feeling that this is not my way. I was doing many things. I had studied physics and philosophy, and was doing amateur theater, writing a little bit, a bit of journalism, but . . . Then I did eight- and sixteen-millimeter films, which were fun. I won a few prizes and decided to try film academy, which is very selective, with a very competitive entrance exam. I decided to try it but I didn't take it very seriously. I was still continuing my university studies. I also felt very disappointed by philosophy in the way that it was only an expression of my argument, reaching only my rational aspect. As a human being I have other elements, other levels. There are so many other levels of communication. I'd like to communicate with people's senses, people's guts, as much as with their brains, and, in that sense, film seemed to me to be an interesting and very unintellectual medium, not expressing arguments and ideas in a clear way."

Zanussi has learned a lesson from physics: "Whatever has not been proven wrong may be right." His films exclude no possibilities in context or in form, they never stop at appearances, at the reductive, pat explanations of human motivation or behavior. His moving explorations of a character or characters take us through many possibilities. For Zanussi, all art has to remain "ambiguous, appealing to our integral personality. All the rest, which are easy to describe in words, are just something unimportant."

Filmography

1966   *Death of a Provincial*
1967   *Face to Face*
1969   *The Structure of Crystals*

1970 *Family Life*
1971 *Behind the Wall*
1973 *Illumination*
1974 *The Catamount Killing*
1975 *A Woman's Decision*
1977 *Camouflage*
1978 *Spiral*
1980 *The Constant Factor*
1982 *Wege in der Nacht Contract*

·2·

CINEMATOGRAPHY

Cinema's primary fascination is its ability to create the illusion of reality in motion. The human body makes that illusion possible with the eyes' ability to retain an image longer than its actual presence, an optical illusion known as "persistency of vision." Despite the fact that the camera shutter is opening and closing, alternating light and dark as it photographs slightly different images at the rate of twenty-four frames per second, we retain each image long enough to create the effect of a continuity of action. If the film strip is projected at a rate slower than it was photographed, the result is an effect of slow motion; if it is projected faster, the effect is one of fast motion.

The image is impressed on film stock that is emulsified to create sensitivity to light. "Faster" film is more sensitive and therefore requires less light on the subject to create an image. "Slower" film is less light-sensitive but produces a clearer, less grainy image with a more balanced contrast of light and dark. Awareness of the various effects possible with each kind of film stock enables the cinematographer to create a variety of moods, even to provide information to the viewer. For example, one type of film stock could be used throughout a film except for a dream sequence, which would be signaled by using a noticeably different stock.

Film is as much an art of illumination as it is anything else; it is light that allows the viewer to see the images composed within the camera frame, and the quality of illumination, whether natural or artificial, gives the image its special character and mood. The lighting design is primarily the responsibility of the director of photography; he determines the correct exposure for an image by computing the rating of the film stock, the intensity of light illuminating the subject, and the opening of the lens. The most critical consideration is to light in depth, that is, to create planes of light in order to produce an image that appears to be three-dimensional, thereby furthering the illusion that we are seeing reality moving before us. The three key elements in illumination are intensity of lighting, by which the director of photography "paints in" relative light and dark areas to create depth in the frame; the direction of light, which has a dramatic effect on the character and mood of the image; and the character of the light, which can range from clear to hazy with red or blue tones, also critically affecting, even creating, mood.

Even before issues of composition and lighting are settled, the choice of lens must be made. The lens is quite literally the eye of the camera through which the image is perceived. There are a wide variety of lenses, including the zoom lens, which contains characteristics of many lenses in one. The properties of lenses include size of lens, which varies from long to short to close-up and is measured in millimeters, and depth of field, which refers to the range of sharpness before and behind the plane of focus. Depth of field has tremendous aesthetic import in that we are not only directed to the areas of the image that are the sharpest, but our affective response to that image is also controlled greatly by the depth of field. In fact, the size of the lens per se is not as important as its effect on depth of field. For example, the wider the lens, the greater the depth of field. A third property of lenses is "freedom from linear distortion." In general, wider lenses create more distortion of the image. Finally, we consider the effect of the lens on movement. Distortion of movement is called the "telescopic effect." As the focal length of the lens increases, movement to and from the camera seems to contract; conversely, as focal length decreases, movement to and from the camera seems to expand.

Because of the possible distortions mentioned above in longer or wider lenses, many filmmakers prefer to stay within what is known as "normal" range, thus illustrating once again the general objective of preserving a look of normal reality from which one departs only with specific aesthetic intent.

The same trend toward naturalness or normalcy holds in the area of lighting. Although elaborate lighting equipment is no exception to the increasingly sophisticated technological aspects of motion pictures, many filmmakers consider their form to be "techno-ridden," that is, weighed down by heavy, intricate equipment. Both Nestor Almendros and Billy Williams, certainly among the best cinematographers today, espouse skillfully used natural lighting whenever possible.

Composition of the elements in motion pictures is continually changing, either through the arrangement of the elements within the frame, through the movements of these elements, through movement of the camera frame itself, or through a combination of the above. It is this unique composition in flux that gives film its characteristic rhythm and continual motion. Since camera technique is as much a function of what the filmmaker wants to say as it is an expression of his attitude toward his art, the filmmakers offer some interesting and often contending notions concerning what is art and what is unjustified manipulation of the viewer through camera technique.

Long shots, close-ups, and medium shots could be termed the visual "grammar" of film. Conventionally, a close-up makes a large comment, taking the viewer right into the actor's face and, thus, emotions; a medium shot is used to establish the scene; and a long shot, including the most material, gives the viewer the greatest amount of information. Cutting from one type of shot to another can be shocking to the viewer, tending to attract his attention and elicit some emotional reaction. In a sense, however, the filmmaker should learn his techniques and then forget them, because he is dealing less with technique than with realizing his vision.

For this reason, many filmmakers scoff at purist notions concerning cinematic technique. For example, some simply believe that shots derive from dialogue. If the dialogue is long, then the shot is longer. They reject "stone age" theories such as underlining a change of feeling or of content by cutting to another shot. Others consider camera movements as coming from something almost unconscious, not part of a rational sphere of choice, emerging as they do from a kind of anxiety within the filmmaker that must be expressed. At the most extreme, a filmmaker improvises his camera movements, finding himself within a situation, within a space, and deciding the best angle, the best way to move, the best time to stop; that is, he relies on his instincts. Since camera technique arises out of what the filmmaker is trying to do, there are no rules, only techniques that tend to create certain effects within certain contexts. But there are issues.

One such issue revolves around how long a shot should be held. Should the frame be held steady as the actors play out the action and dialogue so that the viewer's eye focuses where he chooses? Or should the viewer's eye be directed by the filmmaker through camera movements, change of focus, and cuts that underline every meaningful moment? And is it even possible to avoid manipulation of the viewer in this mechanical art wherein the choice of subject and attitude toward that subject is the filmmaker's, and we, the viewers, have paid money to witness his vision of reality, offered ourselves up, in a sense, to be manipulated?

Another issue concerns the camera frame itself. Does it offer artistic freedom to the filmmaker through its four-sided limitation? Is it a control within which it is possible to create one's vision of reality? Or is that restriction a frustration, a limitation on one's ability to show reality in motion? For some filmmakers, this limit is welcome because it allows for a paring down of material, a means of reducing one's expression to the most essential, thereby giving the film validity as art. It is a means to organize, a way of progressing from frame to frame, offering the viewer new information with each subtle change of image. For others, the frame provides a key for "reading" the film, a way of allowing the viewer to see better because the image is isolated from its context by that frame. Finally, the limits of the frame are what distinguish the image captured by the camera from what we see around us in everyday reality. As Emile de Antonio says, "It's a means of both isolating and bringing together the elements you really want. The frame is like the word in a lot of poetry." And the choice of frame, like the choice of the word, belongs to the artist. It is his means of control.

Rather than imprisoning its elements, the camera frame can liberate them—that is, if the composition is flexible and flowing rather than static. Filmmakers can suggest the world that continues outside the frame by many techniques, some conventional, others unique to their own plastic sense of space. For example, having actors move in and out of the frame while continuing to record their off-frame dialogue extends the frame, as does the device of including only a part of an object or human figure within the frame, suggesting the rest of that presence continues beyond its boundaries. Choice of focal depth often suggests what lies outside the frame: whether or not background is obliterated and the relationship between foreground and background effect our experience of the frame as either contained or expanded. There may be a visual limitation but that does not necessarily imply an intellectual limitation. An exploration of what lies outside that frame can say a great deal about what lies within and may be even more important. By framing things, the filmmaker can make a statement about them; he can explore, choose, and magnify. Through the camera frame—what Nestor Almendros calls "an instrument of analysis"—the filmmaker brings his vision to life.

Since the choice of frames is such a critical consideration, a related issue concerns who has the responsibility for that choice. Conventionally, the director confers with the director of photography concerning lighting and camera position and angle, relegating the actual running of the camera to the cameraman, but opinions range all the way from Perry Henzel's attitude—"I like to take the attitude that it's my job to set up something worth shooting and it's up to the cameraman to shoot it"—to Barbara Kopple's during the tension-ridden shooting of her documentary on a coal miner's strike—"In doing a documentary, particularly one that's a life-and-death struggle, the camera and tape recorder are almost a shield for you"—to Ermanno Olmi's, working in an improvisational documentary-like style, who equates the filmmaker who lets someone else run his camera to the man who lets another man make love to his beloved. One can see that the issue of whether or not the film director sets his own frames and runs his own camera is particularly interesting in that it reveals the differing concepts of the director's role vis-à-vis his subject, his co-workers, and his means of expression.

JEAN-LUC GODARD

The formulation of the framing or simple limitation of space is a question of space and the duration of the shot, where we push the study until the end of the shot. The technique is simply the point of view of the director. Having specific prejudices about certain shots like medium shots is like saying you hate Jews or Black people. You can only say something like that in relation to a specific condition where the shot is of no use.

As a general rule I use 30 to 40mm lenses. That gives the impression of close-up but at the same time keeps precision, focal depth, and perspective. Fifty millimeter at closer perspective already destroys the focal depth and is more impressionistic, similar to Manet, who saw first through "30mm" then through "50mm."

With video I have become interested again in the zoom lens, but in a different way. In 35mm it's more difficult to use because the equipment is so huge. That's why I like the new smaller electronic equipment that you can use like Super 8mm equipment, but with 35mm film stock. The zoom was used mainly by TV people, who used it poorly. You should use only two or three parts of the zoom. You shouldn't use it continually, obtrusively. Sometimes the zoom is a comfortable way and a quicker method than thinking about what to do and it's utilized a bit stupidly because people use it for its ease. Sometimes it is good not to use the zoom but to use two or three cameras, each with their own lens, and to know when they have to close in or to be at a distance. I am more of an amateur from this point of view and I use the means of the amateur, which I try to employ professionally.

Everyman for Himself was shot in 35mm and the zoom lenses in 35mm are enormous. They are bigger than the camera and that stops all possibility to move, to put the camera somewhere or to think even to put it somewhere. It is too difficult and you cannot use the zoom in a correct manner in 35mm.

The zoom can be used in amateur films, where it replaces the various lenses for reasons of convenience even if they don't zoom. They can change lenses without unscrewing one and replacing it with another. This method has come to interest me gradually, after I became disgusted with the way it has been used for television, where it is employed to get closer or farther: to get close because the cameraman is bored or asks himself why he is far away, or when he gets close he asks himself why he's there, as well. The problem is to spend time.

In *Everyman for Himself* there's a lot of movement and a lot of slow motion, and there the zoom would have been interesting because the changing of speed would also have enlarged the field of vision. You have time to see more, and to change the frame as you change the speed would create a different kind of movement. In the editing machine the footage is analyzed and one sees certain elements that belong to the script. For example, in the scene where Isabelle Huppert is spanked, you could see more of the girl than the men. If I had a zoom, I would have wanted to make a sort of turning movement to get closer and to find a good speed, which makes that movement slow down, and decompose the landscape, which has no one in it but has forms and colors.

I also don't like the way slow motion is used, just as tricks, for no reason. Anyone who is running is filmed in slow motion. What is interesting to discover is that the usual speed is just the speed for some. In life sometimes you do something slowly and sometimes you do it fast. You have different speeds. Today, TV and movies are bad because everything is on the same speed, whether it's De Niro in Scorsese's movies or Walter Cronkite on CBS. They're acting in the same speed, so there's no rhythm.

MARTIN SCORSESE

What you put in the frame is a major decision. You can just put an arm in the side of the frame, and the audience will expect something else to happen. Or you could pan over and include the head or pan over to include the whole body, but it's important if you decide to just leave the arm in, or the hand, or the finger, or not at all. I love the restrictions of the frame. I also enjoy putting titles over the picture saying who everybody is, what year it is, where they are. And I'm sick and tired of playing trick games with cuts that will be very, very beautiful but where are we? "Ah ha, flashback!" That sort of thing. The way transitions are shown by cutting to a certain thing and everything goes out of focus and then gets back into focus, or you do a dissolve. There are no dissolves in *Raging Bull;* it's all straight cuts. The title comes up "1956" and that's the best way to do that type of thing. The point is to use it all for clarity, so you can say, "Now here's where we are, let's go."

Similarly, where I place the camera is very often determined by having to relay the right information. You may literally have to show that a person does open the door and come in. It may behoove you to show him come through the door: he opens it, closes it, and sits down at the table. But, who knows, maybe you can do it with sound effects: just have the sound effect of a closing door. It can be done many different ways; it depends what the scene develops to.

But it's really a matter of the angle, even when you're moving the camera. It's important on the level of how much information, how much you want the audience to see, and somehow there's an emotional thing too. I prefer to use longer takes, to let things play out, definitely. The only thing is sometimes I wish I didn't have to cut them up. But I think that's a kind of ego thing; it gets to a point where it's very ego-centered, only because we know that the greatest directors like Renoir, Ford, Hitchcock, and Mizoguchi—all the boys there—very often let it play for a long time. Even Nick Ray and Sam Fuller did that. The rhythm and everything is there in those shots. They're great, but somehow it seems an older style of filmmaking. Maybe because cameras and technique have changed and because we are not the old-style directors anymore—certain groups of us are not, I should say. We don't see things that way. We go for other values. I'd rather cut to an actor if he gave a line better in another take. Even if the inflection in *one* word was better or there was a certain look on his face, I'd rather cut into that shot for that word or that look. So what if we did the master shot in one take and the acting was pretty good? But if the acting was better in another angle, even if nobody would ever know that—the acting was fine in the master—*I* know that it was better in the closer shot, and it made me feel a certain way, so it has to be used.

The master shot is at times almost just for me, so that I can know where everything is, and I often get new ideas from watching it a couple of times. The only things I don't particularly care for are fast zooms and long lens shots. I don't like the impact of that flattened image. If I do use that, it's used for a special effect and it isn't obvious either. I prefer a normal lens, a little wide angle, as long as I don't get close to the person and it makes them look fat or ugly—a 32mm basically, around there.

But even though I try to keep a normal look to dramatic scenes, they have an effect: it's where you place the camera, the lighting, the look of the film; it's what's on the table, it's what's in the foreground, and what's in the background. And if we want to make really tricky shots, we can easily do that. But I don't think it's worth it. Not anymore. In *Raging Bull* the fight scenes move like hell, very fast, but everything else is basically static in comparison, although not completely: there are plans, etcetera, there's a lot of movement from Jake's point of view and the use of slow motion. But I like slow motion in other ways than the obvious, just a little bit of running the camera at high speed, sometimes more so, but it's just to point out how Jake sees things.

Basically, if a shot doesn't interest me, if an angle doesn't interest me, I hate it. There has to be something special for me in each shot: whether it's the size of the people or the foreground or the background or the way people move in and out of the frame. It has to be something special. I just don't put the camera there. It's a strange kind of simplicity at times and also extremely complex. Where I set the camera is just something I feel.

ERIC ROHMER

The director of photography is very important in my films. Usually there are two people who work on the photography, one who does the lighting and the other who operates the camera, although sometimes it's the same person. Nestor Almendros is doing a film in the States right now [*Kramer vs. Kramer*], and the D.P. doesn't do both, he only does the lighting. With me, Nestor Almendros really wanted to do both because otherwise it was very difficult, since he is very precise with the framing, even more strict than myself, a strictness that can be troublesome when the actors are less than familiar with the script.

In my films, it's me who decides on the frame, who places the people, but it is he who performs the finishing touches, who gives the precision. The exactness comes from him.

In general, Almendros is very demanding; he wants something very clear and pure. Sometimes he'll even ask me to omit something, not in a film where there are very few props, as it is already a little bit naked, but in *The Marquise of O*, he left out a lot of things. He always pushes the director towards bigger ideas. I like exactness, and sometimes he made me eliminate things that were useless. That's remarkable.

I don't like diffusion and I use it rarely. I rarely use long lenses; I prefer shorter lenses, usually at the 35mm focal length, because that shows the subject at the same distance as does the eye. One should be aware that depth of field focus is where one places action on two planes or levels, otherwise there is no real *mise-en-scène*, no deeper meaning, and the actors would otherwise always be on the same plane, what we call a lateral *mise-en-scène;* there is no placement of one actor in front or behind another actor.

I like to use the same lens in a film because the audience gets used to the space more easily, relates to it better. However, in *Perceval*, which is more fake than the others since it was done in a studio, I changed the lenses more frequently, using a 50mm often, which I might add is what Bresson uses exclusively. For him, it is the rule because he wants to make the material pres-

ent and that lens brings things closer, makes them more present, more intimate. Thus, in many of the battle scenes in
Perceval, in order that the suits of armor be brought in closer, I
used the 50mm. On the other hand, in the interior scenes, I
used the 32 or 35mm because I like the characters to be situ-
ated in the scene and in full frame, but I don't like to get too
close. The 50mm is used mostly for close-ups, but you can use
it for establishing shots by placing it far away, although I don't
like to do that. I like the lines of energy to run away somewhat;
I like a more open point of view; I like the frame to be more
open.

I don't like static frames, frames that congeal things. I don't
like those perfect compositions where a lamp is placed in the
corner and then balanced with something else. The framing
should liberate forms, rather than imprison them, and should
indicate the lines of energy, not only in the frame but the entire space filmed and imagined—what we call the infinite space
of the film. The interior composition should be flexible, even
flowing, not rigorous.

However, in *Perceval* and *The Marquise of O*, I was much more
precise and rigorous than in other films, because these were
films of the more plastic or pictorial arts, and, consequently,
required much more precision in the placing of the people. In
Perceval, I wasn't so preoccupied with the frame, as it was a
rather simple, classic frame. I was much more interested in the
internal organization of the frame. The problem was to translate the world of the romantic paintings with the miniature
stained glass windows and the sculptured columns, for example, into a rectangular format. At that time, one did not use the
rectangle as much as one used a curved line to represent the
world, or better, a circle or even a spiral, as in those famous
Irish manuscripts that are so beautiful and are used as wall
decorations.

So, one solution could have been to introduce a round frame
inside of the rectangular frame of the screen. But that seems to
me to be a static solution that would have to be reconstructed
to work on the screen. But in film, I don't think you can simply
work on the forms, because it is a realistic art, with realistic

points of view, and when you try to manipulate forms, especially living forms, you end up with something very superficial and old-fashioned. For example, in some expressionistic films there is very plastic distortion, which gives a very artificial impression. I think that rather than working solely on the image, you must operate on the dynamic of the image, that is, the orientation of the lines of energy, particularly where they cross or where they take you on the horizontal surface of the frame. If there is a curved space in my film, it is not the vertical screen that makes it exist, but the space as filmed that is curved, and the "travels" which follow are parallel. In *Perceval*, the shortest distance between two points is not a straight line, but a curved one. In the Middle Ages, when men fought, they didn't go straight ahead, they turned continuously, and that is the solution I found after much hesitation. This solution has stayed with me, and forms a part of all my work.

There are several rhythms: the rhythm of the play, the cutting rhythm, but I take a lot from the movements of the actors themselves. I place the camera and the actors play the scene. I don't think about cutting in advance: the main rhythm is that of the actors themselves within the play.

NESTOR ALMENDROS

I think you do need the frame, otherwise, if there are no limits, there's no artistic transposition. I think the frame is a great discovery. The stone age men of Lascaux or Altamira did not frame their cave paintings. Someone said that what counts is not what you see but what you don't see. What's interesting about the frame is what you frame out, not only what you frame in. By eliminating several things around the subject, you concentrate on what counts. I believe a lot in the frame. That's why I'm against some experiences of "total cinema" on a dome with no edges.

Actually I'm almost as excited when I work with a frame as with the lights, although a director of photography is supposed mainly to worry about the lighting. I do care about the frame on a film, and that's why I like to be my own camera operator any time I can. You're not only selecting, but organizing things in relation to the verticals and horizontals in which they exist. *Then* things suddenly become relevant. I've noticed that every time I see something when I'm making a movie, this something only becomes relevant when I am on the viewfinder and I have a frame. And that is why I think the camera operator has the best job on the movie crew. Not only is he the first to see the film, but, by looking through the viewfinder, everything suddenly takes shape. He instantly knows what's wrong, what's right. It's like a microscope. It's an instrument of analysis: by blocking out everything else, you just focus on what counts.

If I have chosen to do a certain movie with a director, it's because I've already seen a movie or two or several of his and I know what his style is, and I evaluate if it belongs to my way too, because I'm not going to work with a person from whom I'm distant, have nothing in common.

Although the director normally proposes a shot, I like to comment on this first idea he developed and maybe make a change. I will say, for instance, "Well, why don't we use instead of a 50mm lens, a 40 or a 75?" or "Let's get closer" or "farther from the subject"—discuss the shot. There, of course, I have an influence, as in the choice of the colors of the set or the choice of the actors' sides. There's an influence, yes, but it depends on the director too. Some don't like to discuss anything. I have found out in my career that the less arrogant ones are often the best, as well.

Many directors of photography want to make others believe that what they do is more difficult than it is, perhaps to justify their high salaries, and they like to feel important by splitting hairs, but nature is right as it is. Yet they try to have big crews with lots of lights and equipment, pretending that they're doing something very special. It might be lack of imagination, but I get my inspiration in lighting from nature. When I get to a set which is a natural set, I try to use the real sources of light if I can. If the set is built in studios, I try to imagine how it would be lit if it were a real place, where would the light come from in a real situation, and then, starting from that, I light a scene.

I also use a single source of light, because in nature light is that way. Very seldom do you have several sources of light like in the old movies of the forties, where you had a little light in the back, enhancing the hair, and another one on the side, and still another for backgrounds, and one for the shirt. This exists very seldom in real life. Normally, in a room you get light coming from a window or light coming from a lamp, one light or two, that's all. It's analogous to people's criticism of early Technicolor as being too brilliant, but it was gaudy because of the art direction, not because the early color system was gaudy. It wasn't the process itself. It's the same as with early color television. They used to put lots of colors in the costumes because they wanted to get it for their money. In the beginning, if it was a color movie, you had to give them color. You would have in the same frame a woman with pink clothes, another with red, and another with green—hard to believe, especially in a period when textiles didn't have that many vivid colors.

So there haven't actually been that many changes in the technology. Cameras haven't changed basically too much in the last forty years, only in their size. I used the Steadycam/Panaglide for *Days of Heaven* and for *Kramer vs. Kramer;* it's good for certain things but not for everything. It has its limitations.

There have been only two important changes. One of them has been fast lenses, which can register images at a very low level of light. The other is the "pushing" of film at the laboratory, the overdeveloping that allows you to give more speed to the film. That has created some kind of revolution. In *Days of Heaven* I used a fast film combined with fast lenses, the technique also used in Kubrick's *Barry Lyndon.*

I like to compare this revolution of fast lenses plus pushed development to painting. When they started making tubes of paint, painters could go and catch changing light outdoors. That's when Impressionism came in. Impressionism also came out of a technological discovery, which was the tube of oil paint, as opposed to being limited to paint you had to prepare and mix yourself. The tubes were now ready-made, so you just

took them in a box, went any place. You could just paint Notre
Dame at different hours of the day as Monet did, because you
carried your own ready-made paints. So, in the case of cinematographers as well: if we are doing things now that were
not done before, it is not only because of a revolution out of
our genius or intellect, but also because nowadays you can do
things you could not do before. Maybe people in the past
wanted to film with extreme levels of light, but they could not,
especially with early color film that was so slow. Technicolor
was so slow at the time that they had to light a scene where the
characters are carrying lanterns with so much light that the lanterns are just props—they light nothing. Now, as I did in *Adele
H.* and the mining scene in *Goin' South,* they carry lanterns that
really do light the scene as a source, because the filling light I
added was a minor intensity compared to the light coming
from the lanterns.

On the subject of shot length I am very eclectic. I like montage: I like it a lot. I am attracted to it. I think it's a heritage
that we have since Griffith, et al. We should not throw it away.
I'm very delighted when I see a modern movie like *An American
Friend* by Wim Wenders, in which he went back to the editing. I
love the mathematics, the precision, the choreography of editing as it was practiced by those who came from silent cinema,
such as Hitchcock. But I also like very much, for instance,
Cukor movies like *Adam's Rib,* in which there is practically no
editing.

Until now I have preferred to mention films I haven't done
so I have a distance, but in talking about the ones I have
worked in, I would say that Rohmer edits very little and he's
more in the George Cukor school. I enjoy working with him
enormously because of the fact that the actors move in the
frame and create a variety of compositions without the camera
moving. You know, when the actors move inside the frame,
every second they make a new composition; that's why with
Rohmer there's only a little panning here and there. You let
the actors act, without disrupting them by cutting, without enhancing or shortening their performances. It's just the truth,
it's there. If it's good, it's excellent; if it's bad, it's terrible. I

mean, a bad director will do a long take, and if it's too slow or too fast—if the timing is wrong—there's nothing you can do. Because you cannot cut it, you cannot shorten or expand it, so you have to be perfect in directing your actors and their positions in relation to the camera. You have to get it right. Whereas, if you bombard the same scene with the camera, shooting from all different angles, what they call "coverage" in Hollywood, you can always fix it up later on the editing table. "Fly now, pay later." Of course, that's a weakness; it's a weakness on the part of the director if he *has* to do that. Ideally, a director should know where the camera should be at any moment in any kind of situation. There are people like Wenders or Truffaut who use editing, but they don't multiply the angles just to see what they can do afterwards on the editing table. No, they conceive scenes and film them *one* way. The form of the film comes from the concept. If there's no concept to begin with, there's no style.

For example, many times directors just use a close-up because they don't know what they're doing: they don't use it with an idea behind it—alas! Rohmer doesn't like close-ups. He makes very few. In everything he does, he keeps close-ups for a very strong moment and there's only one or two in a whole movie. In *My Night at Maud's* there's only one real big close-up. He knows that close-up exaggerates things. It makes them stronger, more powerful, and if you multiply them in the film too often, the moment you want to stress, to underline something, then it's not effective anymore because you've been underlining all the time. If you use them seldom, the moment there's a close-up, that close-up becomes very powerful.

BILLY WILLIAMS

The frame is the visual opportunity to express the written word. One starts off with a script which then becomes a director's vision. It then takes on life when you have the actors in front of you, rehearsing. Then you have to decide where you're going to put the camera, how close, how far, and break it down into images that will cut together to capture the essence of that scene. So, the frame is not a limitation, the frame is an opportunity. It *is* restricting what you see, you *are* excluding certain things, but it's *what* you include, what you frame for, that makes the opportunity. And I don't like things to be too neatly framed. One likes to suggest that things go on. Take that piece of furniture there [a rectangular chest in the room where the interview took place]. Just by cutting it at a certain point, you suggest that it goes on without seeing it go on, because if you pull back to see how long it is, somehow you might weaken the composition.

I regard a most important part of my job as directing the attention of the viewer to whatever you want them to look at, which is done by composition, movement, and light. This means sometimes you may go for a lot of space with little in it, or you might just place something a long way away in silhouette. But because it's the only thing in silhouette, your eye will go straight to it, although it's very small on the screen. This is all part of directing the audience's attention. What I hate is muddled composition, and one sees it a lot. You're presented with a shot, a picture, and you're not sure of what you're supposed to look at. Obviously, if you're shooting a crowd scene and you're shooting establishing shots, then you'll be more general, but, as a scene develops, you've got to be more specific, to the point where although there might be a lot of other elements in the frame, the eye of the audience is going to go to the thing you want them to look at, rather than the elements that are less important.

By the choice of position of the camera, the lens, the light, you can make the same place look quite different at different times of the day. That's why it's important to make the right selection and not just go to a place and stick the camera somewhere and shoot whatever you happen to have. I think if you're making a film that is relying on strong visual qualities, you have to be very selective.

For example, we shot *Eagle's Wing*, a dramatic film, in Mexico, and one has remarkably dramatic skies at certain times of the evening, very black and blue combined with the dramatic landscape. There was one scene where the character comes upon a strange scene, which is an Indian burial ground where a chief has just been killed and the shaman, the witch doctor, is going through the ritual, destroying all the chief's possessions, and he's about to destroy this beautiful white stallion and Martin Sheen stops him. We had these strange totem poles with dead Indians hanging from them. To have shot it in bright daylight would've meant losing a great deal of the atmosphere, so I shot it over a span of four or five evenings just before it got dark, which was a very difficult matching problem. But the scene, about five or six minutes long, has a very strange, eerie quality. Had it not been done at that time of day, the scene would've lost a great deal of its dramatic energy. It would've been just an ordinary scene. But we shot it just before it was dark because the sky at that time is very exciting, particularly when you're looking west, before it goes orange and becomes all romantic. I could only shoot two minutes a night. And I had a similar experience on *Women in Love* where I had to shoot over a long time a scene that ran several minutes: the drowning of the young couple in the lake where he dives in, frantically trying to save them. It was a long scene and you can't get that sort of thing in one evening.

When I am working on an interior set, I prefer to work from the source, to get the source of the light correct, to make it look as if the light is coming from that lamp or in the window. But I build other light in, so that you don't have tremendous imbalance. I don't like flared-up windows or burnt-out lamps, because I think they take away from the faces of the actors, particularly on interiors or when you're working very close. One doesn't want to be distracted too much from the face of the artist. And, also, I think there's a lot of photography where people are played against a very bright window to the extent that their faces are so in shadow that you can't see their expression. Well, that's fine, occasionally. It's great to use silhouettes for effect, but I think it's very dangerous to play a long dialogue scene like this, particularly when you have to contend with the sort of projection quality we have these days. If you produce a negative that is only just on the edge in terms of exposure, then it's not going to reproduce unless it's shown under perfect conditions. So, you do have to, I think, create a negative that will stand up to a certain amount of imperfection. One does aim for the ultimate, but one has to be very careful not to go to such depth of shadow that a lot of cinemas are just not going to record what you have done.

We're able to go to wonderful interior locations now because more lightweight equipment makes you more mobile. Now with fast lenses and lightweight lights, a new approach has been possible towards filming on location. The film stock has also greatly improved: it has wonderful latitude, good tonal range, and flexibility. But you still have to have originality and imagination or things go stale. Equipment like that does open up more opportunities, but I think we're reaching the point where equipment isn't necessarily the final answer. If you have great locations though—and I don't mean pretty, pretty picture postcard locations, because that's something I always try to avoid—but if you have great exterior locations, they do present more opportunity to exploit the resources that are there than do studio interiors. But in terms of lighting, studio interiors do offer more full control over what you're doing.

It's always an advantage to have sufficient time to go through preparation before the shooting to discuss how the director sees the film, the contribution of the art director, to visit the locations, to see the set designs, because only when you start getting these things together and having discussions with the director can you form a vision of how the film will look. I think it particularly applies to location work because the locations are so varied and you can go to those locations and make them look quite different depending on where you place the camera, the time of day, etcetera. In the same way when you walk onto a set, you choose the angles and think of the most suitable and the most interesting angles. It's an ongoing process that is initiated during the preproduction stage when there's much less pressure on. There's much more pressure, of course, when you're shooting, so that you have to have agreed on certain things before you start. But, at the same time, you should leave room for improvisation, for improved ideas, which should always be incorporated. I don't think one should preplan things so precisely that when something extra comes up, you're not in the position to accept it.

I look upon *my* work as an added emotional quality to the script, what the actors are doing, and the way the director is handling the scene. Through framing and composition and the control of light, one can add an extra emotional quality that can sometimes be very powerful. But, in doing that, one has to be able to control it, so that you know where to use it at its most effective.

But a lot does depend on the director, because if one has a good director-cameraman relationship, a good understanding, then one can create wonderful things. It's very much like a man-wife relationship, where you're stuck together for however many weeks, you're very close, you depend upon each other, you have your differences of opinion, you're a sounding board for each other over the whole visual concept of the film. The director has other areas to which he's responsible, of course, but in the visual area, the director's closest ally is the cameraman, and he must build up confidence in him and they must communicate and express their ideas. Where you really have two people prepared to go for broke, to really go for effect, then you come up with good things. For instance, when I shot those scenes that were the first ten minutes of *The Exorcist*, the rest of the film had been finished, and I hadn't seen it—all I'd seen was a few shots. I had not met Billy Friedkin until we met at an airport on our flight to Iraq. I had been to Iraq once before, so I knew the area, but it wasn't until we got there and started traveling around, looking at everything, that we really got to grips with it. And he said to me, "Shoot this however you want. Make it the most exciting, mysterious, beautiful-looking material you can. Don't attempt to match anything that's gone before in the other part of the film. Don't think about that at all. Just take this ten-minute selection and get the best you can from this short bit." And it stood up in its own right. That was a very satisfying piece, although it was only about ten minutes long.

I think a sign of inexperience on the part of the director is a lack of pacing of a scene: at what pace should it be played, how long a shot should be sustained. A lot of inexperienced directors try to hold a shot too long because they get so fascinated by what they're doing that they don't always consider the audience. If you make a shot slow-paced, in terms of what it has to encompass, unless you give yourself a cutaway, then that's going to be the length of the shot, whether it's the length of time it takes an actor to say a certain number of words or whether it's the length of time it takes for the camera to go from over here to there, or the way in which the camera accomplishes a certain exposition. In other words, you've got to say a number of things visually, without dialogue, and you can do it by a certain kind of shorthand, by choice of lens and setup, or you can do it and make it last much longer, still only telling the same thing. You are saying things without words, telling the audience things by what you do with the camera. You're giving the audience information with every setup that you choose. Now, if you take too long with that, if you're too languid, too slow-moving, then you're going to lower the general pace, you're going to make it longer and possibly be boring. And I think this is a fault with younger directors.

I'm not too keen on too much coverage: there are only so many good setups to be gained from a scene, and overcoverage will often result in a certain number of mediocre shots. But here one is in the hands of the director: there are certain directors who do not cover a great deal. I like to work with a director who's fairly sure of what he wants and doesn't overcover, but they're all different, and every film is different. Some films are more dependent on cutting than others.

Ultimately, it depends on the scene. I prefer to move the camera and create an image that is evolving and developing and introducing fresh points of interest, and I like to move the camera in conjunction with the characters. If you plan these things properly, you can sometimes sustain a shot for a long time without a cut, and sustain it without losing interest. But other scenes are much more dependent on cutting, particularly scenes where people are just sitting down. Then it's better to cut; I don't particularly like the camera wandering around the room too much when people are just sitting still. If it happens too much, it can be a distraction. I do think, however, that once you've set up, at a certain point in a scene you very often have to know where you are in relationship to the geography of a room or the place you're in, so that at some point or another, you're going to "be wide." But there's no reason why you shouldn't incorporate a wide shot by moving in or following somebody, by getting closer and drifting in and out of door-ways or whatever—introducing a flow to things. I think if you just stay back, there are times that you want to get close to the actors. There are certain moments when you want to get close to them to read their expression better. You can't read people's expression if you stay in a long shot. I think one needs fewer close-ups though. It is overused, especially on television, and I don't think one needs such big close-ups, because you're look-ing at them on a big screen. There are huge close-ups that I've seen that should be used very sparingly, but, at times, they can be enormously effective.

Again, it depends on the subject, but I think one shouldn't be too inhibited about using different focal lengths, because you can't get everything with just a couple of lenses. I do have a preference for wide-angle lenses. I'm not particularly keen on the overuse of long lenses; they flatten things out too much, bring things close together, and I like to achieve a greater sepa-ration between the actor and the background. Although they do limit the focus, they sometimes bring the background close to the point where it seems distracting.

I also don't see any reason why one shouldn't change the lighting style for certain scenes, because different places look different. I've never believed in just following a lighting style because that's the way you might prefer to work. Night exteri-ors, for instance, have to be lit entirely differently than day exteriors. And I think there is a whole range of ways one can express oneself by the way that the light is handled, To vary the treatment of ways in which different scenes are lit helps to create an added interest, in that I don't think everything should look the same all the way through. I'm not preaching a disunity of style; I'm saying different techniques can be incorporated into a film that will make the film much more interesting.

JEAN ROUCH

I am very different when I'm with a camera, and this provocation of the camera is very important. So, I must shoot *myself*.

When I shot my first film with Michel Brook in 1960, *Chronicle of a Summer,* at the time we were making a camera which became the Eclair. We were just checking it at the time, and Chris Marker shot *Le Joli Mai* just one year later. But I remember quite well. It was fantastic. We were shooting during the day, every evening going back to the factory and saying to the man, "Well, there's some trouble here." And they were repairing the camera during the night and we were shooting the day after. The camera was born at the same time the film was born. I think that's very important. Of course, a lot of films are not made in this way. I've a lot of admiration for Renoir, Godard, people like that, who are using a very good staff of cameramen and so on, but from my point of view, I was obliged to be alone.

We are all around the world; we are maybe ten people making films in this way: the Maysles, Ricky Leacock, John Marshall, Pennebaker, Timor T. Ash, Sandal Sauzer, a man from Estonia, Buldanski, who's from Brazil. We are a small gang of people doing the same thing, not so many. A small international gang.

But what is interesting in Super 8 is that you need very sharp camera lenses. For example, a man like Bauer, who is a German Super 8 filmmaker, is working on this problem, and soon there will be very, very sharp lenses for Super 8. There will be improvement in the coming years. We need this because—it depends on what we are working—but we usually shoot more with wide-angle lenses in order to be close to the people we film. We call this *"la camera de contact,"* which means we are at arm's length from the subject.

I move with the camera, but I cannot explain the way I move. It's in connection with the subject. For example, I was shooting Margaret Mead in the Museum of Natural History. We were in the department of pre-history, among the dinosaurs, and I said to her, "Well now, Margaret, we have spoken about the past, now we can go outside to the park to speak of the future." Then I was walking with her in this big hall to go outside and she was wearing this big blue cape and on the wall was a drawing of a big prehistoric bat, and it was quite nice. As she was walking by the drawing, I stopped, let her go out of frame, and panned to the bat. I just did it because I saw it in the viewfinder. It's impossible to say to a cameraman in the middle of a shot to stop and go "there." He would never think of it and you would have to stage it that way. I'm sure in the coming years, films will be done this way. There will be some people who are telling the story, and the cameraman will be staging the film itself with a camera. I think that will be the way to do it.

Here at the Cinémathèque at Chaillot they have a wonderful museum made by Henri Langlois, and I wanted to make a film here, starting at Trocadero and following the place, which shows the history of cinema, with Langlois. I wanted to shoot it in one half-hour take, going outside, seeing the Eiffel Tower, etcetera. But it's very difficult to do. I know that the idea of the old tradition is that meaning is created in the opposition of images, through editing, and I agree with them. I prefer to tell a story and follow it. That way, of course, a lot of things can happen.

ERMANNO OLMI

The frame is not a frustration to me, perhaps also because I work without preplanned shots. The frame becomes, in that moment, a way of focusing, not a composition, because it corresponds to the things I want to look at in that moment. It's good that there is, outside the frame, "a discussion that continues," something I can even imagine, desire. As in literature, there are phrases that let you think of an infinity of other words that are even more beautiful because they aren't said.

In pre-packaged films, which are born on the drawing table, planned out by the art director and all the technical-artistic staff, the camera merely establishes a framing angle selected in advance, and all the things written in the script occur within this frame, which may be fixed. My own procedure is different. At the beginning, I don't think about the camera. I think about the ambience and all the events that are to be presented: place, lighting, people, color. I construct the fiction I need. When I feel this fiction corresponds to my needs, then I go to the camera and let myself be dragged along by the event without establishing beforehand that "here" I'll do a close-up, a long shot, a camera movement. With each shot I participate in the event almost instinctively, gathering up what happens. It's rare that I decide in advance. I invent the action at the moment it takes place. I almost always work with a hand-held camera and, having to take direct sound when there is dialogue, I need a very heavy camera since I shoot in 35mm and therefore have to put it on a tripod with wheels. I never do dollies or tracks; I never put the camera at a level higher or lower than a horizontal line drawn at eye level, though sometimes I go out on a balcony, a window. The camera is on this wheeled tripod, but I move it like it was part of me, always at my height.

I always use the camera in an objective way. The difference from the documentary isn't so much in the techniques of shooting because, for example, in a documentary there isn't elaborate lighting, etcetera. For me, the technique of shooting is almost the same. The difference is that in a documentary I shoot a reality from outside my will; thus my critical participation in the event lies only in choosing with the camera the image that, at that moment, I find most interesting in a documentation of the event. In the case of a fiction film, reality doesn't happen outside my will, but is organized by me. Thus, my critical judgment and my suggestion of content lies above all in this organization of the event. Then the approach of the shooting: I do it just as in a documentary, in such a way that I don't deceive the viewer with a suggestion made through certain acrobatics of the camera or the use of a redundant little touch in the lights or the atmosphere.

Even when the camera is objective, the subjectivity is my own. But I never feel alone. I'm convinced that participating with me in the action, in this event, are many others. It's not my personal point of view. Certainly it is, because I decide. However, the sensation as sensation is that these choices of mine are not only mine but that others have them too. I really don't feel exclusive. There is a certain type of intellectual who, either out of presumption towards himself or contempt towards others—which is the same thing—has the ambition to be so subjective, to be the only one, to observe life and events from that isolated perspective. My ambition instead, perhaps because of my peasant-worker extraction, is to look at the world *with* others, not as an aristocratic intellectual, an elite, but mixing as much as possible with others.

However, there are excellent directors who work with camera operators, but everyone makes love like they want to, in the way they feel. It's like going up to a loved person and first thinking, "When we meet, I'll touch her hand, then kiss her like this, then say this phrase. . . ." Certainly we go to this meeting with a whole series of motives, but it is only during the meeting that these motives assume their final expressive physiognomy. There is another reason I'm behind the camera. Because going to a girl it would be like saying, "I love you but now he's going to kiss you for me."

ROBERT ALTMAN

I don't feel frustrated by the frame at all. That's the medium I've chosen to work in. I can't envision a 360-degree thing— you'd have to put somebody in a swivel chair—that would be fun to work in, to deal with, just like theater-in-the-round or horseshoes—all the various things as opposed to proscenium, but I see film as a proscenium. I'm able to turn you to the back, I'm able to reverse the direction. I'm able to pan into a 360-

degree thing, and I think it's very important in film that you don't show everything. The minute that you move off of something, what does the audience know that's over there? Only what's left in their mind, their memory of it. And their memory is not accurate, so you're able, then, to deal with the audience's, each individual's, mind. That's why nobody sees the picture the same way. I can start on a thing and I can hold your attention on the middle of the screen with somebody coming down the stairs and I can start to pan off to the left and just before it moves off frame, you see a shadow cross there, and you say, "Was it a mistake?" Then, all I have to do is keep getting your back to where that shadow was, more and more, until your back is right to it, and I've got you frightened: "Somebody's behind me!" And, then, I make a noise, and the character jumps and the audience jumps.

I think the anamorphic lens makes a better presentation on the screen. I like the ratio, I think it's closer to the eye. The big problem is when you go to translate that to TV or to 16mm, or you get it out to some of these little theaters, your composition is totally destroyed. So you have to ask what you are really making the film for? If television is going to be a big part of the audience, it's going to be important for you, then you should come as close as you can to using that frame—the square. But, I feel that in *Popeye*, for instance, which is not designed for television, I'm going to use an anamorphic lens. The same thing in *Health*, which we shot in a big hotel. I wanted that sense of space; I wanted the audience to feel diminished, that they are in that room. In *Quintet*, I went back to a regular 1.85, because there was a special filter I wanted to use that didn't seem as effective in anamorphic, because we tested it both ways. And, again, I wanted a claustrophobic effect, I didn't want the audience to feel free. The same in *Perfect Couple*—I wanted the story to be more intimate, a little more like television. *Wedding* was anamorphic, a wide screen. *Thieves Like Us* was shot in 1.85 because we didn't have the money. I would've preferred to have shot that in anamorphic.

It depends entirely upon the situation, but I don't use a lot of close-ups, although sometimes I find them very effective. I don't practice things like drawing out little diagrams; I don't do my camera angles or moves before I rehearse or shoot. I just pick my spot and say, "Okay, this is where I'm going to look at the picture from," and then I'll just cover it in that manner. But I'll do that on my feet, and I will not do that the night before. But I'll have some idea when I'm working on the sets, and I'll plan out that scene ahead of time, if I know there's a definite shot. In *The Long Goodbye* I wanted a shot of Elliot Gould and Nina van Pallandt in the bedroom of her house, and, as he interrogated her, to move off the two of them over to her face and then past her face to see the figure of Sterling Hayden walking on the beach and off the beach into the ocean and committing suicide. Well, I had to let them know a day before that I was going to do that in order to get the lighting equipment and everything else that shot would require. So, every once in a while, there'll be a shot that you definitely want to use; you say, "This is the way I want to tell this story, by doing it in this manner." But the rest of it, the normal process of it, will just be done on your feet. I really never know exactly what the actors are going to do or how the scene is going to turn. So, for me to block it out and say, "Okay, that's the way we're going to shoot it and light it," and then have the actors come in and say, "Okay, you move here, and you move there"—I may want to change all that; I may want to change the content of the scene.

I think every situation calls for a different view, and then your overall frame calls for an individual view. It's like painting a picture. If your canvas is eight-by-four feet, it's different than if you're painting a canvas that's two-feet-by-one foot. It forces everything to be different. It could be the same subject, but still it isn't, and you would find no painter working in a different size that would be doing the same painting. So, I don't think there's any such thing as a rule: "I don't like medium shots." Close-up shots, long lens shots are easiest to make look arty. The wider the angle or the more normal the lens is, the better you have to be, the better the eye has to be. Any fool can take a 100mm lens and follow somebody down the street and the cars flashing in front and it gives the kaleidoscopic illusion and you say, "That's terrific!" Well, it is terrific. You have to know that every time you change the distance from the lens to the subject, you're changing the depth of field. Every time you change the lighting or the exposure, you're changing the depth of field, and you have to say, "How do I want this? Do I want this to be clearer? Do I want this to be vague? Do I want it to be very out of focus?" All those things have to enter into it. I mean, it's not a simple thing. But to say that you don't like medium shots; you have to say, "In this case, I don't like a medium shot."

I use the zoom a lot because it's convenient and I like the use of it, I like the movement of it. You know, actually there's no point you can't get, unless you're going for a very, very clear picture that's really crisp, that you can't get as well in 16mm. *Padre Padrone* was all shot in 16mm, and Elio Petri shot *Todo Modo* with a 50mm lens, and at normal height.

Another reason for using a zoom lens or a long lens is so that the camera isn't sitting right up in your face when you're trying to act and all the actor can see are a bunch of guys or a bunch of lights. We'll set up the scene with the cameras a long distance away from the people, especially when we use multiple cameras, and I'll have everybody performing the scene, and they don't know if the camera's on them or not on them, or whether they're in long shot or, in fact, in close-up. That's why I have the actors come to the dailies all the time. Because, they'll say, "Hey, I didn't know even that I was in that shot. You were really close to my face." So they get the idea that when they're on, they don't have to worry where the camera is—they're on. And it kind of gets rid of "I'll save my best performance for the close-up and that way they'll use it in the editing." Those are all those old Hollywood bromides, but people still do that.

R. W. FASSBINDER

It is very simple. I think the frame is like life. Life, too, offers only certain possibilities. Film is like a square of life; it has the same boundaries, but I think film is more honest, because it admits that it is limited space. Life pretends that it offers more possibilities. That's why it's a bigger lie than film.

I always frame the shots myself, but I tell the cameraman what kind of light effect I want. For two films, I worked the camera myself, and I think I can now give the cameraman probably more freedom because I know how to do it myself. I have to try it out. I don't know yet how it is going to work. I hope it will work out. Previously, I set up every shot myself. I looked through the camera, chose the colors—I did everything.

As far as lenses are concerned, I prefer the 32mm lens because it comes closest to corresponding to the visual field of the eye. Longer focal lengths are already an indication of a preconception. This applies to shorter ones, as well. They are all artificial means, and you have to know exactly what you want to use them for, but I will use other lenses if the situation requires it. There has to be a reason to make a change. I have made films with only a 32mm lens, without a zoom, without any other lenses.

Most people reproach me for moving the camera too much, but I direct each scene to correspond with what I want to say at the moment, or how I think I should say it. I don't have any principles in that respect. It is never the same. I made one film, *Chinese Roulette*, where the camera is the main actor. In other films, the camera came close to being an actor, but not throughout the entire film. But it is impossible to generalize, because the camera is, in the sense that it expresses my position, a character in itself. I tried to see in *Chinese Roulette* if it was possible for the camera to actually become the main actor, and it was an experiment that I would not do again. It is not possible, it doesn't work. The observer does not identify with a character's vision through what the camera sees. I would say the camera can be a character *sometimes*. The camera is not an observer either, because I don't make documentaries, so it expresses my personal position towards what is happening, though there are, of course, moments where the camera will show the scene in a way that it can be observed.

In fact, the light is the most important part, more important than the set-up, the position of the camera. Most important, the camera develops things vis-à-vis the lighting.

LINA WERTMULLER

When you speak, when you work in theater, your first communication is the word. In the theater, in the performance, the voice begins. Afterwards, you work with the image as well. I began writing, then directing, for the theater. When I began with movies, it was at first very difficult for me to think through a "hole," because you *have* to think through a hole, one that excludes everything else outside of it. Every moment, every milligram of a movie is a choice. Every choice excludes a world. It's clear. The choices are very committed.

This is a wonderful thing. With one hand over an eye, look at one point in focus, just one point in focus. When you look at me, you think you see everything, but you don't. Your ideas come from many millions of different points of focus in time, but in any one moment you see only *one* point in focus. Your memory remembers all these other points of view, but in this moment you look at only one point. It's the same in movies in a different way because you look at one point in focus and you don't have many, many, many possible ways to direct your gaze. In a picture, there is only one point of view. Our way of looking at life around us is a matter of our memory of sensation. Many different points focused on in one minute come together in memory.

So, you "drive" the audience a little. If in this room, I choose to begin with "that" and "that" and you, I drive the audience to look through my eyes, and this becomes a story. The normal rule of filmmaking is to begin with an ambience, a master shot, and afterwards, you take a shot of "this" man. I'm often told, "Lina, cut," because I use extreme close-ups too much. It's not normal, because you never look that closely at someone in life; it's not normal syntax, as well. So, you really work like a driver with the eye of the viewer. If you go to the country with a friend and tie him up, forcing him to look at the landscape for a number of minutes, perhaps he won't see it, because he's very distracted, he's *forced;* he starts to wonder why he's there, there's nothing to see. But later the country begins to speak to this man. You decide for the viewer. You tie him up, in a manner of speaking.

I don't know if you know the Greek filmmaker Anghiopolous, but he will hold a huge panoramic shot of the country for as long as ten minutes. Some of the audience want to kill themselves from boredom, but he needs this time for his shot. It's very personal, it's a rhythm in time, very intimate for a narrator. You know, it's like a little cabaret story, a showman who tells you a little story while he acts it out. Maybe he talks a lot before beginning: "There is a street full of people." He describes many things before beginning the story. There are many many different ways to tell the story. It's very personal.

For example, I always try to do some *piano sequenze* [long takes], and it's always a crime when I end up cutting into them later. I know how to do them well, I like them, they're very beautiful, but I prefer to cut them up later. Always. They're a kind of vanity; there's a gratification in seeing them; they're a kind of masturbation. That's the sort of thing I force myself to cut against my will. It's a game with myself.

When you are shooting, you have to have the choice, that's absolutely necessary. My ideal is to shoot everything and afterwards to decide. Shoot the long-take sequence, shoot very close, and decide later, because that way you are left with richer possibilities of telling the story. Our war is against money, because money is time, and it forces us to make decisions beforehand. We always try not to make a choice before the editing, but often we do because we have to.

I find a certain type of tension when I shoot that leaves me free to decide later, so I often take subjective shots, for example, even if they're forced. It's not a question of shooting. It's a question of editing. I think that fifty percent of the film is created in the editing.

CHANTAL AKERMAN

I am very close to the camera and I do the filming almost myself. But I'm not at the camera when the actor acts because you cannot see the way they act. You can see that they are organized well within the frame, but not the way they act because you have to look at too many things at the same time. But sometimes in rehearsal I will look to find the right frame.

For my films I prefer a depth of field. I don't like to use a face and then behind the face have everything out of focus. I also don't like to use close-ups, probably because I think it would be very manipulative. I have nothing against the close-up itself; it's just the way it's used. I may want to use it someday in my movies, but so far I haven't felt I should.

Many of the first movies were shot with a stationary camera, but it wasn't exactly the same way as it is done now. The idea of moving the camera a lot came largely from *reportage*, television, and things like that, and also from the idea that in movies you have movement. But that doesn't mean that the *camera* has to move; something can move within the frame. I have done that for almost all my movies. That doesn't mean I won't change, but I don't feel I will.

I prefer that things happen within my frame. When the camera moves, it changes the point of view all the time, so the viewer can see that it's my point of view. I prefer it not so much for a specific reason but more because it gives more tension. When the camera moves, there is less tension, I think, in what I am doing. When the camera doesn't move and things are happening within the frame or outside of the frame, you feel that frame all the time. Finally, it's a tension. I have no idea why, but I can see that this is what happens.

Another reason is that I almost never feel I *need* to hold the camera. You just don't move it for no reason. I have had to do some camera movements, but not a lot. In *Les Rendez-vous d'Anna* there are maybe five or six shots where the camera moves, and there are also traveling shots when a camera was on a train and the train moves, but the camera is steady.

But no one technique is appealing in itself. If I really need a technique for one subject matter, maybe I will use it. But to use it for itself, I don't care. I even don't care if the camera doesn't move per se. It's just that I don't have a need to move the camera and I think a lot of tension is created in one shot when the frame is the right one and there is no movement. It's something strong. And what I'm really looking for in the movie is a kind of energy to come from the frame. It's a kind of restrained energy, but even more, because it's so restrained, because it's so steady. Finally, you know, it's like one line that says everything. You don't need to be stronger. You *essentialise le propos;* make it not like a documentary, not like a report. Let's say when you write you don't want three words where you only need one. It's the same economy of expression.

It's a very strange thing; you have your theme in mind, and then you have your actors and your camera and everything else. And, finally, where you put your camera just works with the space and the actors. What I like to do all the time is to play, not a game, but a relation between the abstract and the concrete. That's another reason why I use that stationary camera: let's say there is a station and a train in the station. If it's done in a way that doesn't look too realistic, it doesn't look like a documentary, it doesn't try to imitate life. It will show by itself within the frame. And if the shot lasts five, ten, twenty, twenty-seven seconds, you have the first information that it's a train in a station, but after a while you see lines, colors, and then you see again that it's a train and then you see the actors, and then the station again. But for a shot lasting only a brief instant, you forget what it is, you just see lines and colors. So, it's a game all the time between concrete and abstract. That is important to me. But, you know, when you do it, you don't do it on purpose. I just feel it has to be done that kind of way. If you feel the shot has to be that length, it's asking from you just your sensitivity, your sensuality, your feeling. So, probably, you can explain it, but I don't really want to.

I'm not covered at all. It's much more exciting to take risks; otherwise, if you are covered, if you cover too much, then you have the design established in the editing and then you have lost your style. Because if you cover like the Hollywood direc-

tors, all the movies look alike. An editor can just follow directions. What you see in my movies is what I shot, and I didn't
shoot anything else. I may shoot the same thing two or three
times, but from no other angles. But for the sound in *Jeanne
Diehlman*, I didn't use almost any sync sound. I rebuilt practically the whole soundtrack afterwards.

All this applies to my movies, but for other movies I think
you can use whatever you want, if you feel it's right. I don't
have any theory about it. For me, it's what I need. But I can see
a movie and not accept the way it's done because to some extent it's pornographic. Not that the subject is pornographic in
the conventional sense, but the way it's done is dishonest, false.

ANDRÉ TECHINE

What I do and what is interesting to me in cinema is that I
do not feel cinema should be a reproduction of reality. I don't
feel film should have as its goal the reproduction of reality. So,
the frame for me is the idealization of what I feel like showing.
I idealize the pieces I want to construct and everything corresponds to my desire.

What is interesting is to be able to play with what is inside
and outside the frame. What is outside the frame is equally
present but in a different way. For example, by the ear, by the
sound. What amuses me in film is to have parallel action outside the frame and in the frame—it's a bit of the combination
of the two that produces a cinematic effect. Frequently in film,
it is the things we hide, what we don't show, what is *not* in the
frame, that is much more important than what's in the frame.
It was Chaplin who said he would rather shoot a face with a
shadow crossing it and add the sound of a train than to show
the whole train station.

I like close-up a lot. It is no doubt where the emotions come
from in silent films. I'm thinking particularly here of *Joan of
Arc* by Dreyer. I adore Dreyer; he is one of the most important
cinéastes for me. I was totally fascinated by the architecture of

that film and by the sequences of close-ups. A face is almost like a white paper on which you inscribe letters, like scenery that changes with the light. For me, it is one of the great strengths of cinema to show faces you can read, or even looks, and then have a voice that comes out of that face, which comes from lower down in the body, and then have that face speak. This is what the great *cinéastes* showed very well, in a poignant way.

I like the 75mm lens, and I very much like to have depth of field, especially when it allows me to establish a contrast, when there is an effect of surprise between the first and second planes, the foreground and the background. I like to use the depth of field to divide the space between what is present very close to the camera, and what is present very far from the camera. There can be a kind of short circuit, a movement of contrast very violent, as if it were divided by the same space.

But you always have this problem of focus; it's quite difficult. In *Barocco* I used the depth of field in a very tricky way, completely imaginary, because we used transparencies. It was the only way to hold focus in foreground and background both. So, by using a transparency behind the window, for example, you could have the scenery in a transparency and the foreground action in a transparency, and, of course, all of it could be in focus. In *Barocco* the whole scene in the luncheonette at the train station was done with transparencies, and I had depth of field through both parallel actions. It's an effect, but it's one which I feel is quite significant because you can have a second frame in the interior of the first frame. This sets up an opposition, a dynamic conflict of two different spaces and actions, and it can be very fascinating, thrilling.

I don't like to be too systematic regarding shot length. I like long takes and also extremely short ones, cutaways of things, objects. I like to play with both forms. It depends on the dramatic situation, and on the actions I want to put inside the scene. And what I like to do is not to mix up the people, but to create an uncertainty in the audience with the mix of artificial and natural elements, comedic elements, dramatic elements, elements of the sad, romantic novel, in such a way that the person is completely uncertain about what is happening. It's much more active for the spectator.

I do only two or three takes of each shot. I don't take several points of view in the same scene. I rarely have shots I can cut away to in the editing. I don't cover a scene from all the angles—not at all. Sometimes I plan to have cuts in a scene with different size shots and so I shoot it in a sort of cut-up fashion, but it's never the same shots, never the same situation from another angle. I don't do double coverage. You never know too much about what you are going to need in the editing. Sometimes it's very tight and I regret not having taken some kind of security shot, but I don't like that kind of security. Often though, I regret it. But it's also a question of economics. If you want to assure that a scene is covered from all angles, it is at the same time a matter of precision and of economy—depending on the schedule of the day's shooting. Otherwise, I feel that once you start covering "for safety," you'll never stop. You can go to infinity with safety shots.

GEORGE ROMERO

I don't find the frame frustrating at all. Maybe I do subliminally, maybe that's why I do a lot of shots. But that's a limitation that you come to know right away. For example, I'll shoot conversations from five or six different angles. I don't use a technique where there's a master shot and then I "go in." I prefer to leave it wide open. I'll shoot a master sometimes, but then I'll shoot individual shots also, then "two shots," then mix them up and play around with them later, in the editing, after I can see it and feel which way it's going. That method also gives you information about the surroundings. It gives you just as much information as looking at a static frame.

I don't feel frustrated, because you can make the frame do anything you want it to do. It's a blank canvas. I find it limitless. It depends on what you put there. I don't think you really get a sense of that until you back off and start getting analytical—looking at films forwards and backwards. I don't think anyone on first exposure to a film really gets a sense of that, unless you're looking at something that's so highly stylized in a graphic sense, like Gordon Willis's photography in *Manhattan,* that it pushes your awareness of the frame. I don't like that very much because it just makes you aware of one of the parameters of the medium that you shouldn't be aware of. You should be kind of "in there." If you're going to make the audience aware of the frame, you might as well work on a proscenium stage where you're always aware of the format. I prefer a more real involvement with it. To me, it's a much more tactile thing, which is why I use a lot of shots and move the eye around a lot and do strange things with that.

In general, I like to take the audience's eye. I don't like to mess with that subjective point of view. That's where you fuck your "graph" up, your moving of the audience's emotions. It's basically information that I want to get out, even though I'm working through characters. Basically, what's happening is *I'm* giving you information I want you to have, and so it's more my point of view that controls than any of the characters' points of view, except internal to a scene, where you need to have a character's perspective on things.

BENOIT JACQUOT

The frame is a means to organize and a frustration at the same time. It's inventive, but the frame fundamentally determines the film because it *is* frustrating. It does place a limit on reality because it hides as well as shows things. It is that fact which creates the fiction and the invention and the cinematic process for me. I try to put as little as possible in the frame and as much as possible outside the frame in such a way that what is in the frame creates questions and suggests the mystery around that which is left outside the frame. That which is in the frame should call to and encourage a sort of mystery about what is outside and hidden. For me, it is not only the resource of what

I try to do, but of all that interests and pleases me in film, as much as in the comedies as the dramatic films—Lubitsch as well as Hitchcock and Lang—filmmakers who always played with the off-frame, that which could at any moment appear, filmmakers who played constantly with surprise. And if cinema is not the art of surprise, I don't know what it is. And the surprise always comes from outside the frame. It's the very nature of film that implies that everything in the frame gives rise to the imagination of the spectator for that which is outside. It is suggested with sound as much as with image, but it could be a color, a voice, a shadow. It's really a more general thing. The entire film is determined by the "off" frame, what goes on outside. And, for me, what goes on outside the frame is much more important than what is in the shot. I direct in such a way that what you don't see comes from the actual material of the film, or what you do see.

Directing is the art of framing things in such a way that a surprise is always possible.

I like very much to use a long depth of field, but it's not a question of focus or of lens. I have a horror of wide angles. But these days, since we have less money to make films, that means we have less material to light with, and the only lenses that have depth of field in a low light situation are the wide angles like the 18, 25, 12mm, and I detest lenses that deform the perspective. Before, when we could afford lots of light, we could have depth of field even with the 50mm lens, and that is really beautiful. Now we can't anymore. I prefer the 35, 40, and 50mm lenses because they distort the lines of perspective the least. If I made big-budget films, I would do what the filmmakers of twenty years ago did: use 35, 40, and 50mm with lots of light so I could have that depth of field, because it plays upon the effect of surprise. It can give you a whole series of little tricks, little hiding places, little hooks in the image where you can hang surprises, places where they can suddenly appear, just like that, within the frame itself. You can create the off-frame within the frame.

Until now I have tended to prefer shots with long duration, but I don't want to do them anymore. I've done enough of them. They became a mode, a style, a rhetoric—a kind of new academicism. On the contrary, I would like to arrive at a very accentuated kind of cutting, with very rhythmically cut films, with a rhythm from shot to shot, rather than rhythm within the frame. I like cuts to shock the audience. I like violent cuts where the spectator is totally caught up in it. I like it when you are not aware of something right on the spot, but after it really works on you. That's what I try to do.

I like to use close-ups because they fragment the totality of the scene. I don't like them for psychological reasons, but really for emotional ones, like when all of a sudden you cut to a big close-up of a face, it is almost dizzying for the spectator. I like to do things like that.

I have a lot of trouble using zooms or dolly shots on static actors. I like to move the camera only to follow someone or something. I like camera movement to be determined by the action of a character, and it should always be an accompanying movement, never a movement while the actor is immobile. I have my own personal allergy to this kind of camera work, but I think everything is permissible in cinema. It depends on who is making the film.

But I hate effects. For example, you always use subjective points of view in films; it's done all the time, with Hitchcock for example. But a whole film like that doesn't interest me. *Lady in the Lake* was interesting enough, but a bit empty. It's forced, it's an effect, like long lenses or opticals in the editing. It's also a kind of imperialism of the point of view, and what's interesting to me is to have the points of view constantly change, cutting into one another, and the drama of the film comes also from these different points of view, which reflect each other, break one another, diverge and converge. It's more dynamic. But I think anything can be done in any way if that's how the filmmaker wants it done.

JEAN-MARIE STRAUB

The frame has been talked about a great deal. André Bazin said the frame in cinema was assumed to be like the frame of a painting; it limits it on all four sides. But, on the contrary, he said that in film, the frame is a mask, a screen, a hiding place that hides the off-frame space while illuminating what's in the frame. It fragments the space in the middle of the frame. I think it's both at the same time. Some filmmakers work with it in one sense; others in the other. Me—I think no matter how you view it, the frame illuminates *and* safeguards the off-frame space. You must do both. I don't think the frame is only a visual element, but is also the result of the position of the camera and the choice of the lens, which further implies a responsibility of a moral and political choice taken by the director. Because it is at least as important to know what one doesn't want to show as well as what one wants to show, and at what distance, what angle, etcetera. I suppose it comes from a long tradition of filmmaking, American films and others, that everything in the frame is not seen as equally important. Most American films are humanist, whereas we are trying to make films where the men in the frame are no more important than a small stone, rock, or a blade of grass, a breath of wind, a cicada, or a bird that passes.

In some of our films we have less than one-second takes [fourteen frames]. Some takes are short, some are long. It depends. It's a question of construction and rhythm. You must give some pieces of reality a certain block of time to vindicate themselves against the film, and for the audience just to see. At first, they might not see much or maybe they see a lot, and then, as the shot goes on, they see less and less and then they see more and more. But if the shot stops too soon, the audience doesn't have the time to make the curve. Or the reverse: one can see nothing in the beginning, perhaps, but if the shot continues, one sees more and more, and if the spectator is tired, he sees less and less. Again, it depends. In general, if one interferes either at the height of the curve of the tension or at the bottom of the shot when it goes down and the shot continues past that point, it's not good to cut into it. You can do it, but you should know why and how.

CLAUDE CHABROL

Sometimes the problem with the frame is like that with a second language: you have a dictionary but it isn't enough. When you do a certain shot in a certain way, it means something. It worries me. It's just like a period or comma in the sentence—it's the most important thing. What's important in the frame is what you don't show. You have to *choose something* and sometimes the frame comes to mean all the things, even those you left out, the context, what the dictionary doesn't give. In one film I asked the director of photography to do a very unusual thing. He was upset because he was not used to it, but it was very simple. There was a big table with three people on one side of the table and they were in the camera frame—just in the middle. Then there was a very short dolly shot that put them on the right. There was now nothing on the left. And from the left, a man entered with a jug of orange juice to complete the frame. "Well, you cannot do that because it puts what's in the frame off-balance," he said. "Yes," I said, "but I do it deliberately because the real use is an element of the balance." So you are waiting for the element that will restore balance and the jug of orange juice is an element of the balance. It's really important.

At this moment the frame was exactly the most important thing, as important as the pace of the actors, the speed of their movements. For example, very slow movement can give significance to an ordinary action. That is why I sometimes like to have three people in the small frame. I try to give meaning just by the speed of how they do things, sometimes very slowly, sometimes too quickly, sometimes they move at a realistic pace. I think that for me it's the purest way to express something, because you just have people in that frame.

DUŠAN MAKAVEJEV

It's very important to realize that many people believe that
the frame contains part of a larger reality. What is important to
understand is that in movies there is nothing else—whatever is
in the frame is all there is. There *is* nothing else. Everything
else is just fantasy, and what is outside the frame does not
really depend on what was outside the frame during the shooting. What is outside the frame is something we create *by* the
frame. And the image creates the fantasy about what is outside.
But it's very important to realize that the only thing we really
work with is what is within the frame. So, framing things in
means drawing attention to, embracing, taking care, and incor-
porating something, but whatever you frame out means you're
depriving people of it. Now, when I speak of something being
"framed out," I don't speak of "real" reality. I speak of what
you *believe* is framed out. When you look at the frame, what is
within is all you're getting as the spectator.

There's incredible erotic tension in the edges of the frame.
There is an incredible tension because the frame—these four
sides—is incredibly active. There's a real castrating action
going on there. You just cut out everything else, so it means
whatever goes on inside is this piece of living flesh inside this
four-sided frame. Let's say we have reality—and I know from
my documentary experience that documentary is a fiction. At
some point, what you see changes. Now, if it changes by your
look, if it changes by your selection of the space, then it
changes by your selection of the frame. So, as soon as you
frame some piece out of reality, and you get it on the stock,
there's several processes already finished. One is your gesture
of selection, which creates this magic moment of turning something real into an image of "reality." So, the selection is a carv-
ing out of one piece—it's highly creative because as soon as you
carve, everything else doesn't exist and the lines that are the
frame are creating this new reality. What is the eroticism of it?
You know from Hitchcock movies if you have a person and
he's not filling the frame, there's a space behind, you know a
knife is coming. Now, this knife is not a real knife—it's just a

danger that starts with framing, let's say, two actors, in a slightly eccentric way. An incredible tension builds. There's this kind of deprivation of "good" composition. You deliberately don't compose well. It always means something or you're embarrassed. Life is not symmetrical, so you pick it up, you forget the symmetry. It has incredible force.

Now there's another step—the first is the frame—this second step is the shot length. You keep a shot on a window a few seconds longer, suddenly all kinds of things are happening behind. Or, if you keep a shot on a house, you expect it to explode. You need three seconds to perceive the house, but you place it for five seconds, so it means you wait for it to explode and then nothing happens. But, then, people carry that expectation of explosion into the next shot. So, next time you have another shot, you make it a little short, so they're expecting something in there. It's like rugs being pulled out from under them. You see something and you don't see it well. So, then you get nervous. Then you get another shot—you give it just the right length. People get happy watching it, not only for what is there, but they're relieved that there are no surprises. They get a kind of subliminal gratitude when you do something nice and calm, etcetera. And there is always a constant excitement or embarrassment when you do something shorter or longer or abnormal. So, you work with these compositional ingredients to create this space. And the space is psychological.

·3·

SOUND

The emergence of sound in film is one of the most interesting episodes in the brief history of motion pictures. The technology that brought sound to the image was developed after movies had been successful as a mass communication form and conventions guiding the ways in which it spoke to its audience had been established. Silent film had its unique forms, its own symbol systems: it was a language without sound. So, as Michael Powell recalls, for a period of ten years after sound was first introduced, cinematic art came to a standstill:

> "When sound first came in, we regarded it as a tragedy, a barrier, whereas before, if you made a good love story, it would go all over the world. It didn't matter who was playing certain parts as long as they were good: Czechs, Russians, English, Americans, it all was a marvelous tapestry of movement and people and fabulous personalities, and then, all of a sudden, this terrible barrier of sound came in. For ten years it was the dullest business you could possibly have been in. I can't tell you how dull it was. But gradually a few pioneers got hold of it."

Filmmakers were completely stymied. Having developed a means of creating images whose eloquence more than compensated for their silence, they simply did not know what to do with this new, added element. It seemed at first to threaten the visual-poetic nature of film art, the dreamlike quality of people opening and shutting their mouths without sounds coming out, the magical ability to express so much meaning through one beautifully packed image. However, as some filmmakers note here, sound always played an important part in the film experience, as did language, because there was always the accompaniment of a piano or organ, as well as the explanatory titles.

It seems, with hindsight, we can say that the early filmmakers actually undervalued the poetic capacities of film. As Mark Rappaport notes, film is "an ever-expanding envelope," and sound, when used artfully, can only enrich the experience, because, more than the visual element, sound is emotionally evocative. The films that really carry the viewer away, such as some of Hitchcock's best, are those that use sound cleverly. Sound does much more than give information; it can totally change the way the viewer relates to an image.

Sound consists of narration and voice-over, lip-synch dialogue, music, special effects, and the absence of sound. The conventional soundtrack is used in film either as reinforcement or as counterpoint to the visuals. The relationship of sounds can be vertical, that is, relating to each other in terms of sequential order, what comes before and after a sound, or horizontal, the mixing together of several elements of sound simultaneously. Sound can be taken during the shoot and organized later, or the entire soundtrack can be built after the shoot during the editing stage, as is commonly practiced in Italy. Most often, however, a combination of both methods is used.

Whether it is ambient noise evoking an atmosphere, affecting our sensibilities and our sense of time and place, or dialogue, sound gives the image more power, more credibility. But the soundtrack can do more than merely convey information and relate to the visuals in a direct manner: it can extend the action beyond the limits of the frame, by including on the track sounds that originate from off-frame sources. This not only enhances film's ability to suggest a world that continues beyond what the viewer can actually see, but also reflects the ways in which we experience our own aural environment, thereby strengthening the credibility of the entire cinematic world of the film.

The soundtrack can establish, not merely follow, the rhythm of the visual images, so that the correspondence between picture and sound is either perceived by the viewer consciously or, at its most subtle, with the expressive force of the subliminal. It can enhance the reality expressed in the images, or it can shatter that illusion. At its most bold and suggestive, sound can seem to go its own way, expanding the total effect of the film by bearing its own freight of feeling and meaning.

Some filmmakers are more interested in exploring this aspect of film-making than any other. It is thought by many to be the gateway toward a "true" cinema, toward discovering more refined, less literary film forms. Through creative use of sound, film art becomes more than an assemblage of the scraps gathered together from other arts, stuffed into a plot borrowed from a best-selling novel, and illustrated by the camera.

JEAN ROUCH

I was violently against anything other than live sound for years and years, and I discovered this year when there was a festival in San Remo with the old Roberto Rossellini films that although, of course, I knew all the films were, in fact, post-synced sound films, all dubbed, I saw a classic shot where Anna Magnani is arrested in *Roma, Città Aperta*. Well, when I saw the film I had already seen three or four times, I realized that you could not have this sound in sync sound, live sound. It's impossible. She is shouting, "Francesco!" You cannot have this kind of sound any other way than dubbing it in later in the studio. Then I thought that I'd better rethink about this idea of using sound. And I hope that this spring at the summer institute of film at Harvard, M.I.T., and Yale, where I hope we will have a regular international meeting with our small group of people who are making our kind of films, that this time I'll ask some Italian filmmakers to come and explain the way they are doing sound. For example, the American films shown in Italy were always dubbed, and the public knew it. They knew that Humphrey Bogart was always done by this one wonderful Italian actor and they were going to see it not only for Bogart, but for the man who was making the voice, who was also a very good actor. That's a very important thing, and so I have to think about this issue again. The whole time I was seeing these Rossellini films I was thinking, "We are crazy to say that it is only the real sound that is important"—why? In fact, I made a film about lion hunters, for example, and I put a sound effect of the arrows as they were shot which was not on the live soundtrack. You cannot hear it in life when the people shoot the arrows, so in a way, you have to make the reality by these kinds of effects. Maybe it's the same thing with the voice. To give an example, the success of the disco music, which started supposedly in France as a means to cover very bad singers. They put a very strong beat on a very high level behind it to cover the bad voice. They recorded the beat separately to have a pure drum sound, so then what you hear in disco music you could never hear in person. There are very few disco concerts because it is always tricky with the tracks. They have maybe forty tracks just to put sound effects on. And that means it's a new kind of music, and maybe we have to do the same thing in film. But I have to think more about this.

I hate music in film. You know, I had a very big discussion with Jacques Cousteau about this stupid music he puts on his films, with the bubbling water and things like that. It's a shame, but he said, "Well, if there isn't this music, you cannot sell the film to TV." What kind of sound can you put on a film under-water—only the bubbles? No, of course, when I think of those old Westerns, the role of the music is fantastic, but I try to avoid music myself, although sometimes I cannot. Very often I just fall into the trap myself. I made a film about hippo-potamuses and I put music in the film. When there was a cli-max during the hunting party, I put a very lovely song on, which was a kind of a war song. When I showed it for the first time to the hunters themselves, they said, "Well, Jean, you are wrong. The hippopotamus can hear everything when he is un-der water. If you play music at this point, he will come out of the water." And it's true. Why put music in the middle of a dramatic thing like that? I don't know, we have to think about it, we have to experiment with different uses of sound. To give a summary of my position, I think that we have to learn all the time. When you have finished learning, you are good only to be a spectator. You are no longer a creator. Creativity means to learn something. After, of course, you can make films for TV and for the film industry, show business. But I'm not very in-terested in that.

BENOIT JACQUOT

I think what is risked in the game of cinema, as much by the director as by the spectator, is their regard. By "regard" I don't mean simply his look; it means something that comes from the eyes materially, but which only puts into play the entire body. So, for me, the sound is only an element of the spectator's regard. But the sound, paradoxically, has a rapport with the regard. For example, if you put someone in a screening room and made him listen to a soundtrack of a film, that isn't a film. But if you shut off the lights and project a simple white light on the screen while playing the sound track, it starts to become cinema. So in order for it to be cinema, the regard must be put into play at one moment or another. If only the ear is being used, it's not cinema. So for me, first it's the regard, then the sound, and all the rest is organized concurrently to engage the regard of the spectator. It is not vision; it's not the fact of seeing. It's rather the engaging of something that comes from the body as a whole but is determined by the regard. There is a difference between look and vision: in French *regarder* means to engage a desire in what you are looking at. But *to see* is just to put your eyes on an object.

Up to now I have done sync sound because it allowed for the surprises that occurred during the shoot to manifest themselves the most. All of a sudden a baby cries or a plane goes over, and it curves the meaning of a scene, and it can be very beautiful. But now I wonder if it's so important or even interesting.

Before, sync sound was almost a religion. You had to do it if you were honest. If you started to tamper with the sound, you were a liar. But now, since I realize that to make films is to lie—it's in fact the only way to arrive at some sort of truth—I don't care about sync sound anymore. Cocteau rejected all that; his soundtracks are totally fabricated, no sync sound; the same with Bresson.

The best way is to use both. If there is something in the sync track that happened unexpectedly and is very beautiful, something unplanned, you can keep it in the film. But you can also correct and manipulate things. That's the best way to work for me.

WERNER SCHROETER

You can go far back to see movies like *Jeanne d'Arc* by Dreyer—the silent films that don't need sound. Otherwise it's ridiculous to refuse the possibility of work with a more complex medium, which means the forty years in which we have had image and sound. So it's particularly important to me.

But if we didn't have sound pictures, cinema could be as intelligent and could transport as much message and image and idea as it can with sound. It's only nice to have the more complex sensual material and there is no doubt that, if you use it right, a sound picture has more sensuality than a mute film.

In my earlier films, I used sound mostly in the way of juxtaposition to the image or identifying ironically the sentimentality of the image. So it was something added to the image and was also a counterpoint to the image, more or less. Then, later, I used direct sound and dialogue, approaching what you would call "normal" cinema, instead of having the sound contradict what you see in the image, which is unused in Italy. Italian cinema doesn't use the technique of direct sound. They dub everything. And that is a much more difficult situation because you become very tied up in your possibilities of "do you use direct sound," and the actor feels tied up too, because if an actor misses some words, the whole take has to be redone and redone. And it's not only necessary that the image be beautiful. But I like Italy, and the Italians have a natural talent. It's a cliché but it's true. The Mediterranean people have a natural talent for self-exposure. They are not afraid of cameras. So, with people like that, you really can work with direct sound, which I prefer because it's much more beautiful to have the sound integrated with the image.

If you transport the meaning rather than the aesthetic innovation of your own idea, it means that there is a better possibility to have an integration of direct sound because it's more the image of the whole person—the face and movement, everything goes together. But I understand why people don't do direct sound. It's much more stressful for the filmmaker because so many technical difficulties do occur.

YVES YERSIN

I have a lot to say about silent films because many of my documentaries are silent. For the producer this was for economic reasons, but for me it was interesting to have the limitation in order to better understand cinematographic grammar, and because a silent image can make a lot of noise. It's interesting to work with the visuals only because you can better understand the importance of the other elements when they are used.

But I do work a lot with the sound. I do the sound myself and edit the film myself because I can control the sound more. I very often work on the sound equipment myself in the studio. I take direct sound, but after, I do a lot of building on the track. There's a scene in *Les Petites Fugues* with three people singing. These three people take power in the scene. To show this taking of power, first they are playing cards and singing. It's late at night, and the people who previously dominated the place have just left. It's important that they take power not only of this specific place in a physical sense but that they take power by making noise, by dominating the sound environment, as they were always oppressed before.

I took direct sound, but in the editing I began with that direct sound when they started to sing. There wasn't much noise. Little by little I took other recordings of direct sound that had been made with the other takes, and I mixed them so the effect became that of twelve people singing, not just three, as there still is in the image. And the spectator doesn't realize this, but it's powerful. The sound takes over in impact, at this point, from the image. It's another way of focusing the spectator's attention. For me, sound works enormously, deeply, and it doesn't always travel through the intellect. It's a poetic way to speak to someone.

ANDRÉ TECHINE

It all depends on the director's imagination. There are some filmmakers, like Bresson, who have worked on having the picture dictated by the sound. It's very striking when you see a film of Bresson's to realize that all of the images are completely dictated by the sound. The sound dictates the action and what the camera will show. His work is rather extreme in this regard. Antonioni worked a lot on the sound also, the sound of the sea in *L'Avventura,* for example, tells a whole story in itself. The perspectives of sound are very refined, and often we reduce them a bit too much. I think it was Godard who said the sound was a slave to the image.

What I try to do, not in any systematic way, because I don't want to do theoretical films, but when the situation presents itself, I try to have the frame say something, like a face, and the sound say something else. I don't like to be redundant. When I have a close-up of an actor, I try to have his face communicate something different than his voice. I try to do it when I do sync sound as well as in dubbing, to have the voice that comes out be something of a surprise, an effect of contrast to the face. I always try to make the sound and the image differ.

R. W. FASSBINDER

It is impossible to talk about sound, the subject is too vast. Bertolucci said that the spectator has become conscious of the images and soon he will be conscious of sound. That is when sound will start.

Before Godard, the film was developed from a story. Godard started to develop a film from images. He did not want to tell a story in the first place. One can ask the question of whether it is possible to develop a film from what you hear. So far, sound was only just there. It was not something you would work on. The sound was not really a major part of the film.

I want to see if it is possible to develop a film from what you hear, which also means from what you think: a completely opposite position from a silent movie, which tells or writes a story in chronological order with pictures in between. I would like to find out if film could be understood as, let us say, a symphony. If film could no longer be a means to tell a story but be something with which our sensibility deals in the same way it does with music.

DUŠAN MAKAVEJEV

First of all, sound doesn't automatically belong to the frame, and, so, direct sound can be an awful thing. Direct sound can be okay, but it's an additional illusion that "this is a piece of reality." So it's very important if you do direct sound to undermine it with all kinds of commentaries. All these realistic Hollywood movies always had one thousand violins playing and no one ever commented on its unreality. They're overpowering emotion with sound all the time, pretending that it's reality. But it's like painting everything pink, without using any other color. Sound is very important, but it's another construction with which you can do anything. I remember one beautiful piece with Oliver and Hardy talking as women. It was terrific. It is very rare that sound is used dialectically, that sound is used for its own value, not with the pretension that this is reality. So, very often sound is used in this servile role. Sound is just used as a slave, and *real* sound is a great thing.

Sound can be almost as important as the visuals in some places—not equally important though, because you don't need sound at all. But then you have silence that is sound. So sound *is* there all the time, if you use it or not. In silent movies, you hear the projector running: you always have sound. Sound is an independent ingredient. That's why I like to cut sound in, not to mix it in—to *show* cuts, for sound to appear, for music to appear suddenly. Mixing is also nice, but everything's legitimate. You play music, you cut, a second later, you continue. For years we allowed this to happen only in theaters. Theaters were always chopping film, but this kind of chopping effect of sound you never had in the original film. They would edit them additionally, like in Godard's *Breathless;* those kind of jump cuts came about after several thousand showings. So, normal city kids who don't have money for the premiere showing always see films this way: you know, there's a horse, and suddenly, there's a guy on the horse. It's normal. Why should we be nervous about it? It's an additional cinematic quality. I like scratches too. They look like rain. In childhood we believed that in American Westerns it always rained, because these were B movies shown in B theaters, and they were always scratched.

ROBERT ALTMAN

Jack Warner once said of me, "That fool has actors talking at the same time." I think I've always been interested in that kind of presentation. And we've gone more towards this as an additional tool. And once you've got a tool and you know it works, it gives you a little more courage and you can say, "Sure, let's do it this way, and we can also do so and so." But I don't believe I started using overlapping, multiple soundtracks because the technology was there. The egg, the idea to use it, came first.

"Unmixing sound" is literally what using multiple tracks is. In other words, you are miked, and me, and there's a mike out the window getting street noises, and I put a mike on the clock, or in the kitchen. If there were only one microphone, some of the street noise would leak through, and some of the kitchen noise would leak through, the clock may or may not, and the sound mixer would be trying to take this one mike and getting a balance between you and me and he'd have to ignore those other sounds. And when he would finally go to put this on film, those sounds would have to be gotten rid of or covered up by putting a higher level on them so you couldn't hear them. Consequently, the whole background level could come up, which we don't necessarily want, and it would not be a realistic background level. Now, if we can get enough isolation when we finish with all of this, what do we have? Well, we have the sound effect of the clock, we have the sound effects of the street, of the water, of the noises in the kitchen, and they're live sound effects. So if we want to use those, say, for the master shot, which would be you and I sitting here, talking, that street noise could be brought up to exactly the level we want and it would be in sync with us. If we made cuts, we could also continue that level, and even though you get an overlap in the hammering, you would not notice it. So it gives you a little more work in post-production. In other words, you have to do more transfers. On the books it would appear to be a little more expensive. But, on the other hand, I think we're saving money by not having to worry about shadows and lighting for mike booms and having to move lights. In other words, we never see a boom in the place: there's one take we call a "master coverage boom" we do to pick the whole thing up in case something goes wrong and we have to loop the thing. It used to be that we'd have to rehearse the scene with the boom man in the shot and the lighting cameraman would have to change his lights and various things. This way I can let everybody go, and we can separate those tracks, and I can raise your voice and bring mine down or whatever I want to do. It's like doing music.

I think some people also do it now in certain cases, but I don't know anybody that does it as a general production philosophy. In other words, they will say, "There's a certain scene coming up and it's going to have a lot of things in it, so let's go for an eight-track or a multi-track in that." But then when they get into their normal scenes, they don't bother with it. We use it because it's our standard equipment, so we don't show up those tracks that we don't use. It doesn't make any difference, we reclaim that two-inch tape anyway once we've finished with it, so it doesn't make any difference if we only put one track down or two or all seven.

We're improving our equipment and our use of it constantly, and so are other people, and other people will definitely go

into it. In a way, it's the way Europeans have developed dubbing to such a fine extent that we have not over here. They
couldn't get what they wanted so they just did it all afterwards
and became very expert in dubbing in sound after the shooting. Now, if they can change their habits, in a while, in Europe,
you should see people going for this sort of thing. But the very
fact that they're so good at the dubbing and so many filmmakers like Fellini and many others get their scene and are
rewriting after they shot the picture, they get used to that. But
I think eventually the technology is going to get to the point
where you don't have to worry about lighting too much or anything. It gets easier all the time: the lights we use get better, the
lenses get better, the cameras get better. In fact, the lenses are
so much better, we have to spend a lot of time putting gunk in
front of them so it gives an effect look, so it isn't too absolutely
brilliantly clear.

HENRY JAGLOM

I surrounded the individual characters of *A Safe Place* and
Tracks with symbology of their individual oppression. One of
the main things was the music. In *A Safe Place* there's an old
jukebox, a Wurlitzer, beautiful, deco, gorgeous, and it's playing
"Someone to Watch Over Me," "La Mer," and "These Foolish
Things," and all kinds of songs about being taken care of,
about sitting back and waiting for "Some Day My Prince Will
Come." Slowly, I use the jukebox as a starting-off point and
then throughout the film interweave snatches of music into the
moments of her life, because pieces of music that come to the
surfaces of our minds are a very strong conditioning for most
of us and affect our perceptions of time. For instance, in the
middle of a scene with Jack Nicholson, Tuesday is about to go
to bed with him, and he's doing a particularly male number to
her, and the conscious mind realizes that there's something full
of shit about what's going on, but when she hears Dooley
Wilson singing the theme from *Casablanca*, "As Time Goes By,"

then the conditioning moves her into a different mood and she starts acting out the image of what she's supposed to be, the child-woman, and she gives up control. In the same way, in *Tracks,* Dennis Hopper carries the cassette player, and he listens to all the World War II songs, "Praise the Lord and Pass the Ammunition," and "We're Going to Have to Slap That Dirty Little Jap"—all the real songs that a person Dennis's age and that soldier's age heard very early in life from the "good" war. I think we can't understand who we are now without going back to what conditioned us. Movies conditioned us and popular music conditioned us enormously.

I think you create the heightened subjectivity that only music finally can give you, when it comes on top of a certain kind of acting.

MILOS FORMAN

I don't think sound ruined movies at all, especially because I like to treat dialogue as another equal, not less, not more, but part of human behavior. If we see human beings on the screen and they behave, it would be silly if they don't talk. I don't like discussions. I don't like disputes instead of dialogue. I like people when they talk, not when they discuss. And sound effects are, again, part of the behavior of nature around us, so they're natural. In my opinion, sound effects can enhance or strengthen moments of surprise, moments of fright. They're very helpful to create the mood for a scene. For example, silence in the sound film is the greatest help to create tension, suspense. But that's only in sound movies. And, of course, music has been with film from the beginning. They figured out that it's good to play piano during silent films. Music is as essential as photography. It's something very aesthetic and emotional. Again, it's very supportive of the mood of a scene, the dramatic flow of a scene for tension, for suspense. And, in the case of *Hair,* in the case of any musical, the lyrics took care of the message of the film, which was a big relief because then I could concentrate on scenes in the plot that are seemingly very unimportant, really behavioral dialogue. The characters are never discussing big philosophical issues of life and death and war and peace because we have all those songs to do it. I didn't have to get across any philosophical issues of that era, I didn't have to translate them into the dialogues. I could just let the kids react to normal situations in the story without suddenly having them discuss the question of life and death. Why not? Because we had a beautiful song about it. Of course, when you're working on the script, you have your record player or tape ready when the musical number comes. You hear the songs again and again, over and over. You go with a vague idea, a small idea of what should be there, but then the rhythm of the song, the lyrics of the song, dictate what should be there. They dictate the imagery.

I was just trying to find a little different way of approaching the songs so no two are sung exactly the same way. So sometimes you illustrate, sometimes you just hear the music without the lyrics and go with the mood of the tune, sometimes you go against the lyrics. It's important for me to try to find as much variety in staging musical numbers so that every musical number will be slightly different or bring in something new.

When you know the music beforehand, of course it influences your usual preparation for the shooting. For me, it was absolutely essential to solve the first moment when somebody opens their mouth and starts to sing. Because that will either turn the audience off or it will hook them. If they accept that right in the first number, then they will accept everything. The "Aquarius" song and its introduction really helped enormously in finding what kind of imagery to use.

JEAN-LUC GODARD

In *Everyman for Himself* I wanted people to *see* the music, not *hear* it. I started using music quite late. I did a bit, but I did not quite understand when I did use it, such as in *Breathless*. I thought it was a movie like Preminger's.

I did not understand how I, with my hands, my eyes, my past, how I could have done something like that film, my other films. But they were me, and that is why I am interested in film history. It is also a means to see my own history and to interest myself in others' histories.

I learned by chance that music accompanies things, that one needs company. Even big industrial societies call themselves "Peugeot and Company," and I think that the company is music. One also says "women of good company"; in military art they call groups of soldiers "companies." "Companies" is like accompanying. I always used accompanying music the American way—voice-accompanying music. In a movie scene when one hears music, in a love scene or the passage of the Red Sea by the Egyptian army, the moment there is music in American films or by those that imitate them, it is simply as background. One "sees" one hundred and twenty musicians of the Boston Pops who accompany the images because their music is inside the film, and I am one who always pushes things further; even if it is the subject, it is also the accompaniment.

In *Everyman for Himself* we have only two tracks, but we put everything on the two tracks, and so, the editing and mixing is done differently. We don't have one track for the effects, one or two for the music, one for some lines. The two tracks are completely full. And we work with only two tracks in the editing. You have to work more like a musician in the studio.

For those who know a little of the technique of moviemaking, usually films have one picture track and then on the editing table there are quite a few soundtracks. There is one direct track of people speaking and when they do not speak, there is nothing on the track. At that moment, if one is on a farm, let's say, generally the director or the editor suggests putting in the sound of a chicken or a car in the street, etcetera. It is not that one is interested in the sound of the car, but for background. So, one can have a large amount of tracks. Martin Scorsese in his last film had forty-nine tracks, and, of course, the tracks are like steps, and then the mixing is well-organized to balance well so that sounds of the chickens don't cover the sound of the farmer woman who says "I love you" to the milkman. On this film we tried to have only one track. We did not manage that; I had to put in two, but they are stuffed to bursting. When there is a moment when one says there should be music, then we simply stop the dialogue. In this film we did not feel that the dialogue was missing. If we cut the "I love you," it would be because I found that it was more important to put music in. At that moment in a regular film the way I used to make, the music would have come on top of the "I love you." In *Everyman for Himself* we did sound as if we had two tracks; we did not want anymore because the machine could not take more than two tracks. We already have a picture; there cannot be thirty-six million sounds. There are one or two sounds, or we should have brought in the orchestra on the spot and do it at the same time we filmed because we could not do it later. If we did it later, we start to think in heights, like skyscrapers—and I think skyscrapers are a bad system to inhabit apart from a few places—rather than in terms of length. We had a very good sound engineer who was used to forty-nine tracks who felt very lost with only two tracks. He felt lost because he had a sound in the right track and the sound disappeared. There was only "I love"—and the "you" was replaced by music. He was completely perturbed because he had to listen to what he was doing and not function like a computer.

EMILE DE ANTONIO

"Filmic" is the quintessential property of film, which is simply the ability to express action and character through motion: action, characters, images, and sounds in motion. And sound in motion is correct, is the correct formulation for that. Sound is not just an accompaniment as it was in the beginning. *In the Year of the Pig*, in the beginning, there's a mix as Cage would use the work "mix" in his music. I asked myself, "What one sound separates this war from all other sounds?" The helicopter, and the helicopter is a moral proposition because without the helicopter we would've had mutinies, we would've ended much sooner since we didn't have what it takes to go into the bush and fight on a man-to-man basis—forgive the John Wayne language. So I took helicopter sounds from many different sources: newsreel footage, mostly Vietnam, mostly from ABC. Then I put them on different tracks and made a mix of them, and played with the levels, so the sound begins very low, and by the time those minutes are over, the sound is supposed to cream you, deafen you, make you unhappy. But, instead, what projectionists do is turn it down so it won't affect the audience.

But it's what sound and image do together that matters. The sound isn't realistic in a Hollywood film; every bit of that sound is totally controlled in a studio atmosphere. And the so-called reality films, fiction films, still have to mix and mute out stuff and amplify some material. So, Jackson Pollock is the opposite of what I see in film: that whole idea of putting the canvas on the floor and throwing the paint around—your unconscious expressing everything. Maybe that's why I like that kind of painting, because I don't feel competitive in any way. I look upon film in a totally different way: all that sound is contrived. You're working with machinery, let's face it. You're not working with a floor and a canvas and a brush and paint. And you're not working alone. It's a social art in which more than one person works. It's an art that must use a machine: the camera, the Nagra, the Steenbeck are all machines. All your data are processed through machines, so it becomes a romantic and ridiculous piece of pettifoggery to say that it's anything but those things.

The ultimate test of anything, and this is true of painting, writing, film, is if it works. If something doesn't work, it shrieks at you. For example, I don't use too much voice-over; in fact, *Point of Order* was the first full-length documentary made with no narration, but nothing would be wrong with using it if it works.

I also like to make the audience work. In *Painters Painting* you don't have to be very smart to know that when you go into a huge studio like the one Jasper Johns had, which was an old bank three and a half stories high, that you're going to get reverberations. All you have to do is to listen. I always do listen to the Nagra, just as I always look through the camera. And you don't have to be very clever to know that because a radio is on, you're going to have a lot of interference, but when Mary, the soundperson, said, "Should I cut the radio?" I said, "No," because I wanted the audience to strain because Johns is one of the most intelligent painters of his time. He's an intellectual, he reads Wittgenstein, etcetera. And the film experience, which obviously antedates the television experience, is basically such a passive experience—it's a cliché, but it's true. You go into the warm, darkened room, lights go down, and there you are, returned to that inner experience, of things happening *to* you. And there you are with all the perfect sync sound, and all the effects easily penetrate your system. Well, I don't like that. I want people to work, so in the case of the Johns interview, I intentionally made it hard to hear. You have to listen for it, you have to strain. And that also sets you up in the whole film, because if you strain for Johns, you're going to relax a little afterwards, but then maybe it keys you up in general. I don't make films to entertain people. I'm not against entertainment films; it's just that I'm not interested in them, in making them.

·4·

THE ACTOR

An aspect of movies that has no real equivalent in any other art form is the presence on film *of moving, breathing, talking people. Though they are photographic representations, these iconographic images are given a heightened reality by cinema. Unlike ordinary people, they defy normal physical limitations: they move freely through time and space; they vary in size from the minuscule to the immense; they can reveal to us all or only part of their bodies; they can move in normal speed or in the camera's speeded-up or slowed-down motion; and they can be transformed into images of inhuman beauty or ugliness by the willful distortion of the lighting pattern and the lens. But their magic is not always so flamboyant. Cinema's most special gift to the actor is simply bringing the viewer close enough to see the blink of a lash, close enough to see the character think, close enough to enter into the character's inner life, to discover the motivations underlying his behavior. Above all, it is the actor, that presence which is both less and more than human, which links the viewer to the events pictured on the screen. Because it is the actor who creates the fascination and the seduction, few filmmakers would deny the critical importance of choices in casting and working with the right actors.*

Traditionally, the director attempts to cast according to type, but many films succeed because the director followed a canny hunch that at first may have seemed to be improbable. A classic example would be Dustin Hoffman in The Graduate. *Though hardly the image of the blond, preppy dreamboat of the source novel, Hoffman's off-beat swarthy looks were largely responsible for lifting the film out of the ordinary and giving it special appeal.*

Film acting differs greatly from stage acting wherein the actor remains life-size and, though physically present, is removed by the proscenium from the audience. His actions, voice, and facial expressions must be magnified to be perceived, whereas film acting is done for the hypersensitive camera, which demands subtlety from its subjects or they become grimacing clowns. In fact, a good film actor doesn't "act" as much as he simply thinks and trusts his mobile actor's face and body to reveal the thoughts of his character. Often an inexperienced observer on a movie set has mistakenly thought the actors were doing nothing.

Many issues surround the role of actor, and once more the issue of control versus improvisation is at the core. How does one conceptualize a role? Is this the actor's sole responsibility or the director's, or is the realization of a role a cooperative venture? Should the actors be allowed to improvise their dialogue, at least in part, or must they follow the script to the letter? How far should the actor's cooperation in the total film extend? Should he be involved in the writing stage, even in the edit, during which, countless actors have complained, their best moments were left on the cutting room floor? Is it preferable to use the naturalness of non-professionals or to rely on the skills of the professional actor?

The truth is, one can never completely dominate an actor, professional or non-professional, and this is another element of surprise that makes film so exciting. It is undeniable: actors are the life and breath of a film. As far as veteran Michael Powell is concerned, the problem of actors is very simple: "An actor only needs a sympathetic director who's got the camera at the right distance. Everything is in having the camera at the right distance."

JEAN-LUC GODARD

In the United States the system is so corrupted, the actors are stars and they cannot act.

"The star" is a cultural problem or phenomenon. The star represents something that belongs to people. They are happy to see that in close-up: they can criticize it. That is something in film that has always astonished me. The spectator pays ten francs to see a film. Alain Delon or Barbra Streisand earn in one day or one hour what it takes people one year or even more to earn, but they don't mind that at all, whereas in a factory or office they do mind that others earn more than them. But there are moments even with Alain Delon and myself; there are parts of Alain Delon I detest, and these parts are mine, and I cannot blame him for these parts, as if he was some kind of a king that he represents. But as long as he does no harm, he furnishes an hour or more of doing something that I don't feel like doing. It's okay.

In my films I often had to use people, such as Marguerite Duras, who could speak their own truths while being in my fiction, and their truth supports my fiction because without them, my fiction collapses.

It's impossible to work with actors who are stars because they are like presidents or chiefs or governments and they are afraid to lose their place, to try something else. Maybe in a country like Poland; the way they work, you can have someone starring in one picture and then in the next picture they can be an extra and there is no hard feeling about it. Polish actors are very good this way and you have a feeling you can work with them . . . in Russia, too.

If you're working with someone who's unknown, you should at least have a common relation to what's in between the image or the camera, but since the camera is unknown, you have too much unknown. If he doesn't know me, it's a problem, and if he does know me, he knows me too much and that's too little also, because then it's corrupted by the way it's coded or symbolized.

I wish I could work more now with actors. I'm more able to

bring something of the story, but you need to work more, and they should bring more, and they don't know what to bring. They are waiting for genius and they don't know what to bring. You have to train, and to train means sometimes to run, to swim, to go to another country just for fun and to talk to the people so you can study. That's training, and actors don't train in life. They pretend to imitate it and sometimes it's very poor, so I just try to make them *look* natural, but it's such work that sometimes it is too difficult. I prepare, but somewhere else and not with the actors. I attempt to make it spontaneous. It was good earlier, but not now, after twenty years of making films.

MARK RAPPAPORT

I always used to hold actors in great contempt, and then I made *Local Color,* which involved eight large speaking parts, and I realized how hard it is to act and what is required in directing actors. I think that what actors can do is very wonderful and I think working with actors is great. I don't let actors improvise. I write dialogue. I think it's a rare actor who will come up with dialogue that is as interesting as what a writer-director can come up with unless the actor is *very* good. After seeing *Last Tango in Paris,* I would trust Marlon Brando to do anything, but generally, it's a very heavy burden on an actor. I wonder when you're acting if you can really think, "I've got to make this line funny, too," and it's sort of having this double vision: your eyes are always cocked on a double response: "How am I doing as an actor and how am I doing as an actor-writer, and am I getting the lion's share of the laughs and the attention?" In that kind of situation, it's really the very fabulous actor who doesn't go for the immediate laugh or the immediate *zoftig* line. Maybe one day I'll feel freer to improvise, to let actors be more in control of their performances, because I think it's probably very tight-fisted of me. I don't want actors doing *everything* they can do. I don't think that I make those kind of movies where it pertains, in any event. At least not right now. I think part of directing actors is making the right choices in casting, such as a movie like *Citizen's Band* by Jonathan Demme in which the acting is great and the movie works partly because of very canny casting. That takes a lot of time. Half to three-quarters of a director's job is getting the right people.

I'm working on very low budgets and that's a little harder because you don't have access to agents: you often don't have access to union actors or well-known agents. You don't have access to people who require a lot of money. I think that for low-budget filmmakers it's a little more difficult, so you try to concentrate on the kind of film where acting is not that important. But it's not true of the films I'm making now, especially this new film that I'm writing which is, again, very precise, very specific, and very talky, so I need very, very good actors. Since I've written lines to be said a certain way, I need actors who will be able to hit certain points in the way I intended them to be read. That gets a little tricky, and in the films I make it's a question of tone, also. So the important thing is getting actors to understand the tone properly or the proper tone of the film or the scene because it's very tight-ropey: Is it funny? Is it intentionally funny? Is it unintentionally funny? Is it ironic? Is it played straight? Well, if a scene has all of the above in it, it's very tricky for an actor. On the other hand, you don't want actors experimenting with it and maybe never getting there. So, in a certain way, I like to clarify my intentions almost at the very beginning. I first let them do what they want to do, and then I say, "I'm glad you got that out of your system. You'll never have to do *that* again." If you come to a script cold, there's a lot of possibilities of misunderstanding simple sentences. Or, if one word in a sentence is supposed to be underlined, you wouldn't underline it in the script because that makes it too emphatic. It's not good to hide your intentions from actors and hope that they're going to arrive at the point, because it's not fair to them and it's not fair to yourself. On the other hand, I'm not into giving line readings, as when you tell an actor, "Do it this way," except when it gets very critical. Then I tell them, "What the line means is such and such, not the way you're doing it."

ROBERT ALTMAN

Actors are, without a doubt, the most important element, because they're the ones who are performing. And if it really came down to it, where we didn't have a set, we didn't have any lights, and we were sitting on a beach with a camera and four actors, we still could do something. So, the actors are the real artists and everybody else is in support of them. Now, if you're dealing with a film without any actors—*The Life of a Squid*—that's a different kind of film, a documentary, and then the squid's the most important thing in the film. It's the living, moving presence. Sometimes the most important thing can be the sun—where is the sun? But, by and large, the sun is going to do the same thing every day and it's not aware that it's being photographed. The actors are. They have to behave in a manner to express a combination of what I want and what they want.

The first thing you have to understand is, what are we doing? I mean, *why* are we doing it? Are we doing this because we're getting three thousand dollars a week? You're never going to get a group of actors or even two actors who totally agree on what they're doing, and you don't have to because people don't either. But they have to be true to what they are in that film. I try as much as possible to let the actor draw as much of his own life and his own experience into the character he's playing and encourage him to use that mainly because it gives him less to think about. You don't have to say, "Jesus, what would he do if his grandmother died?" Well, he doesn't have to think about it because his grandmother *did* die, so he knows what to do. To use those kinds of things means they have less to concentrate on and that is the actor's art: to slip into a character, to make himself someone else. But it's all drawn from themselves; it has to be; it's the only frame of reference we have.

I'll do whatever the actor wants to do. I have written or talked elaborate back stories. In *McCabe and Mrs. Miller* we had a situation where I wanted to use a little speech in the book that I thought was marvelous, very poetic, and in the writing of the script I tried many times to get that same material in, but it doesn't work when a person thinks to himself, "a stream of consciousness," because those are things he can't say. So, when Warren and I started talking about it, I said, "Let's take a chance. We can have the character talk to himself alone in a room." And Warren said, "That's pretty dicey." And I said, "Sure, it's pretty dicey, but let's do it." And then we said, "Let's set it up, let's have this guy mumble all the time, talk to himself." And we set it up in the very beginning. And Warren said, "You mean, I'm just going to walk around, mumbling all the time?" So, we set up this whole back story that created the character, that he was never the top dog. He had a friend named Frank, and Frank was the sharpy. Frank was McCabe. Frank was the real good gambler. Frank was the guy that killed Bill Roundtree. And Frank had said, "Listen, we're going to get out of San Francisco, because the money is up in this place called Presbyterian Church up near Bear Paw, and the electricity's coming in and zinc's really terrific. And we're going to go up there and we'll open ourselves a whorehouse and a gambling house and we'll have it set for life." And McCabe says, "That's terrific, Frank." So, Frank is the leader of this whole thing. Now, Frank picks up a girl and they're all in San Francisco and McCabe says, "Let's get going." But the girl doesn't want to go to Bear Paw, she wants to stay in San Francisco. So, Frank says, "in a week or so." Finally, McCabe says, "I'm going tomorrow and if you're not going, I'm going by myself." And he makes kind of a weak stand, and Frank says, "Okay, go on by yourself." And McCabe goes to bed and he's not really going to go, but when he comes downstairs in the morning, the girl and Frank have checked out. Now, he goes off somewhere for the first time in his life, not as second banana, and the first thing he says as he comes into this town with his derby, and he looks over this hill and he sees those huts, he says, "Six of 'em, Frank, I told ya, six of 'em." So the idea was that he always had that reference so that everything he did was imitating his best friend, who he couldn't live up to being.

The audience doesn't know that—all they see is McCabe coming in, but he has to have some background. It gave Warren a place to work from, and it gave all of us a place to work from. The only thing that didn't work as well as we thought was that Warren got nervous about the mumbling to himself, and he didn't want to carry that through as much. But he did enough so it set it up. And he may have been right. I may have wanted to go too far.

Actors always say that their best scenes were cut, and they feel that because they have never *seen* those performances, but they felt something. They performed something, and for them, the full center is around them. And that's the way they see it. Burt Lancaster in *Buffalo Bill and the Indians*—he didn't like the film at all. We left a party afterward, and he was walking down the stairs with his son, and I just happened to be walking directly behind him, and he said, "Well, they cut at least eighty percent of my stuff, all the best stuff has been cut. And," he said, "it's a different picture. It's not the picture I made." As a matter of fact, Burt Lancaster played the narrator in a way, the Ned Buntline character, and every single scene and footage we shot on Burt is in that picture. But to his mind, it was not. But an awful lot of stuff we did with Paul Newman is not in the picture and an awful lot of stuff we did with everybody else is not in the film. And yet Burt had this thing about, "Well, they cut most of my stuff." And he's not lying. He believes that.

ELIO PETRI

I think the filmmaker should be good enough to use the actor's humanity for the purpose of making a film, but you mustn't go against the actor, as often happens in the theater.

I improvise in front of the camera because I think the actor influences the camera, its movements, and that the camera influences the actor. And this is also true for the sets: I think the thing must be born on the set.

The actor is a very important figure in Western culture, in all our culture. Our culture is based on a split inside us that is very important insofar as we're not based on an integralistic process,

an autistic process. So, within us there's the possibility of having many "I's." That is, within us there's a process of splitting
that doesn't finish if one can get control of it. It's schizophrenic
in an active sense. In a way, coherence is a word you apply to a
state of madness, incoherence to a state of normality. The actor
is a projection of ourselves and the audience is a projection of
the actor. If you take this as a principle of departure, you can
understand many other things about society. If you start with
the principle that society is a theater, a principle so elementary
that it seems banal—but it's true nonetheless—then right now
we're acting a scene: I'm in one role, you're in another. It's not
a role we have inside us. The movie theater becomes a liberat-
ing moment in which the viewer finally has no role to play and
in which the actor chooses the role. In fact, it's not by chance
that the English and American theater has a great tradition: it's
the one place where people finally accept this split and abandon every form and every role. But this takes place in accord-
ance with social rules. The theater is always an officially
designated place. In cinema it's even more complicated because
of the solitude occasioned by the darkness, the lack of form
because the spectacle is continued. The rite is less formalized.
And then there's a magical-technical element that in some way
leads to dream. However, there is in some way an element that
lessens the other three: the camera is objective. So these three
highly subjective elements: darkness, solitude, and magic, are
fused with a strongly objective element. Because if I were to
photograph you as a mask, you are a mask, it's clear you are a
mask; while in the theater it's different. The magic works in an
absolutely different way. In the darkness of the cinema, there
is the solitude of the spectator and the solitude of the actor
who doesn't, after all, act in front of an audience. So there is a
confluence of solitudes and an element of splitting that has a
very different meaning from that of theater.

DUŠAN MAKAVEJEV

In the beginning I was afraid of actors. Now I'm much more confident in myself and in them. Professional actors can do a lot because they carry a lot. They carry their own charisma, they carry their own aura. And if they know what you're doing, they're terrific. I feel they're my assistants. Sometimes they should do exactly what is written, but the best thing is to get them to relate and to create. And professional actors have a great sense of space: they use their bodies. They know where the lights are; they know that they're used to produce images, so they shouldn't be treated as illiterates. They're highly professional—they know everything about movies. So, tell them what you want and they'll do it.

With Jimmy Dean, we understood for the first time what an actor is: a guy who put his back to the camera and mumbled. He knew that it's important to place obstacles between himself and the public. He did it the same way as Brando, who said you should act forty percent. You create this big aura, you create this incredible tension. This is what I was saying about creating that tension with the frame and the shot length: they do it with themselves. So, when they slow down and there's something not normal, suddenly you almost jump in to see what's happening. Or when they drop something. It's very important for them not to try to be perfect and not to imitate even themselves in reality. This is movies. Unfortunately, some actors are afraid to use their bodies. They're ready to give themselves completely in the medium shot, but they're embarrassed about close-ups or about everything that's not the face. So, they're ready to show a naked face but not a naked back or a leg.

I think our sight is highly censored. The face is seemingly highly legal, breasts are not, etcetera. The foot is not sexual, but you rarely see people's feet playing in movies. For example, there's a beautiful number in *Hair*, "Black Boys," using feet. It's a fantastic piece using legs and feet magnificently. People are infinitely rich in what they have, but they are used so rarely.

JACQUES DEMY

What I like to do is just to set up the scene without the camera, just the actors and myself all together, and we play. But we play like children when they play a game: it's to have fun and get the best out of it. And we give each other ideas, and I'm open to any suggestion as long as we're going in the same direction.

Anouk Aimée's character in *Lola* is a beautiful study of a certain type of woman, and she plays it with a charm. Hers is the most beautiful face I've ever framed; that was a pure joy—just to look at her through the viewfinder. She's really beautiful and talented, but lazy. She wouldn't bother to learn her lines, and the dialogue was just so. I had spent a long time writing it, and very precisely. So she had to say the lines and, in the end, she did it. But I had a problem at the beginning of the film and I didn't know how to deal with that. Anouk was marvelous at the first take, but the male lead was good at the tenth one and bad on the first one. Fortunately, I realized it on the very first day, so I worked a lot with him before, just to get him ready, and then I would call to Anouk, "He's ready!" She gives everything on the first take, which is fabulous but difficult to work with, even with the crew, because everyone then has to be good on that first take and so many things can happen. So, then she would take a rest and would be back for two or three takes and be good again. She would find the mood again.

You cannot ask for that because it depends on the sensitivity. You have people who cannot control that. It's more difficult, but when they give it, it's so beautiful. Jeanne Moreau was more professional that way. She's a marvelous stage actress, so she knows about that. One day we had fun because she was so good that I said, "Jeanne, that was so good, could you try it in exactly the opposite way?" And she gave me exactly the opposite and as good as before.

ERMANNO OLMI

I use non-professionals for more or less the same reasons I choose a real landscape over one reconstructed in the studio. For *Barry Lyndon* Kubrick looked over half of Europe to find the countrysides and atmosphere that corresponded to his expressive needs. Within this countryside, this choice that he made from the real, he grafted on the actors. I prefer to continue this relationship with reality, not reconstructed in the studio. The real tree is continuously creative; the artificial tree isn't. The fake tree responds to the creative needs of a fact already laid out and defined, and stops there. The real tree has continuing virtues: it responds to and reflects light in an ever new way. When you shoot in the studio, you've set up the lighting in advance; the lights are the same from beginning to end. You can shoot the same shot a hundred times and it will be the same. The real tree, on the other hand, is in continual evolution, modifying itself inside the situation, so much so that you become anxious lest you not be able to capture a particular moment when the light is changing. This, too, is very beautiful, because between the first shot and the fourth and the fifth there are variations—it is continually palpitating. Thus with the actor. Maybe there exists an extraordinary actor, but really, I have always felt in them a bit of cardboard in respect to the great palpitating authenticity of the real character who was not chosen, as the actors were some time ago, for a certain face, beauty, or because they characterize a certain type. For example, in a film about peasants I choose the actors from the peasant world. I don't use a fig to make a pear. These people, these characters, bring to the film a weight, really a constitution of truth that, provoked by the situations in which the characters find themselves, creates palpitations, those vibrations so right, so real, and therefore not repeatable. At the twentieth take the actor still cries. The real actor, the character taken from life, won't do more than four repetitions. It's like capturing a light: either you get it at that moment or you don't get it at all. But it isn't that he exhausts himself; he becomes something else. So, my emotion lies also in following these things.

MILOS FORMAN

You can see small, unrepeatable moments in films, for example, in Italian neorealistic films, in the beginning of the French *nouvelle vague*. You can see those moments occasionally in American movies. This is something I like very much because that's probably the only thing that distinguishes film from any other medium. You can have it on television, but usually not in dramatic form. You can have it in direct transmissions of sports and things like that. But as part of a dramatic story . . . theater is rehearsed, but if you're a great master, you can master that. I saw Dean Martin in Las Vegas and I would've bet all my money that he was drunk, and then I saw him again two nights later, and he was exactly the same. It was an act. He's such a master that it seemed spontaneous. That's one of the advantages, on one hand, and one of the disadvantages, on the other hand, of being a filmmaker: that you can see through things, unless it's a very good movie that sucks you in. Otherwise you just sit there and see how it was done. I know how thrilled I am when I see a moment where I wonder how they did that. How did they get this from the actor? I am fascinated by that, so I try to do the same thing.

You use a lot of tricks, psychological tricks, on them. Also, in the case of Ivan Passer's films and my films, we worked in Czechoslovakia with a lot of non-professional actors, not for artistic reasons, but for very practical reasons because there the actors act in everything, and if someone's good, they are so busy. They might do one hour of radio in the morning, go to the studio to shoot for five hours, then go to rehearsal in the theater, and in the evening, play on the stage. So, if you're an unknown, as we were when we first started, and you're doing a film miles away from Prague, you don't have a chance to have a good actor. Nobody will disappear and let all the other jobs go to be with you, especially when it's not sure that you will turn out a good movie. So, rather than work with mediocre or bad actors, I turned to non-professionals. And you can't over-rehearse with them. You rehearse very little, and then you must start to shoot, even if you consider it as a rehearsal, and through *this* way of shooting, you suddenly got very exciting moments on the screen that I didn't know if I wanted or could repeat if I wanted to repeat. This practical experience revealed for me the way to provoke these kinds of moments, even with professional actors. Or you just start shooting: "Okay, let's do one more rehearsal. Oh, let's just put it on film, but it's just a rehearsal." So, sometimes you use tricks: you tell an actor, "Now you are here, you do this, you go there, and you say this, and then you do this. But 'this' is not really important. Now, when you get to this point, then you say this, and do this—and this is important. And you know I will not use that, that will not be in the film," but that makes an actor concentrate very heavily on something I won't use and go very easily through things I know count. For me, the credibility of human behavior on the screen is very important. The moment that credibility is shaken by feelings such as, "This is rehearsed and they are just doing it without thinking," I am turned off.

I understand using non-professional actors very well, except that sometimes you are just lucky enough to find a professional actor who is so close to the character you need, that you can use him without suffering this cringing embarrassment when you see somebody pretending something when it's not real. In *Cuckoo's Nest* all the doctors are real doctors and some of the aides on the maximum security ward were real, but I think it was very proper to use a star for the lead because it is a story where somebody from the outside world, which means a world familiar to *us,* is entering an unknown world. So I wanted that everybody there is unknown to us, but I felt it was right if the person who was entering was someone with whom we can identify, which means we know who he is. He has our confidence already. Besides, I think Jack Nicholson has very many aspects of the character to play. With Jack—I still don't know today if he's so smart or so crazy.

HENRY JAGLOM

I encourage actors to do the scene and when they finish the scene just to keep going and then to do the scene again and keep doing it over and over again, but in their own words, as they feel it. I'm not enamoured of my words. Frequently, I think actors—if they stick closely to the reality of what I'm trying to do—will give me more with their language than with my words that I have written for them. Dennis Hopper gives me a look and it is more moving than ten pages of dialogue because it is *him*. I cast him as a soldier for reasons that were clear. So I could throw away ten pages and I could play around and just have the actors try this and that and discover all the wonderful accidents that happen. If you're painting and you make a mistake—there's a drip—now you've got to incorporate the drip into the painting. It forces you to rethink. It's wonderful. And it gives the actors a chance to really contribute an extraordinary amount more than film acting usually allows them. In *A Safe Place* the same thing happened between Tuesday Weld, Orson Welles, and Jack Nicholson by casting people close to their characters. It's a nice reason for using stars, if you cast someone that the audience knows about.

I also like to use real people who are available to fill in the landscape around the actors; it helps their reality. I think that surrounding good actors with real people, non-actors, is very valuable. In *Tracks*, we were on the train and we used a real soldier as the Mexican-American soldier on the train—he's not an actor. I found him on the train. He said, "What are you doing?" We were having a break and I told him. He said, "I had a cousin who came back from Vietnam." And I said, "Do you want to tell me about this?" And he said, "Yeah." I said, "Not now, on camera." He said, "Sure." And I just took the cameraman and I said, "Turn it on and focus it on him, no preparation." The result is, I think, that you get a much more natural look. My cameraman on *Tracks* told me at the beginning of that film that none of it would come out. We shot across country for three days and he was convinced that none of it would come out because he said, "You can't shoot without lights on a train." The soundman said that I wouldn't be able to hear anything. The conventional wisdom was that since nobody had shot live sound on a train before, it was impossible. I had been told this all over Hollywood. Producers who had done ten movies told me you can't shoot live on a train because it won't come out. Well, of course it does. All that happens is that when a train noise occurs, the actors have to talk louder, and it resembles real life, just as when you're on a train and you go over a bridge, it's louder, a louder environment, so you talk louder to compensate for the noise. What they meant when they said you can't do it live is that you can't cut it, they think, because they're thinking of logical cutting. Lights are changing on actor's faces, but that's wonderful for me. You've got lights changing on people's faces and the feeling of real movement on a real train with real noise—changes and everything.

Once a conductor came and said, "Do you have a permit?" And I said, "Sure!" And he said, "Where?" So I sent one of my assistants back to an imaginary car to get an imaginary permit, and while they were looking for it, I shot the rest of the scene and we got off the train. And you know it works better that way. In the last picture we did that same thing. In *Sitting Ducks* we went into Howard Johnsons and Holiday Inns and shot freely real backgrounds and real people. If you get permission you're comfortable and you start filling the place up with extras instead of real people. Extras act like extras, you know? The actors start thinking that they're actors and they're not people any more. The cameraman thinks he's got time to light and suddenly you're making a "movie," and you're not revealing some sort of behavior, and it just doesn't work for me.

Actors are wonderfully capable of doing something that real people aren't. Real people are very self-conscious about being themselves. Some, very few, can do it, but for any prolonged period of time they start becoming their *idea* of themselves, and that stops them from being free and flowing. For instance, it's much harder to get a real person to cry, because crying is a private behavior for most people, and an actor knows that his private behavior is his public behavior. So, I don't think you can ever do away with or should do away with actors, but what you should do is help them. First, you have to choose good actors who are also real people, and there's a lot of actors and actresses who are and a lot who aren't, so you have to choose those well. And, second, if you surround them with real people, you surround them with enough surprises. Zack Norman in *Sitting Ducks* did not know that Patrice was going to pour the water on his head. Michael Emil did not know in *Sitting Ducks* that Zack Norman was going to get into the bathtub naked with him. And knowing that Michael Emil doesn't like to have too close proximity with another naked male—that's something I know about him. So I tell him, "Okay, you sit in the bathtub; what we're going to do now is I'm going to send the girl, Irene Forrest, in and she's just rejected you in the scene where you explained sex to her, and she's going to come in fully clothed and sit on the edge of the tub and you're going to have a conversation. There's just one rule here: you can't get out of the tub. No matter what happens." And then I arrange with Zack to go in naked. Michael, all he remembers is that he's not allowed to get out of the tub. He's in complete shock at this. So that helps them. They're very good actors. But this helps them get to their own surprise.

Non-actors would just turn and not know what to do. I love surprises because you give the actors the advantage of surprising them. There's all different ways of doing it. I usually conspire with one actor against the other to sort of constantly have private little deals, so that they're surprising each other. It's a game.

But I'm talking about the *film* actor, because none of this applies to theater, where you have to do the same thing night after night after night. You have to be precise. On film, all you've got to capture is a *moment*, and any way you can capture that moment obviously is legitimate.

JEAN ROUCH

I filmed a twenty minute segment for *Paris vu par*, a sketch film with Chabrol, Godard [the Godard segment was shot by the Maysles, who came to Paris], Rohmer, people like that. My piece was a fiction film about the Gare du Nord. The story was done in one shot, twenty minutes. Of course, we had to stop after ten minutes to change the magazine, but we did that while we were in the elevator, in darkness, and we tried to keep the continuity. The story was what happens in the twenty minutes before a suicide. There were three actors: one was professional; the girl had acted in two of my films but she was not professional; and the third was Barbet Schroeder, who was the producer. And in the Gare du Nord, in the last part, the guy who committed suicide was the actor and he was very bad, not *very* bad, but the others were so good. But, if you use only non-professionals, only one take is good: take one. You can never have a take two with a non-professional. That is the difference. Actors can repeat takes. With the others, you have to take take one. But it's really thrilling to make a film this way. You have suspense, you are making your film, walking with the camera, you don't know what will happen, you might just fall down because of a stone, or you are very tired or very tense and the actors are too. And this contact of people who are making something in ten minutes—if during the last minute you have something wrong, you have to do it again from the very beginning. *Then,* the tension is fantastic. That's the way I like to make films. Of course, you never have these kind of relationships in real life. Maybe when you are trying to catch a plane and you are late and you are on the highway going quickly and it's very dramatic. But, in fact, it's not really drama; it's just fighting against time. The contest is not good, but in filming, the contest is good because you are just doing something, and minute after minute something is being born. You are procreating something in this bloody small machine that makes noise and you know you have to go to the end. And I think that is the way to make films.

GEORGE ROMERO

The actors are very important. I'm not one of those people who say, "Forget the actors." It's unfortunate because for all my films, I get the attention, or the film itself gets the attention, and really, the cast is important. The cast in *Martin* is a really good cast, as is the cast in *Dawn*. I cast just by looking at people, and we play around and do improvs. I'd rather see things that they know rather than give them a sheet and say, "Read this," or "Go learn this." I'd rather just play around with things that they know and just talk to them. I'd rather be sure that they know what I'm about and what we're trying to do—that's the most important thing to me, and that they're bright enough people to know what we're about rather than just technicians or commmodities.

They have a lot of input, though if you look at the script for *Dawn*, a lot of the dialogue is set, although I don't consider that sacrosanct in any way. I'm not at all insistent that way. I'm more insistent on an attitude. I just want people to understand the characterization, and I don't care about the words so much as long as it's in the right vein. Sometimes when you're doing really melodramatic comic-book stuff, people want to back off and make things a little too naturalistic, which is weird, because I thought that if anyone would say anything about the cast in *Dawn* they would say that they overacted. Instead, they're saying that they were wooden. And they're anything but wooden. They're very broad. It's strange sometimes the way people perceive things. It blows my mind sometimes. But if you go down to the theater and watch the audience getting off and cheering and going crazy, one of the single elements has to be that they're behind those four people, or at least understand them.

And the cast looks like real people. I think that they're very important that way. And that's something else in terms of working within the mechanism, because when you're working with melodrama, or any of the genres, it's very important to have actors about whom you don't have any preconceived notions. It's a very important element. You know, can you see Richard Thomas as Martin? But there, again, unless you want to keep working with low bucks as a sub-independent, nobody would ever let you get away with that. And that comes down to economics, because I've had people say to me, "If I spend two million dollars on a movie, I'll lose every penny, whereas if I spend six or eight, then I buy Anthony Quinn and get it all back: three million from television, twenty-five percent from European sales. I'll blind bid it and get my money back from theaters before I ever open the picture, and I'll be out. Because if you tell me to put a million or a million and a half on this movie, you're asking me to gamble on a *movie*." Nobody will gamble on a movie. Everyone wants to gamble on the deal. And that's the stuff that I go apeshit over.

But I cast non-professionals a lot. I like to do that. It's more fun and you get a certain honesty from them as long as they're uninhibited enough and as long as they can say lines without being outrageous. There's a certain texture in that that really works for me. Sometimes not. It depends. If it's a really structured thing, it can become jarring. The one-legged priest in *Dawn of the Dead* was some guy who's a stagehand in a little theater that I used to work with, and there's a guy that's literally right off the street in the film. There was a lot of impact from him.

JOAN MICKLIN SILVER AND RAPHAEL D. SILVER

J.S. It seems to me that most directors permit the actors to rehearse both from the rehearsal space and the location, then determine angles and coverage and so on. It's especially hard to pre-plan outdoor scenes because you don't know what the light is going to be. I understand on television all those things are pre-planned: the actor is told, "All right, sit over there and say these two lines and get up and go to the desk and say . . ." because they don't have time, and everything must be thought out ahead. I understand that some films are shot that way too, but I can't imagine working that way. One of the things that keeps changing is your perception of the actors. Actors continually surprise you, and you realize, "Here is a side to this actor that's a marvelous thing and I want to get it," so you're constantly adjusting because you know more on day ten than you knew on day one.

In rehearsal you might explore the aspects of a scene: you

might try to take the scene in a different direction, you might try to play the scene from the opposite point of view, anything to illuminate what the scene is and what the actors know about the characters. Then I would personally rewrite the scene, and they learn the rewritten version, so they're always working from a written version.

I don't believe in improvisation in front of the camera. First of all, I couldn't afford it; it's a very expensive way to shoot. Second, it's so rarely effective because it's shapeless; it meanders and it makes you want to run it over with your blue pencil and cross some of those things off—get it together and get more dramatic coherence. I don't think actors are writers. It's as simple as that. I think you should go by your script.

R.S. Improvisation can be helpful sometimes to help the actors loosen up and get into it, but when you've got them in front of the camera, you want them to stick very closely to the script. It's a very different quality. When, in some films, a scene is drifting to improvisation in the midst of structured dialogue, it's very noticeable. It's a very different kind of thing, a conversational dialogue that is free-form and something that is dramatically formed. I don't think they blend at all; unless the entire structure of a film is based on improvisation, the film's structure becomes erratic. So if you see a film that's ninety-five percent structured dialogue and somewhere along the line some scenes are improvised, you're very conscious of it and it throws you off. You lose contact with the story in the middle of the film and think about the device that's being used, which I don't think is effective at all.

On the other hand, if you're dealing with an inexperienced actor, as in *On the Yard,* where a number of inmates acted small roles in the film, I asked them to familiarize themselves with the dialogue in the scene and what the scene was supposed to convey. But, if they felt more comfortable using different words to express those feelings, I told them to feel free to do so, and I asked the professional actors who acted with them to stay with the dialogue so there would be a basic point from which the non-professionals could wander a little bit, but the scene could be brought back to the structure.

J.S. Some filmmakers don't believe in improvisation. There are good filmmakers who absolutely don't believe in it. It depends on what technique works for them. It also depends on what kind of actor you have. In *Between the Lines* we had an extremely young, very loose, very gung-ho group of actors. They were just dying to try all sorts of permutations in every scene—about one-third of the final film came out of the work that they did in rehearsal, in improvisation. They wanted to rehearse at night, on the weekends. On the other hand, there are a lot of really wonderful actors who cannot improvise one word, who fall apart unless they have written dialogue.

As far as how you work with actors, I don't know, I think every actor requires something different. It's your personality; sometimes you find that you can be very helpful to one actor and there's something there that's stopping you from giving the same kind of support to another actor. I find it terribly hard to generalize about those things.

R.S. It's also partly trying to understand what the need of the particular actor is. Some of them are desperate to talk out forever the role interpretations, etcetera. Some actors really have to work to get it because they want to block; they have a different conception of the way they want to do the role. They really don't want to share it with you until they're in front of the camera. That's a big risk, so you somehow want to find a way to penetrate and open up the dialogue and find out what they're really thinking and try to make adjustments and changes if they're necessary. The experience that I've had is that every actor is very different and wants a different kind of relationship with the director. Some are very comfortable and confident, and some are very confused themselves and distrust themselves and distrust you and are never sure even when they're told they've done a marvelous job and everyone else tells them. They'll say it's terrible. But they also realize that the director controls what the public is going to see, both in the shooting and the editing of the film, and that their interpretation of the role, and more than that, is really in the director's hands and much harder to control than on the stage where every night they can modulate their own performance and experiment. The director is always the one that's really doing the experimentation once he's got them on film.

J.S. I think there's probably never been a film in which some actors didn't forever feel that the director left out his best work. I heard a great story about someone coming in to dub his dialogue and when he saw how the scene had been done, he was so angry about what had been taken out that he pulled the phone out of the wall. That's a common kind of reaction because they don't think in terms of the whole. They don't actually have access to see everything that you see. It's also very exposed, and the hardest thing is to make actors feel that they can really make mistakes on film, and that you will never let them make a fool out of themselves. Because if they can't get to that point, then it's going to be a very tight situation—they're never going to give very much of anything if they're that worried about what you're going to do with it.

One thing different about the way we cast, I'm beginning to realize from what people say, is that when we can, we'll ask an actor to improvise with us, playing the character that he's trying out for. Not because we want to find out how he improvises, but because it gives you a much closer look at how he views the role. So that whether or not he's an adept person at improvisation, he will somehow give you something more of himself there than he will in the tense situation of trying out, where he's worked very hard on the scene and has come to present it to the director and producer. And you often find out very surprising things—that this actor views the role one way and you didn't understand that at all from his reading.

The thing that every director worries about when he's casting is, "Have I really given this person a fair chance to show me what he or she can do?" And some people do very well in auditions, some people are notoriously bad in auditions. Some people read well, some don't, and if you reduce your consideration to how that person came in and read this particular scene, you don't know as much about that actor. It's a way of helping you understand more, getting more of a sense of what the actor's scope is and other things the actor can bring to it, that maybe he or she didn't do in the audition situation, which for many actors is not a comfortable one at all. I still to this day run into actors who say, "Oh, I could have read better for you." You know, they keep thinking it over—the ten, fifteen minutes they have to present themselves. And as much as the actor worries, that's how much the director worries. There are directors who don't read people at all; there are directors who simply look at some film on people and cast from that. There are different ways of doing it. Some actors had much more than we were able to grab onto in the audition situation, and you go later and see that actor in something else or in some play, and you say, "Wow, where was I when that actor . . . why is it that I missed so much?"

R.S. If you have a preconception in your mind of what you want the person to look like, I think you can end up with a pretty dull movie. You can look and not even listen to the people you don't picture in the role, but sometimes they have extraordinary things to contribute. So, I think, we spend a lot of time talking about what we're looking for, but I think what we're really looking for is a kind of quality—an approach to the material, an ability to deliver the material through improvisation, or from reading the script, and a certain degree of conviction about the kind of character that we have in mind. You don't even get to that point if you're looking for a six-foot-two-inch guy with broad shoulders who's going to have to convey a notion of masculinity—it's really terribly limiting. However, in *On the Yard*, the character that was played by Mike Kellin—I wouldn't say it was typecast, but I was certainly looking for someone who could convey what you would hold in your mind as someone who had been through the mill for dozens of years, in and out of prison. So that eliminated a great number of very competent actors who could have acted the part but couldn't have looked it.

·5·

STRUCTURE AND RHYTHM

For some filmmakers the form or structure of a film is based on conventions shared with literary arts: a character or characters is in conflict with someone or something in the environment. The conflict builds to a climax and then winds down toward some sort of resolution. Traditionally, the writer conceives of a story, dialogue, and characters, and then the director decides how this is to be filmed: camera movements and angles, lighting, staging, cuts, actors' expressions and movements.

Other filmmakers, either auteurs *or those working in close collaboration with the writer, conceive of the story with the literary and visual elements planned simultaneously. The script, however, is almost never finished until the film itself achieves a final form. Rather, it serves as a blueprint of theme, mood, and story for those collaborating in creating the film. Though a film may be planned in every detail in its creators' minds, the script generally is not cluttered by specifics of camera work, editing, acting instructions—the details of the film's style.*

Some filmmakers reject the need for a conventional story totally. For them, the open-ended, ongoing nature of real life reveals the well-made, neatly resolved plot to be a reduction and an evasion of the truth: filmic structures do not develop from an illusion of human order and logic at work in the universe. Instead, images and sounds borrowed from the known world are coaxed into a form shaped by a control derived partially from the nature of the medium itself and partially from the intuitive, emotional, and intellectual insights of the filmmaker.

The process of making a film is simultaneously analytical, self-conscious, and intuitive.

A shot is a section of film exposed during a single take. A scene is comprised of one or more shots occurring within one time and place. A sequence is composed of a group of scenes having dramatic unity. These three elements comprise the conventional structure in film, wherein the visual progress of a story and/or action may be interrupted for dramatic effect by a single shot, perhaps changing the angle in a startling manner, or even by a scene or a sequence that relates events from a past or future time. Conventionally, sound is used to reinforce or counterpoint the rhythms created by the camera, the action, and the editing. Thus, filmic structure is comprised of images relating to images, images relating to sound, and sounds relating to each other.

Form and structure do not always develop from purely aesthetic considerations; the need to simplify either for better communication or, perhaps even more frequently, for economic reasons, often leads a filmmaker to use, for example, a tracking shot that would give the audience the same information as several shots with separate (and more costly) setups.

Finding the form of a film, then, is often an intuitive process confounding the aesthetic and economic aspects of this art/communication form, reflecting its unique blend of the crass and the sublime. Chabrol describes his experience:

" *I find the form, but I'm not sure of it because I'm not alone. There are the actors; they are what the audience will see, but they are not there yet. So, I have the structure in mind but I don't know yet. Sometimes, on the first day of the shoot, when the actors are there, you see at once it's impossible because the actors don't fit that form well. So you have to change. That's why the first day of shooting is very important to me. It's very difficult, I don't sleep, I try to resist. It's awful. I don't want to begin that first shot. Sometimes I have to begin at nine o'clock and I finally say "Action" at twelve. We may have been working on that scene or on other scenes, but finally at twelve, I say "Okay, we must go—action." So I put the camera somewhere—before the actors, I hope—and from this moment I begin. I just have to follow the feel of it. It's like fishing.*

You follow. And sometimes I find a way back to my first point of view, my first idea of the form.

So, you can have a wonderful formal idea, a form, in mind, but then your actors are not right for that. And you cannot know because they could be wonderful, perfect in this kind of form, but not for this *story,* this *character. It's very difficult. And so, you must have them on the set. And even rehearsals are no use because they don't play the same way. You need that set. So, the first day is crucial. "*

It is clear, then, that whether or not a filmmaker follows the more conventional notions of form and structure, meaning in film is created only within a specific context, that is, from the joining together of all the elements in a particular way and in a particular time and space under the guidance of a particular consciousness. Perhaps it is also the movement of motion pictures that is the glue that unifies and breathes life into a film, that allows it to take its form.

Film is characterized by motion and change, which imply rhythm, as much as it is by its photographic element. But from where does that rhythm come? Internal rhythm is created within the scene by elements such as camera movement, lighting, action, dialogue, actors, music, and the number of events occurring within that scene. External rhythm is determined by the editing: scene length, the method of cutting from one scene to the next, and by the relatedness of those cuts.

Some filmmakers stress the infiltration into the film of the more ineffable rhythms of the surrounding culture. For example, if one is filming a scene that occurs in New York City in 1985, the cars, the people in the street, the rhythm and mood of that time and place are stamped indelibly onto that scene. Other filmmakers stress that rhythm and form follow from what they consider the single most important element of any film—the emotions depicted by the actors. But all would agree that everything contributes to the rhythm. Finally, as Jean-Marie Straub notes, "Everything is rhythm because everything is form," and structure and content, in the end, are not divisible. Whether structure develops to serve a predetermined content or content demands its own structure from the inception of a film is probably unanswerable, but it is clear that they are inseparable aspects of the same creative process. Perhaps *structure could be viewed as the filmmaker's attitude toward his content. Emile de Antonio describes the perfect melding together of structure and content as "that thing that happens when two elements come together and a magic third presence asserts itself. It's that moment in between where all art takes place. There's that flash in the middle somewhere."*

In film, structure reflects the filmmaker's attitudes toward himself, his subject, and his art form. Structure is essential not just to art, but to life, to creation. It allows for and expresses the creative force; it is, in fact, the life force fulfilled. And like all life forms, as Benoit Jacquot points out, "The film has its own breath. It should come from everything. A film is the bringing together of a series of parameters in which the actors, the sound, the text, the colors, the editing—all must enter into the game plan and work as a unit, not necessarily homogeneously, but in concert, like a musical score."

MARK RAPPAPORT

For me, a film that's unified by mood is not interesting, or a film that's unified by an actor's performance is somewhat more so, but I think that films are a little more intellectual than that. You need idea as expressed through script and then all the other elements follow. Even the most beautiful visual experience becomes very tiresome and tedious if it's not hung onto some other structure.

The structure comes out of who the characters are. It comes out of what the dialogue is like. It comes out of ways of simplifying things. Ultimately, I will probably look at this script and make it more compact and say, "Well, if I had this as an image or this tracking shot, I could do away with that whole scene." I think that's how the structure will emerge. I'm not worried about it in the script I'm working on now, because I know there's enough solid stuff in it to come by itself. It's like sticking all these grapes into a bottle and hoping it will be wine.

Film is really everything. It's an ever-expanding envelope. It can be anything that anybody who is really good makes it. A dozen years ago one would have said about Eric Rohmer's films that they're not cinematic enough because they talk, but this is nonsense. I remember a long time ago when the New York Film Festival showed Dryer's *Gertrude*. People said it wasn't cinematic because people are just hanging around, staring into space, *kvetching* at each other. It's a very great movie, so what they mean by it's not cinematic is it puts a great strain on them to find the resources within themselves to experience the film on its terms, not on their preconceived terms.

A few years ago everybody thought the editing in *Easy Rider* was cinematic: flash, flash, flash—five-frame cuts. That's trend, not cinema.

GEORGE ROMERO

I'm very idiosyncratic about dialogue; I'm very paranoid about what I write in terms of dialogue. That's probably why I like working in genre, because I feel safe. I can write really melodramatic tongue-in-cheek genre stuff. But I love situations; I love to develop situations, like the situation in *Martin* when he stalks that woman and then shows up at the house and the other guy is there. The situation is very important to me, in the sense of a certain logic from situation to situation and how one thing leads to another. Even though *Dawn of the Dead* is a fairly long film, about two hours and six minutes, for what it is, within the basic situation of the shopping mall, there's almost an hour spent on little contrivances like going down to the boiler room, a whole little set of situations that would happen to you if you were in that basic situation, rather than trying to introduce a scientist and contrive crazy things. I like dealing with little subtleties, things that would happen to you, particularly in an action melodrama. I don't think you need to have extraordinary things happening, because the subtlest, most ordinary things become extraordinary if the people are interesting and if the basic situation has a certain internal logic. Rather than extraordinary situations, I love to play around with that.

That's my favorite thing in terms of what a film needs to do. And I think a combination of a good, believable situation— even if you're dealing with a fantasy, even if you're dealing with zombies, people coming back to life, a basically unbelievable situation—once you get past that, within what's happening to those characters, if you buy those characters and you buy the place that they're in, then you make very ordinary things happen. Its own internal logic keeps you going. Now, if you can give a good rhythm to that, you keep the interest going. *Dawn* is just a matter of something happening and people moving to correct it. In the meantime, simultaneously, you see something else beginning to happen and it's all kind of woven that way. Getting it down to that rhythm is almost braiding. That's what I was doing with the final cut: getting it down to that rhythm.

And then I played around with the sublayers, like the protagonists change, or at least your attitude towards who the protagonists are changes about three or four times. I dig that, too. The same thing happens with *Martin,* because you're with Martin on the train and you don't know what he's about yet and see him do this vile thing and then the rest of the time is building sympathy for him. And then people around him start affecting your impression of him, but then, pretty soon, you start focusing on the people around him and you realize how fucked up they are, all for their different reasons. And then you almost forget about Martin for a little while. He becomes a constant. And I like that. He should be the threatening, menacing character, and for a long time, he's not. You start becoming him; you look seriously at the other people.

DUŠAN MAKAVEJEV

I find it very strange that things we allow literature, painting, and drama to do, for some reason, we don't allow film to do. Film is supposed to be simple, but I don't see why.

My dream, for example, would be to use more architecture in cinema, architectural structure. Unfortunately, most people who work on the structure in films have nothing to say; those little flickering underground films, those guys who are just playing with pure form. I find it very exciting and stimulating to structure story, to structure meanings, to play, to create a counterpoint between different contradictory situations, contradictory ingredients, and just enjoy the visual contradictions in movies as we enjoy them in life.

In life, let's say you exchange a loving look with someone, and then you eat something, and then you buy a ticket for a bus, and then, when you buy that ticket, you might not even look at that person. Sometimes, you don't know if it's a man or a woman. And you make all kinds of switches every day, all the time. But we never discontinue this discontinuity all our lives. We never really acknowledge that. You can read something theoretical and have a toothache and, at the same time, listen to music—the Beatles or something—and on all three levels be quite intense. But reading something theoretical can also include your thinking about your mate and doing one thing doesn't preclude thinking about another. And we do this all the time. But somehow these reduced films—like classical Hollywood films, those melodramas from the forties, the genres of the forties, fifties, and sixties, those clear genres where someone's killed and you look for the murderer, or someone's in love and you wait for the happy ending—these films are so reduced that they are like zero to one percent of what life is.

So when I speak of architecture, I mean the general structure of the whole film, not about specific breaks. I like buildings with a lot of staircases and separate exits and small balconies, and I like films made the same way. Some classical films are like a huge house with one staircase, and you climb once and don't want to do it again. When you have the "real" house, with every new visit it's different. It's the same with film. If you create films on multiple levels, then people come again and see it from another angle, so you can see it any number of times. It's like you never enter the same river twice. And with this kind of "real" house, this "real" film, you never enter the same film twice. The second time you already are carrying *your* experiences from the first time.

When I'm making a film, in the beginning there's maybe thirty percent I really know, so I tell a scene to people maybe ten times—it's always the same scene and it gets better and better with each recounting. Whenever you tell the scene you get a few more "eyes." It becomes funnier and funnier, so the scene goes on—it's great. And when you know there is a scene, it's short on paper and you know there's a greater one there, but you don't write any more because you'll get questions about it and people will spoil it. So I know there are places that are going to grow. Then, I wait for the right moment. And then when some things grow, they reorganize other stuff. Say you get a very good initial scene and then you go with the film and you get other scenes and suddenly you get one gratuitous scene that happens out of beauty. For example, there's a great sunset and you have "the two of them" and the cameraman brings it to you. You say, "Okay, put the camera there and we'll get the two of them watching the sunset." A great shot, okay, but you don't know what to do with it. But, later, it can become the last sequence, with the music going on and it's the last shot. But then you still have the shot you made for the last sequence. Now you have two last sequences, so one of them has to be placed in the very beginning. So now the first scene becomes the second scene. Now, it's not the same because film has a cumulative effect, so the scenes that are later carry all kinds of meanings. They have to be able to conduct all kinds of meanings that accumulated during the previous part. So all later sequences have to go in the beginning. Sometimes you do things against any logic. And people watch, and they don't see anything illogical. That's the moment when you know the film is finished, when you have this unconscious emotional flow and you've made all sorts of tricks manipulating the plot to stay superficially logical. For example, in *Sweet Movie*, I was never asked about the woman on the boat, but there's another one, and you see her in a number of scenes: when they wash Clementi, and then when the children come, she was part of the bigger scene. But then, it wasn't important, so she was cut out. But I did not worry about her being there sometimes only, and it seems that nobody worries about it. The story goes, it moves, and nobody really questions it. I'm unifying it, and you're unifying it.

ANDRÉ TECHINE

For me the rhythm of film is in the narration. It's entirely the function of the drama. Otherwise, it seems to me to be abstract. Basically I do films that are based on scenes in sequences, and the rhythm is in the continuity of those scenes and sequences. It's the opposite of the rushes. The rushes are totally out of continuity, like the shoot, and what puts them in order is the continuity you find in them or the discontinuity, if you want to create that effect, like Alain Resnais or Godard. So the continuity is in the relationship between the different blocks or sequences that constitute the story. I like contrasts, so I like these blocks to be in contrast also. This I do somewhat like a painter: first, a dark scene; then a bright one; a gentle, soft scene; then a more serious one. I like to alternate between luxurious moments and rather austere, naked ones, sterile almost.

I'm very respectful of the classic Hollywood cinema and it's why I don't see myself as a particularly avant-garde filmmaker, because I give great importance to the scenario, to the text, to the dramatic situation, and to the story that is being told. So, I am totally for a cinema that tells stories. If I can make films that tell stories, while keeping a certain taste of the experimental in sound and image, well, that is my program, my ambition. I don't ever want to renounce telling stories, being narrative. Quite the contrary: I want to attach myself more and more to telling stories with characters with feelings.

JEAN-MARIE STRAUB

Rhythm unifies a film because rhythm is a structure and things must be structured. If not, they don't live. To live is to defend a form, and to fabricate an audio-visual object that one could call aesthetic, other than the sound and the image, consists of establishing a rhythm, within the sounds, to help an actor say the text with a certain rhythm, with certain pauses, certain liaisons. The same thing applies to the image. I think everything is rhythm because everything is form, and without form, there is no life. Just as the soul doesn't exist without the form of the body. The body is rhythm. An actor saying a text immobile in the frame doesn't exist unless the text and the body are in rhythm.

YVES YERSIN

Meaning, the form, comes from the sense of what we want to say. In *Les Petites Fugues* I'm not looking at the psychology of the characters. It's a film built on a meaning expressed *through* these characters. The film is a fable; it's not a psychological exploration. The sense is mediated through the characters, my sense of meanings generalized to everyone. We speak about something more abstract than psychology of individual characters.

If I cannot manipulate sound, time, and space, film does not interest me any more. A very specific example is a scene in *Les Petites Fugues* that shows how the main character, the worker, discovers his solitude. There are three shots: first, we see him and his boss in the real space, a kind of master shot, an objective shot. We can see that the boss is twenty meters away from the worker. The second shot shows the way the worker sees after discovering his solitude: the boss is two hundred meters away. The third shot is from the audience's point of view: we see them together separated by only twenty meters.

EMILE DE ANTONIO

I think film is essentially structural. Just in the fact that it is made up of all those discrete phenomena—twenty-four frames per second. In a sense, the conglomeration, the abstraction of their coming together, creates a social fact that is divorced, that denies any other kind of abstraction. It has to do with movement towards an end, an end greater than just what is on the canvas itself. My favorite paintings are paintings by people like Stella and Pollock, whose ultimate purpose is defined on the canvas. I think film is a different form of art whose ultimate purpose is defined on the screen but that purpose on the screen has to move to some kind of conclusion other than its just being on the screen.

Film joins at all these levels: the mind, the eye, and, in most cases, the maker wants the viewer to see or to experience or to be moved, and, if he's a serious filmmaker, in a way that the person hasn't been moved before. If he's a frivolous filmmaker—and frivolous filmmakers make films for money, like on the stock exchange—then he's interested in cashing in on a mass experience at the expense of his individuality. Film is a

much more fragile art than it seems because of the whole business of balancing those things—of balancing the needs of film
to express yourself. It's a juggling act and it's unrealistic to pretend it isn't. I get somewhat annoyed when I read of film experiments somewhere in northern Canada where they mount a
camera and let it turn a three-hundred-and-sixty degree arc, as
Michael Snow did. That's like all conceptual art. Conceptual art
has no concepts. I mean, what it is is a gimmick. Once I read
about it, I don't have to see it, it's all over. I know if you go to
all the trouble to produce an electric impulse that will rotate
the camera three hundred and sixty degrees within a certain
angle of declination per minute, I can visualize the film if you
show me an aerial photograph of the landscape. And so can
anyone else. I mean, it's not very important.

So, if it doesn't move the eye, it doesn't move the head, but if
it moves the eye alone, then it's titillation. But if it moves both
the eye and the head, then it's film. And it works. That's not a
childish distinction because you can just move the eye—it's
what most Hollywood stuff is about. It moves the eye, it's brilliant in the sense that the eye is moved and the mind is shut
out, totally closed out. That's what *Star Wars* is about. The
mind is shut out. There's an unconscious message there and
the eye is titillated. I don't think that's what any art form is
about. Finally, there's more than that superficial layer. There's
something else that happens and *brain* isn't the right word and
mind isn't the right word. It's complex, and I also hate the word
gestalt. Maybe if you and I talked enough, we'd get to where it
is, but it is a kind of conjunction of receiving and understanding. There's a conjunction there in which that magic third is
that which Eliot talks about in *The Wasteland*. Who is that third
who is always among us when there are only two? And it's what
Eisenstein writes about, too, that thing that happens when two
things come together and a magic third presence asserts itself.
Funny things make it happen. For instance, in a commercial
but effective film, *The China Syndrome*, Fonda makes it happen.
Sometimes her presence with the right words and decent camera work is extraordinary. Everybody thinks she's a great
actress, but still they underrate her. There's something—a kind

of magic. It's that moment in between where all art takes place. There's that sort of flash that's in the middle somewhere. You have a great sense that she's aware of what she's doing without making it boring or vulgar.

The fact that you really want to say something is *not* content. It has to do with structure and the form. The fact that you believe also personally in your own ability and yourself is not being outside that film—it's like Jane Fonda being able to act so well—it's that thing that brings them together. Form and content are Matthew Arnold, nineteenth-century concepts, because when they work, something clicks and they're together. When you're deeply aware of form, there's something thin and superficial; then it's like Louis B. Mayer: when you want to give a message, send a telegram. It's somewhere in between the two. I think it occurs frequently in films by such people as W. C. Fields, the Marx Brothers, Laurel and Hardy, Chaplin, where it belongs so totally in the time—forever.

MARTIN SCORSESE

In the case of *American Boy,* which has Steven Prince as the subject, you get the structure by working on the treatment of certain stories he can tell about his life. I knew about him and asked questions so he would tell us the stories. We talked about which ones, in which order, and I chose the order that these stories would be in with a friend of mine. You see on the credits a friend who worked with me a long time. He researched it for a few years. We then thought about it and decided "this" story first, "that" story second. And then in the editing, it worked out okay. We might have lost a story or cut out half of one, but it *is* plotted, there *is* a climax, and there *is* a resolution. The resolution is not very happy, the resolution is called "surviving." He keeps stripping away things, but you're also stripping away things about yourself just by the fact that you're there and there's a rhythm. The viewer is participating.

An old friend of mine said the other day that many of today's films don't seem to have resolutions, don't make a point, don't take a stand. Maybe that's one of the problems, why I don't find them interesting. When they do take a stand, it's a very obvious one: "Thank you very much, we know that, see you next week, lunch Tuesday." You know, such messages as "War is bad." Yes, I know, the war is bad. "Racial integration." Yeah, I know, you're right. We know all these things. "Let's be fair." Okay. "Extra-marital affairs. No good, not fair." Yes, but it's complicated, as is everything. Each thing has its own reasons. So, either they are simplistic or it comes to the point where, partially I think, some of it is hopelessness. How can you make a resolution to something that is totally hopeless? Who has the fucking answers? So, what you can do is show people going through an attitude change but basically remaining the same person. People who change like Saint Paul, who went from being the biggest persecuter of Christians to the man who organized the Catholic Church, I mean, there's something wrong there. The man is off the deep end. But there are people who change *a little bit*. But they're basically the same person. It doesn't mean they're going to be saints the next minute. *Raging Bull,* the Jake LaMotta film, is basically like that. It's about a guy who goes through life, battering and being battered, back and forth.

JEAN-LUC GODARD

I think one should follow the line of a story, but not in the sense that a screenwriter would have it. But the line can come from the line of a landscape or the line of a story can come from the shape of a tree or the bodies of some children—that's a movie. That's the way they saw it when the movies were invented—it's a summing up of everything.

One project I have in the States, a movie, is called "A Story" and it deals with the audience of a story, with the invention of fiction and why we need a story.

Movies are not one image after another, they are one image

plus another, which forms a third image. The third one is formed by the spectator at the moment when he sees.

The film is an image that becomes more and more precise, like the work of the musician and the painter. Once one starts something it will finish in a certain way. Each beginning defines within it its own end. That is only logic. The doubt is to be alone and unsure. It doesn't bother me to be unsure but it bothers me not to be able to confront this uncertainty with other colleagues and co-workers and to confront this uncertainty with their uncertainty. At the moment when one makes the image follow the script, there is a certitude, like a frame, like a piece of paper or a canvas. It is a momentary certitude, like a film image or like other arts, a moment of visual certitude that represents but which is unreal. But it has a certain reality in that one can represent a moment, a moment real in its uncertitude, but which is everyday life, scientific and logical, which is a moment of certitude. In film like this, or the note of music or the touch of color in painting, this moment of certitude is suddenly shown.

There is no more rhythm in movies now; that's why they are bad. They are flat, TV too, everything. There is a need for rhythm and we have to find it again, even if it's a technical gate you go through to find rhythm, even if you do it through new techniques, it's a way, a gate. Maybe, for example, with tape, since there are no rigid laws, maybe you can work with it like one did at the beginning of the movies, when there were no laws as yet. It was more like a baby who has a chance to find his own rhythm.

It's very difficult to find the rhythm from the actors today, when the very good actors are stars and you don't know what you can expect from the other actors.

In society a certain amount of money is delegated for research in such fields as science, but it's not normally done in film. It's been ten years since *La Chinoise*, but it's not because I didn't have the ideas; I have researched so what I have studied would be used in *Everyman for Himself*.

But it was also a bit of a commercial film when we looked to see which actors would insure the budget and make sure the

film would go to Cannes. We gave ourselves a number of obligations that are no more or less than other obligations and
challenges, neither worse nor better. There are other people
who have the same problems I have—I am only representative,
and it is to them that I speak. I cannot join them because the
circuits of communication do not exist. It is like a painter when
he researches the theme; it doesn't stop him from doing
sketches. This theme must be created in the production. My
ten years of work between *La Chinoise* and *Everyman for Himself* was research comparable to those sketches through which a
motif is worked out. In a film I did, *Tour de France*, I was
attracted to research of rhythms to discover that through
rhythms movies represent so-called life, that they march to
rhythms, that sixteen to twenty-five frames is a bit artificial, but
there are more rhythms than that. One sees changing rhythms
in silent movies that are obtained completely by interaction between great actors and directors. It is in the frame that they
created different rhythms. Today all the rhythms have stayed
the same, but I think there are infinite worlds. Movies do not
"land" on them. This is what is difficult and what interests me.
I had the intuition that I could not go any further, that one
could create a slowing down—slow motion—and changing of
rhythm—what I call decompositions—before the cinema techniques that arose out of the interaction between cinema and
television. When we did changes of speed—half-slow, half-ac-
celerated—all different possibilities happened, because when
one stops the image in a movement, one perceives a change,
one analyzes the motion of, let's say, a loaf of bread; one perceives a whole lot of other worlds. When a rhythm stops, you
see different worlds between the actual image.

·6·

FILM AND REALITY

In 1896, the audience jumped out of their seats to avoid an onrushing locomotive filmed by the Lumière brothers in Arrival at the Station. *Film may not seem as vividly real to today's audiences, at least not in the same way, but the relationship of movies to its raw material, visible reality, is as ambiguous as ever.*

Unlike language, the symbols of film—images and sounds—bear a strong resemblance to what they refer to. To some, this tie to the concrete precludes abstract, conceptual notions as a proper subject for movies. How do you film an idea? Should abstract notions such as "All men are equal" be left to language-based forms of communication such as literature and the theater? Or can the iconographic, dreamlike nature of film dive deeper into feelings and ideas that evade the naming of our language system? Is film's picturing of our world's surface appearance more suggestive, therefore, than literary forms?

It could be said that the source of art in literature is the need to break the binds imposed by the arbitrary symbols of language, to transcend the conceptual in order to approach the perceptual, while film seeks to go beyond the perceptual in order to reach a more conceptual, abstract level of expression. The ease with which film offers images so close to what our own eyes can see gives those images an aspect of triviality. They can seem merely representational, unrefined by human intelligence. In the same way, language's specificity is also misleading. It pretends to name the unnamable.

Many filmmakers feel that anything the mind conjures up can be imaged in a film; that the challenge to cinema is to interpret ideas and concepts into cinematic forms in terms of things we can see and hear, things that move dramatically through time and space. Film's apparent reflection of reality, then, is a deception of sorts, but it is also an opportunity: within that gap created by the departure from reality is where the true expressiveness of film may lie. Film's ambiguous tie to the mundane world is the wellspring of the filmmaker's creativity.

Film is the most inclusive of the arts: it contains not only pictures and sounds of the world, but also verbal language. It gives information in both simultaneous and sequential ways. It has elements of all the other arts, and yet it is itself and holds a promise of becoming even more of itself, though primarily because of the camera's unique ability to communicate that illusion of objective reality in motion, that talent for capturing specific physical detail. The camera eye does more, however, than simply reflect life in process as we see it; it inevitably selects from and rearranges that reality to express a subjective vision: that belonging to the filmmakers. In fact, despite the sense of depth projected by the various focal lengths of lenses, the architecture of the composition within the frame, and the reality-enforcing effect of sound, the two-dimensional film image is hardly an exact replica of what we actually see and hear. A great deal of artifice and selection can go into this creation of the illusion of reality. At best, it is analogous to our experience of the world where seeing lies somewhere behind the eyes. The film artist perceives the distortions, subtle and obvious, wreaked by the film process upon its source material; he either dismisses them as irrevelant to his purposes, or reveals them as they exist, or he may choose to magnify them.

The ambiguity of these camera-narrated images of reality accommodates film to a variety of styles and purposes, allowing for the exquisite artifice of a Jean Cocteau film, as well as for the immediacy of the direct cinema pioneered by Jean Rouch.

Just as the boundaries between the novel and the journalistic report are fading, the distinctions between documentary and fiction film are becoming more and more difficult to establish. Film is no longer defined as either "celluloid dreams" or "reality at twenty-four frames per second." It is both—often within the same film. Consider, for example, the films of the Maysles and those of Emile de Antonio. The work of each is labeled documentary, yet they each have radically different intentions, points of views, and cinematic styles. Their films have less in common with each other than they each have with some fiction films. In addition, just as literature has relatively new genres, the non-fiction novel and personal journalism, there are instances where documentary and fiction merge, an example being Ermanno Olmi's Tree of Wooden Clogs. *Though the basic storyline is pre-planned fiction, the actors are non-professionals improvising their actions in front of the camera, which follows them in a documentary style. In fact, there have always been elements of documentary and of fiction in all films. Whether termed documentary or fiction, a film is inevitably filtered through the eyes, ears, and mind of the filmmaker, and of the viewer. It could be said, then, that there really is no reality in film, at least not "raw" reality. Film is an art form even in the hands of the unartful. When you film an event, unless you show that event on film from beginning to end without cutting the camera or cutting the angle, you are imposing your vision. Merely pointing the camera at something makes that event into something bigger as seen through someone's vision. In that sense, any film could be termed a subjective fiction. Likewise, all films can be considered documentary in that they always reveal something of the world, even if it is only a small piece: a glimpse of sky, a small part of the human body, the chirp of a cricket. Any film is necessarily a document, evidence of the real world, even if this apparent reality is intended by someone to be taken as a symbol of something behind it.*

Of course, there is a difference between the extremes of the relatively unadorned reality of a Jean Rouch film and the artifice of a Jean Cocteau, and there are as many reasons for choosing to work anywhere along the spectrum as there are makers of films. Film can be anything that anyone who is gifted and conscious makes of it. Choice of form is just as complex and mysterious a process as choice of subject. "Choice" hardly describes how and why one fixes on and interprets certain aspects of experience in a certain way. The process is sometimes conscious, sometimes not, but always inseparable from the filmmaker.

ERMANNO OLMI

Since all manifestations of life are life, it's not that there is more life in a man than in a frog or a tree. Life is life represented in all its forms of expression. It's so extraordinary and mysterious that we don't know all these forms of life. Truth is the same thing. It's not true that there is more truth in dialogue between real persons than in a poem, a fiction. It depends on the presuppositions that have generated the thing, the truth of your authentic emotions. False emotions are always discovered.

Some would say the raw material of film is the image, but it's not just the image. Today we have the image, sound, rhythm. All that is so simple, and, at the same time, complex, which is really the unwinding, the development of life. While sound is one moment in this, while the image is another, cinema is this extraordinary instrument that allows you to reproduce—but reproduce isn't the exact work—to *repropose* some of the moments, some of the fractions of life, to choose and compose them into a new mosaic in the editing. This operation is choice, synthesis, image, sound, rhythm.

In the case of my films, it is a reality taken entirely from the real. Within this is the echo of the documentary, but, at the same time, critically penetrated and sometimes put at the service of the content presented.

In a certain sense it's a contradiction to use cinema as a substitute for literature, for music, for the theater. Even when we want to make film full of conceptuality, it's obvious we make choices of representation—for the image, sound, rhythm—of life to express these concepts. It means the image, the music, the action aren't by themselves sufficient vehicles to express that concept. They become significant, if at all, all together. This is why I must express a concept through the dialogue between the main characters, their faces, how they move, in what situations, in what light, with what rhythm. It's not that one thing repeats the other; but, as in literature, I choose this word rather than one that closely resembles it, so in a film I choose precisely that word because only that word can say that thing.

Then that image because it can say something better than anything else, that sound . . . You see? It's as if it were a language
that instead of having only words, had words, images, sounds,
a language that is the language of life. We speak with gestures,
with looks, with the sound of the word, as well as with the word
itself. If I say "Good evening" to you three different ways, the
sound is different each time, as is the facial expression. This is
cinema: nouns, adjectives, parts of sentences that have a special
syntax and organization.

NESTOR ALMENDROS

I think that the transformation of reality is automatic. That's
what's exciting about making movies. It's a very generous art
form. Things are always better, more interesting in film than in
reality. Anybody can take a camera and film, and with just a
little knowledge of composition and lighting, turn out something interesting because of his frame.

The medium conforms things. It's a little like engraving. You
take a piece of wood, and you scratch with a tool—make some
drawing. You put ink, you get the paper, and you print it, and
it's something. The same drawing made directly on paper
would be nothing. The reproduction gives some kind of en-
hancement to the drawing.

There's magic in movies; a camera enhances everything, and
I notice sometimes I even like movies made by people I don't
like personally. Movies are often superior to the people who
make them, which proves that they are helped by something—
the medium.

ERIC ROHMER

I make films perhaps because I don't know how to do anything else. I express myself most easily in film because its my

nature. Certainly, there were times I would have liked to have been a painter or a musician, but I also try to include these arts in my films. Although I'm not a designer per se, I design the "decor" of the people and choose the musical themes; thus I participate in other forms of art. Also, I have a literary background, and film is equally a form of literature, as well as a theatrical expression, in that it is more difficult.

I still cherish André Bazin's conception of ontology of the cinema, that cinema has its relation to reality the way other arts do not. What I consider important is penetrating reality, not translating it.

There must be something physical, something concrete in a film; that is, the degree to which the film is instructing us should not be carried too far—but there are a lot of concrete things inherently in film. For example, in *Perceval*, I was aiming for something neither theatrical nor realistic, something different. There's no realism in that decor by itself, and if it resembles anything, it's miniatures that I found in paintings. I felt that in art direction, we had to invent something new, and the man charged with that actually brought his personal vision of it. For example, I told him I wanted spring flowers for the set at one point. So what did he choose? They were done in rubber, pieces of rubber. So it was a personal interpretation of what would fit, rather than any realism. But there are many concrete things in *Perceval*, such as from the point of view of the image, the human beings, the horses, the costumes. I am also very interested in the voice of the actors. And then there is another point as well. Even if it is a shot of space, there is a reality to that space and the people in it. I fear that the mistake people make in films about the Middle Ages is that they show the people glued to the background whereas here I have given them much more air, and I think that's important.

BERNARDO BERTOLUCCI

Film shows reality *in progress*. When you film from nine o'clock to nine o'clock, there is a reality going on that is in progress, that is moving. There's a very beautiful and famous Jean Cocteau statement: "The cinema is death at work." Because when you show the face of an actor, the time can be ten seconds or three minutes—but time passes in his face. "Time is death at work."

The moment you show a certain kind of reality, sometimes there is an immediate association in your mind with a concept. In cinema with an idea, that idea can be suggested by the reality you show. The difference that comes to mind immediately between, let's say, the cinema and poetry, is that you say in a poem, "the tree was yellow and brown in autumn," so everyone has the right to imagine his own tree, his own yellow, his own brown. In a movie you *show* a tree that is yellow and brown and it is the same tree for everybody—almost. So *apparently* this is a very huge difference, because a word means different things for everybody and a word makes a reader much more active; whereas a movie leaves less freedom to imagine, and, so, makes the spectator more passive. But, in fact, when you come out from a theater, if you talk with people who saw the same movie, you would think they saw one completely different from the film you saw in spite of the fact that the film is one, the screen is one. I think that in the darkness, in the darkness of that movie theater, this amniotic darkness, we want to see our own film.

JACQUES DEMY

I feel you must start from a very realistic basis, and then you take off and do whatever you like. You can transport your audience into a fantasy world or whatever you wish. But you have to really start with very realistic feelings and people: the basic truth has to be there. And it's there in every good film. The films I've really liked always had a basic realistic point of departure.

You have to believe in your characters; if not, the audience isn't going to believe in them. If it's a pure fantasy, nobody is going to accept it as such. It has to be credible about the characters to start with. Then, even if you paint the streets, as I did for some films, then it's a point of view, it's a vision. I think it's art. The visual side of filmmaking is very important, so you must bring something. I'm not very interested in a realistic film where they shoot in the street. That's okay; when it's good, it's fantastic. But it's not my work. I stroll around and have my life in the streets, but I like movies because they're something else, it's another world.

BENOIT JACQUOT

Documentaries about war, etcetera, are no longer cinéma: it's news, journalism. That's an ethical question, the work of a journalist not a *cinéaste*. I think that if you are talking about truth, it is through fiction that you can reach it. It's by inventing fiction stories told in films, like stories told to children, that we can touch the truth.

Yet film's connection to physical reality is where the fascination comes from. In order not to participate in a film, you have to leave the room. If not, even if you laugh, or make fun of the film, you are staying in front of the screen and aiding the process of fascination. That is not the case when you look at a painting or when you listen to music. Film is the most perfect copy of reality we have, the most perfect representation of the physical world that we've found, so that you can sit in front of a film and become totally involved in this almost real world. It is the most refined lie there is, so it's the closest to the truth. Cocteau went very far with this illusion, reality, lies, truth, and, in general, mystery and ambiguity. He had his finger right on the essence of cinema as far as I'm concerned.

Film is a lie because it *so* resembles the supposedly real

world, and it is the most perfect lie but that's not why it is a lie. It's a lie because there is always someone behind the film, directing it, organizing things, calculating the elements of the *mise-en-scène*, and it's this person who is the liar and makes the film a lie. He's a liar who tries to tell the truth while lying.

No one can use such a close copy of the real world to make his personal statement, his own individual fantasy, without necessarily lying while manipulating the elements copied from reality to try to attract the spectator to enter into his game. It's an operation of seduction, of showing off the techniques of the lover, of the director trying to seduce the spectator. And seducer's techniques are always based on lies.

HENRY JAGLOM

To try to capture that subjective moment, that inner landscape, is what really affects me a great deal in film. So I use music very much as a trigger to change the images. When Dennis Hopper hears a snatch of a World War II song in *Tracks* or Tuesday Weld hears a snatch of a romantic ballad from childhood in *A Safe Place,* the scene changes. It can change in time, it can change in reality; we are not exactly clear whether what we're experiencing at any given moment is real or not real, or whether it's happening just now or if it happened and we have a memory of it or we have the anticipation of something that *may* happen.

To get the totality of our experience on screen means to try not to show that hard-edged external view that almost all films show: this is the outside of the person and we are watching them cry but we're not feeling what it's like for them to cry. We are watching them, we can get sad out of empathy with that crying, but we are not seeing as *they're* seeing, their view of life completely falling down and breaking apart. So, one of the main things for me is to try to get film to become a subjective medium, which I think it's ideally suited for. In her review of *A Safe Place,* Anaïs Nin says that "From the beginnings of film it was clear that here was the perfect medium to depict dreams, fantasies, the surreal aspect of our existence." She quotes Antonin Artaud about how film should and could capture the combination of reality and fantasy, of music, of past and of future. It could do everything. But very soon it became a medium of entertainment, of narrative story, of what she called one-dimensional stories.

DUŠAN MAKAVEJEV

For years even the light in Hollywood movies was this kind of zero light. It's like no light. It's like what's on television. Everything's equal. So, it means the furniture and people are of the same importance, and gravity is always respected, as well. Everything's placed on the ground and the horizon is always horizontal. Now, obviously, you have to do that if you're dealing with reality, but, you see, when you're dealing with *images*, you can do anything. But they didn't dare because they believed in reality. It must have some kind of relation to commodities, which is the principle American religion. And then, the clarity: you know the first problems Altman had in Hollywood were because he had people talking at the same time. They said, "That's not correct because you have to hear everything for your money. You buy every line, you have to hear every line." It's robots delivering lines, not as people really relate. So that was the explosive meaning of Cassavetes's *Shadows*. This was just raw New York. It was just what happens. Everyone was carrying existential insecurity, angst, of the city. The only things I recognized when I finally came to this city were what I had seen in *Shadows*.

ANDRÉ TECHINE

I have nothing against documentaries, nothing against "witness" films. They can educate, bring information, but since you asked about reality, I think truth always is advanced through a mask, as in a fiction. For me, there are many more moments of truth in a fiction than in the pretended objectivity of a documentary.

Film lets us carve reality according to our own desires. No one ever sees the same thing in reality—we are captivated by one thing or another. But film lets us isolate those things we want to emphasize, to give value to. So, in a way, we can idealize. I don't believe in an objective reality. Like with a camera or with a tape recorder: what's incredible is that if we are listening, all the noises taking place are of the same value, but if we are listening to our conversation, we don't hear the noise of the people sitting next to us, etcetera. So, for me, reality is tied to our desires, it's never really objective.

There is a rather naturalistic school of thought in French film just now, which doesn't interest me, doesn't speak to my sensibility. There is also in European films in general a very formalistic school—I'm thinking of the Germans—which doesn't tempt me in the least. I believe more in a dialectic between artificial effects and natural ones. It is something like the Eisenstein montage theory, only within the same frame, where you have the effect of a montage between two actions, two spaces. I feel it gives more intensity to the film, gives it more possibilities.

The trap of the cinema of ideas is to make films with a message, a theme. A film that is made to prove an idea as a pure and simple demonstration, a film that serves a cause, like the militant films, always seem to me to be a reduction of cinema. If a film can be reduced to a speech, it's not worth the trouble to make a film. What is so fascinating about a film is when it shows something you could not say in any other way except in cinematic terms. As soon as you can say the same thing in a tract or a thesis, I don't see why you would use the specificity of film—that bothers me very much.

The most defendable analogy is with architecture. I don't see cinema partaking of the language of photography at all, nor of the other arts, literature, etcetera. I think it's more specific. The language of cinema depends entirely on the filmmaker. It's quite individual, very difficult to talk about in generalizations. I feel you rediscover cinema with each individual, single filmmaker. The more singular he or she is, the more you discover.

I think it's good to talk about architecture in cinema because it is much closer to architecture than to the other arts it is often compared to, like literature or theater, because the space is defined by the cutting, by the changes from frame to frame. For me it is the architecture of the labyrinth that is evoked in films, where the spectator looks for the exit. A good example of this I find in Orson Welles's film, *The Lady From Shanghai,* which for me is practically pure cinema.

KRZYSZTOF ZANUSSI

For me, the raw material of film is reality. We are just reproducing reality in a photographic way. We create something, but within the limits of reality, and compared to other disciplines of art, I feel very poor as a filmmaker. I can't create my own space or time in such a free way as I could in literature or in painting, and especially with space we are very limited. The limitation is very painful.

But I never like to make negative statements that exclude any possibilities. This I have been taught as a physicist. Whatever has not been proven wrong, may be right, though it's hard, for example, to express concepts on film due to its slowness. Its language has developed in such a way from Eisenstein's time. There is always a strong feeling of limitation. I try to make my films possibly intellectual; I try to convey ideas. Conveying ideas by dialogue is not really a cinematic way. They should be conveyed by images, by events, by characters, not simply verbalized, and here is a danger for any filmmaker trying to deal with ideas: often we get trapped by words instead of dramatizing ideas, instead of creating emotions in connection with problems we reveal.

This is an important point: the theme cannot be expressed in words. It can't be an argument. If it could be an argument, then I would write an article. I don't make a film. The theme is something that I feel. I have no courage even to put it into words because if I succeed, it makes no sense to make a film. It would be more appropriate to write a statement. So, in a way, it has to be ambiguous.

Literature is even more intuitive. The reality of literature is only hints, it never really exists. When I describe a woman, I tell you, I may put some lines about her on paper, but still you have to imagine her. In film I give you a ready image. It's still different from an existing image of a person.

Film does what the philosopher tries to do but on a different level. And this is a very important difference. That's why I have finished with philosophy and I have switched to films. Our communication cannot be just verbal. It cannot be just rational; it would be very poor.

I think all art has to be ambiguous because it doesn't appeal to our rational level. It appeals to all our personality, our integral personality, and art is most precious when it conveys feelings and ideas that you can't express by direct words. These vibrations, these emotions, whenever they appear in art, are most precious. All the rest, which are easy to describe in words, are just something unimportant.

What I express through films is in a way unique. I know that I wouldn't be able to express it other ways. It's impossible to define. It is the mystery of art, this level of communication, this sort of vibration, this opening of other people's imaginations to my vision, that I can't argue. I can convey it sometimes, I feel it, but I can't explain it in words.

I think my expression is in transforming by elimination. I choose certain elements of reality, and I focus on these elements, and my choice is the creative process. This is what attracts me most. I don't try to create a world that would look very different from the existing world. I know that some peo-

ple try to do this in cinema. But it is not my vocation. I like it
for Fellini very much, but the biggest attraction in filmmaking
is just the point of choice. And since writing films interests me
a lot, so there is the element of choice in writing: in which
event, on which element of the story I concentrate, what I tell
you, and what I don't tell you. Choice seems to be the most
important, but my preference is not necessarily true for everybody. The image is always analogous, in a way, to the world,
because it is two-dimensional and it is arbitrarily chosen, so we
never see in film all that we could see in life. And, above all, it
is framed.

JEAN-MARIE STRAUB

Even a film like *Intolerance* was a film about concepts, or any
of Fritz Lang's films. Concepts are transmitted by emotions and
emotions come out of concepts. Films have the advantage of
being able to convey concepts by the emotions, as does music.
We don't usually think of it as conveying concepts, but it was
made to do so. Even painting can convey concepts. Cézanne
did. Concepts move through form and why not through film?
Film is more an art of time and, consequently, it is like music
and can express concepts, even if these concepts are transformed by feeling or come out of feelings. But film is also a
spatial art, so if painting can express concepts, why not film?
Maybe the obstacles you see are actually virtues, because it's
better to have concepts that come out of material form than
from the air. I think concepts are things that come out of experience and, consequently, through the forms. They come from
life experience and the struggle for existence and the class
struggle. These concepts are conquered and so they come out
of the violent opposition of forms. I believe the only concepts
that really exist are those that come out of the class struggle.

Above all, the filmmaker must know how he confronts this
reality. In ninety percent of the films made today we don't
know what the author thinks. We don't know where he stands

or what he is showing or making for us here, because he doesn't even take the trouble to know himself. You must always know what you yourself think. Otherwise you can't frame. And it's only when you know what you think that you have the right to show a film to people, so they have the chance to know, by the distance and the frame, what you think of what you film.

PERRY HENZEL

I think abstract thinking is in the realm of the theater. That's what's so wonderful about theater. I wish I knew more about theater, but that much I think is true. I have never been affected emotionally by abstraction in film, and I've never been affected emotionally by reality in the theater.

The difference between film and theater is the difference between a photograph and a painting. If you go to the theater or you see a painting, you think about the playwright or the painter. Whatever is there was put there by the artist—there's no other way. The power of the theater is the power of the individual artist projecting. In a photograph as opposed to a painting, you don't think about the photographer. You think about what he shot, the reality that he captured. That's the difference. The power of the theater is the power of the individual artist projecting. The power of film is in the spontaneous moment. So, in every scene I want to capture the spontaneous moment, not coming from me, but coming from the situation and the actors.

R. W. FASSBINDER

Literature has its own forms and they are okay. It is a medium that allows many things. Literature has found its forms over thousands of years, and there are many ways of handling those forms. Film is not there yet.

Film is maybe not yet an independent art form, but it certainly will become one. So far film has been an assemblage of other genres of art, but I think it will become one in itself.

I want to try to make a kind of film that doesn't carry an idea or the idea of a story like a traditional novel or a traditional theater piece. I want to find a new kind of film. Simply said, a kind of film that is like music or philosophy. I don't want to say that film should be like music, then I could make music or philosophy. Film should be something that is exclusively film. Like music, it should be considered as something independent. You listen to a symphony independently from its story. Beethoven, for example, took certain notes after which he composed his symphonies or concertos. But we don't need them when we listen to music. You listen to it independent of anything literary. In my opinion, film also has to be freed from literary moments, as well as from the moments when music is only an emotional support. Film should really be something independent. The notes are not what is communicated. When Beethoven wrote, "Night in a forest . . . lightning over wide fields," or whatever, if his intention was just to convey that idea, then he could just have left those words on paper. But he made music out of it and everybody understands it in a different way. Somebody really understands night in a forest, and someone else something else. It is the deliteralization of a medium. Literature is literature, and that's okay, but film is not film yet. It is still a mixture of many different genres and generally has a story, and that is a mistake.

It is also a mistake to talk about what film is, something in which I am not really interested any more. It is a kind of film about which I can talk, but I am not really interested in doing so: the more we talk about the characteristics of film, the more we consolidate the traditional notion of film.

GEORGE ROMERO

Documentary is a reflection of what's going on. It's a very different exercise. When you sit down to watch a documentary film, even when it's on television, you have a whole different attitude. You're still functioning, when you watch a documentary, on some level to find what someone is about, to find out what this issue is about, to find out what's going on, where. You're still functioning, and you perceive this as the real world.

I do come from a documentary background, so I love accidents. I love to play around with the elements in my fiction films. When we were doing commercials, everything was by the sweep hand and everything was technically perfect. You sit around and pour four, five hundred glasses of beer to get exactly the right shot—what bullshit. And the most fun I've had in making films has been documentaries, so maybe I resist that kind of control in the films I'm doing now. Documentaries are all accidental—it's what you do with the material later. It's a very instinctive way to work. I think that adds to the spontaneity and it leaves a wide opening for creating something that has its own movement and form. You can really choke something up when you do it the other way, unless you have the money to do it right, or you're really brilliant with those other things. Maybe I'm just too lazy.

I think people used to think film reflects reality. I don't want to get into a semantic trap, but I don't think people know anymore. You can only gauge it by what happens to yourself in the movies, and from watching audience behaviors. I think people expect film now to exaggerate reality. We've been so conditioned by the music revolution over the last twenty years, and the evolutions in design, fashion, and everything else, which is all exaggerated reality, that people operate with a very defensive attitude towards this rough, realistic world where nothing is right, nothing is working anymore. And so, you have to be defensive and you have to learn to take care of yourself. I think that's gone so far that no one is willing in their private lifestyle or in any kind of relaxed thought—*any* kind, whether it's buying clothes, listening to music, or going to the movies—to deal with that anymore.

I think film works best on a feeling level. Again, I'm speaking from personal experience, but rather than *see Autumn Sonata*, I prefer to *read* it. It almost goes by too fast on film. To me, there's almost no reason to make a film of that. There is in that it is a way to record it, and that's okay. I liked being able to watch the faces of those two women, the performances are good, and it's an interesting piece. I'm not making a judgment about it, good, bad, or indifferent, for what it is, but it's a written piece with two good performances. It's not a film. Even with Sven Nykvist shooting it. There are some very beautiful-looking frames, but it's not a movie. It's something else. I have a little bit of an aversion to that. It's not using the total medium.

It's not a movie, and I mean on a lot of levels, not just visually. And it doesn't move you. Ben Berenholtz of Libra Films said that movies are like jazz music. Basically it's a popular art form meant to communicate with many people at one time, and our best experiences with movies are in that big room with a lot of other people sharing this communal experience and this bigger-than-life thing that's doing this to us all. That's an important element. A lot of films don't ever get there. I think that's why there's a whole alternative attitude developing towards movies and that's why we're starting to venerate genre things because they do that even though they might be outrageous. And also the timing right now—the seventies going into the eighties. We are almost ready to use movies as a chemical stimulant, use them the same way we use another kind of stimulant. It's like "get away from the shit for a minute and go into the theater and let the movie do something to me." You are taken out of where you are by those kind of movies. You are not by *The Deerhunter*, which is a kind of throwback. And you're certainly not by *Autumn Sonata*.

BARBARA KOPPLE

Every situation is different and part of the responsibility of the filmmaker is to make characters come across, to have a dramatic story, and to be able to reach as many people as possible. As far as point of view is concerned, documentaries cannot be objective. I've never seen one that is, and I think it's very important that you discover what that point of view is that comes from the majority of the people you're working with. People have to decide in their lifetimes which side they're on because it's important to stand up and fight for what you believe. In doing documentaries I'm going to put everything that I can possibly put in that's going to get out to the largest amount of people, move those people, let those people understand who the characters are, what they're fighting for, what their backgrounds are, what obstacles they confront, and how courageous these people are.

However, I tried to cut out my voice from *Harlan County* whenever I possibly could. But there were two or three circumstances when you heard it. On *Winter Soldier,* which was made by a collective, the press was trying to get more information about what it was like to live with Vietnam veterans, who we were, what our backgrounds were. But we decided that the work we were doing was much too important to let any press interview us. We wanted them to just deal with the content of the film and its issues, and, in fact, none of us ever signed the end of it. We just put "The *Winter Soldier* Collective," and that's how the film stood. People really don't want to deal with things that are real and to start connecting issues. They just want to let all that slide. So for those of us who worked on *Harlan County,* being in the film is just garbage. Yes, we were there. People really trusted us, they really cared about us. We lived with them for thirteen months, the entire duration of the strike, but we wanted to not be there. We wanted not to be in anything in the film. We wanted things to happen naturally and spontaneously, as they would without us.

WERNER SCHROETER

There is no physical reality in the image. It's an image, not physical reality. It does resemble it closely; it's more analogous.

If you see the structure of cinema in the forties and fifties in America, when people were doing experiments with abstract subjects, I think this works as well. There is always the fact that you have to recognize something, but if it's a moving line or whatever in the image, it's as much recognizable as the human face. For me, film is absolutely abstract as material, like a canvas, blank paper. I don't do structuralized cinema. I like to work with people; my movies always have people and faces and everything resembling what you say is reality, but, for me, film is an abstract medium of art.

I don't believe in documentaries, only in the case of an event strong enough even to overcome the medium of cinema, like the movie *Winter Soldier*. Otherwise, I don't believe in it. I remember in the late fifties, early sixties, there were several films from Poland and Czechoslovakia about the German concentration camps. You had these horror images of thousands of people pushed into the mass graves like skeletons, absolutely dead, and then they tried to give the images cynical value, to point to the fact of how cruel the people were to those other people, and they put on the soundtrack the waltz of the Nazi singer, Zara Leander, who sings "Only Love Makes a Woman Beautiful," and you see those skeletons. It is the wrong way. You have to create your own reality in cinema and you have to control it intellectually, have very, very high control of yourself, over what you are saying in cinema if you want to have a bigger audience. Because everyone is very weak anyway, everyone is weak.

MARK RAPPAPORT

The art of film lies in its ability to distort reality. If it were just to photograph reality, neorealism would be the answer. To say it cuts across time and space is just not getting to the point. I've always loved films, but I could never see the possibility of it for me until Godard. I thought you had to make story films, and I never felt I had a really comfortable sense of the well-upholstered story the way they made them in Hollywood. I loved/hated Hollywood movies. What I loved was the texture of them, but I couldn't stand the plots and the minor characters, and the walking up and down stairs, the mood music. I could never stand those extracurricular things.

Making movies is so difficult, it's so stylized. What's real about deciding to put a camera "here" and put a light "there" and telling the actor where to stand? None of it is reality; it's all .artifice; it's as stylized as any opera or any Mannerist painting. Even Impressionist painters didn't think they were getting reality. They were capturing some aspect of it; they were finding a new kind of reality for themselves. They were just getting out of doors, using the reality of light rather than a studio light; the reality of movement of a body in motion, rather than the look of posing. But it's very studied spontaneity. A great deal of artifice goes into creating the illusion of reality, which is what film is essentially about.

It is also about selectivity and inclusion. For example, films that pretend to be real—two people sitting at a kitchen table. There's a whole lot of things on the table: boxes of cereal, salt and pepper. If you don't choose the right angle, the right position of the camera, basically you're obscuring the characters with everything that's on the table. I've seen this in lots of movies: I pay attention to this and that's reality—to see a kitchen and see all the brand names. But part of the reality *of movies* is stripping all that away and making the stuff that's essential visible.

EMILE DE ANTONIO

I think *cinéma vérité* is a bankrupt concept. Finally you're confronted with the fundamental question, "Whose *vérité?*" And

once you ask that, you're surely answered by "Me, my *vérité.*"
It's "I" who has the camera pointed, it's "I" who edits, etcetera.
The great contribution of *cinéma vérité,* particularly by the Maysles and Leacock, was the light equipment, light-synch sound
equipment. But it's why Leacock isn't making films anymore,
and I think the Maysles films are an embarrassment, their embarrassment at not doing fiction films, because they let the camera run on, but they dominate everything; only they find it
easier to dominate the weak, unhappy people they're filming
instead of dominating actors who are stronger people. In the
case of *Salesman,* what is more wretched than these guys who
go around selling Bibles? And even that wasn't true because
they moved the guy down to Florida because it was more interesting than his normal sales beat. And in *Grey Gardens* there's a
kind of necessary cruelty in making a film like that. I can see
the necessity of being cruel in a film, but then I think you have
to have a higher purpose than the Maysles had. Because it's not
an aspect of truth; it's just as manipulated as any films edited in
a Steenbeck. It's why most of these guys end up making films
about rock music. This is what Pennebaker did with *Monterey
Pop* and what the Maysles did with *Gimme Shelter.* All of it is an
evasion of where documentary really is.

A documentary can be didactic and exciting at the same
time. What the Soviets did in the early days was didactic as hell
and exciting. I think the documentary can be boring when it is
explained, when it's condescending, when it's like network documentaries. They rarely deal with genuine personalities. They
deal with performers like Dan Rather, who are symbols. The
documentary is the one form of art that is really connected
with struggle, with society, with change. That's why it's par ex-
cellence the Marxist art. It is no accident that I'm a Marxist.

Nobody ever really believes the subject dominates. They say
they do, but no thoughtful person can say that, because in
every case, the filmmaker dominates the subject. I think the
tradition of Flaherty is the curse of the documentary. Nobody
really understands what that tradition really is. The tradition is
that every one of those films is a sponsored film. *Nanook of the
North* was sponsored by Revillion, a fur company. And

Louisiana Story was sponsored by Humble Oil. So when you have all those charming images of oil rigs, and the little boy and the bayou, it's finally a taking of no position about the way that oil rig is changing the lives of those people. I'm not saying that film should shed tears about the destruction of the natural landscape, because cameras don't shed tears, but the maker of that film must have some feelings, not about the ecological imbalance, perhaps, but about the profound changes that are made by that oil rig and the people who operate it and what its future will be and what that little boy will be. *Nanook* was filmed twice—that's your *cinéma vérité!* The negative of the first film was totally burned, so he had to go back and do it over again. It's brilliantly shot, a brilliant picture, of course, but the very premise and supposition of *Nanook* was so incorrect. Already the Eskimo wasn't hunting like that anymore; he had been using the rifle for a long time. And there is in our cruel, rich, expensive industrial society a ridiculous thing; there is this bogus, cheap romanticism about nature—a phony view of nature, about Nanook and his harpoon. A wonderful image, but simply not true. And all of Flaherty's films have this same blemish of romanticizing what appears to be a primitive experience, but in essence isn't. And it seems to me that the documentarian has to be involved with truth. The films have to stand or fall, not only on art and what they look like—and that's why it's a conjunction of all those things—but by truth, by dedication, by purpose. With all the differences between Chris Marker and me, we still both see film not like some mythical Communist party, but as something committed to change and basically an optimistic view of the world: that the world can be changed, that people can be changed, and that *I* can be changed. The important thing about it is that we're not journalists: we make a commitment to the event.

All the films that interest me do look like reality because they also deal with reality. I don't mean just the films I make, but the films that interest me. And this would include everything from Renoir's *Rules of the Game* to D.W. Griffith's *Birth of a Nation*. But you don't have to define reality; I just prefer this to the kind of things that bore me in film like animated abstract things bouncing around to pseudo-contemporary music. That to me is a non-art, non-film experience. I think abstraction doesn't belong to motion pictures in that sense. This isn't a value judgment. All film that has any audience—the audience itself isn't what it's all about but it sure is a part of it—has to deal with some aspect of reality. Marcel Duchamp said it about art and he's right: just as important as the art is the audience. Does a man on a desert island with no audience at all make art? I don't know what the answer is to that, but I suspect not.

JEAN ROUCH

My style is exactly what we call *ciné-vérité*, which is not a film on the truth but the truth on film. And the difference is there. When Vertov was speaking of *"Ciné-Pravda,"* of course it was a joke, because *Pravda* at that time was a newspaper and he was making a kind of newsreel film for the newspaper, but, in fact, I think he was right. He meant that for him the truth you can see on the screen has nothing in common with the Truth. It's what we call the "ciné-truth," the *ciné-vérité*, which is something very different.

When I am making a film with a camera, which means with a mechanical eye and with a mike and a tape recorder, which is an electronic ear, I am using an eye that is not an eye and an ear that is not an ear. It's something different and the truth that I show in the film is different from the Truth, of course. It's something different. *That's* the truth of film.

I also like very much to make fiction films with people I know very well. My best actors are Africans because they like improvisation and we have been friends for a long time. I will say, "Well, the situation is this," then I discuss it with them. We have dinner. We decide to make the film. We decide what will happen and we'll start and maybe there is something wrong, it's not exactly the situation we were supposed to find, and then they change it, and we do it another way. Sometimes it works and we know it quite well. Sometimes it fails and we decide to stop and get another idea. But we never do it over, only one take. But it's a very amusing way to make films because very often I don't know the end of the film. Maybe it's because I read somewhere when I was younger that the people who were making the first Western at the beginning of Hollywood didn't know the ending of the film when they started. They had three days to make a Western and they didn't know what would happen. I thought it was a good way to make a film: not to know the end before. For that reason I often have trouble because the people who have seen a script and then see the film see that it has no connection with the film itself.

AL MAYSLES

For a number of reasons all the great moviemakers have had to make films within the customary genre of fiction. And it's interesting that the great writers of today have moved on to non-fiction and the moviemakers are still stuck with this harness around them which is called fiction. Nevertheless, guys like Fellini are great and his films are extraordinarily good. I would say my favorite film is *La Strada*. But I also know that I had an uncle who used to sell eggs from a special kind of station wagon, and I used to work for him summers for twelve dollars a week, and my uncle was just like that guy in *La Strada*. I know it would be a far better film if it were my uncle who was the character because I don't think that any maker of fiction is capable of recording and transmitting the complexity or the potential of what a real person is. Because, you know, that's imitating something that history or God, or whatever you want to call it, has been required to create in a very complex way. It has had a long history going back through centuries, civilizations, and so forth.

The very name of the Bible company in *Salesman:* Mid-American Bible. If that were Fellini's experience, that it was Mid-Roman Bible or whatever, if he wanted to be that truthful about it, he couldn't, because he would say to himself, "They'll never believe it. It's too pat, it's too cliché." There is nothing we do that is restrained by that sort of thing. Also, because an author of fiction has total freedom, he is absolutely bound to abuse it. Because he can and always does resort in the end to a kind of hyperdrama that is not true to life. I mean, it's true to life that people die, for example, but why is it in every fiction piece it's taken literally? Whereas true death in its complex form is part of life that is going on with it every single moment. So, when you see *Salesman*, every single frame of that film has the sense of death. You never see Paul die at the end, although you do see Willie die in *Death of a Salesman*. Willie has got to die if only for the fact that the playwright has the opportunity to heighten the drama that way.

You know, it takes all that time up to the moment that you film that person, whether it's a person of two or a person of fifty, for the real person to form into all those particulars that he is. Inevitably, to shortcut it or to fabricate it is to create some kind of stereotype, which I don't think can stand the test of time. I mean, *Gimme Shelter* is over ten years old now. I've heard and read all kinds of accounts of the events of the day—none of them can hold a candle to the film.

When you come back with this kind of filming, you can't ferret it all out of the film—there's so much more in the film than you can imagine. Compare that scene in *Blow-Up*—the man in the bushes—with the complexity of the killing scene in *Gimme Shelter*. We had to slow it down in order for the viewer to catch it. I've looked at those three or four seconds in the film where it is slowed down. I've looked at it for hours and hours and hours, and still there's another hundred hours of looking left. So, in terms of power and integrity of the genre, there's so much there. Someone once said that the essence of tyranny is the denial of complexity. It's so easy to oversimplify in fiction, but it's very hard to deny the complexity of the material that you have when it's non-fiction. Having said all this, if a great director comes along, I won't deny him his day, but to me he's fighting an uphill battle.

JEAN-LUC GODARD

I think pictures have been hurt by the comparisons to the Seven Arts, but painting and music take their forms from the movement of a tree or the wind and movies can do that also. Painting is more taking the story from one tree and film takes it from two trees, moving from one to the other.

For me, cinema is a bit the image of the world. This is why it was immediately a popular art. Painting, music—not even that much music—film is simply that one which opens one's eyes, one sees.

To me there is no difference between documentaries and fiction films. My pictures have always been both documentary and fiction. I have always tried to shoot the fiction films in a more documentary way so they bring what they are, the way they look, to the picture. I tell the actors to speak the way they usually speak, not to try to speak another way. It's true that it is an impossibility to avoid reality in film; only your incapacity or your weakness or being in society makes you transform, manipulate without even knowing or wanting it. Making pictures is to clean, like a window you clean to be able to see.

MARTIN SCORSESE

I guess the ideal for me is to blend documentary and fiction. Nothing is real: once you put the camera before anybody, there's no reality, but there's an *illusion* of reality. And certain things can happen sometimes if you work with certain kinds of people and if you work in a certain way. It may seem to be real and yet it's not real. It has a kind of immediacy that makes it seem to be happening for the first time, that that actor never said the line before. Sometimes it's true—he never did say that line before—it just happened right there and he stayed within character and the other actor responded within character and you're cool—but that's highly dangerous, a dangerous situation that you can play with a little bit. And documentary is fictional in the sense that you're making it say what you want it to say. So you're manipulating the film. Even when you just point the camera it's a manipulation, what are you going to do? You can't be ashamed of it. In the case of documentaries, it's your point of view of a real situation. That's how you make documentaries. I like to make them. My documentaries, *An American Boy* and *Italian-American,* were released in Paris last week [April 4, 1980] as movies and they got great reviews, but nobody sees them in this country. I think they're mainly for non-theatrical audiences, not for mass audiences. But I like those films the best. I don't know why, maybe it's the way a person moves their eyes or turns their head. I've heard the story the guy's saying on film a few times before, but somehow there's another element involved because there's something more honest involved. Maybe "honesty" instead of "reality" is the word. There's less between you and the subject.

Film is a manipulation. All I'm trying to do is put on the screen what I see and, therefore, if you want to call that manipulation, it's manipulation. At the same time, there are other people who manipulate film for other reasons. It's how *I* look at reality. The very fact that the person knows the camera is in the room—it doesn't matter if you move it or not, tilt it upside down, whatever. All you can do is get some sense of honesty about it. It's more a question of honesty than of reality. It comes down to one person actually, how he sees it. Most films do today, anyway. It's interesting, though, how the old films sometimes had four directors on them, but one director signed it, and yet there's a clarity, a style.

CLAUDE CHABROL

I try to go from the appearance of reality, of course. In fact, reality is not realism. In film you find reality more by significant detail. Somebody lights a cigarette in one moment, and it can mean so much more. That's the real reality. In the street it's just the appearance of reality, but it gives nothing of the links, the meanings, which exist between things. You cannot find that when you look at the real world. It's very rare. Sometimes you can find that looking out the window, but it's much better with the screen because you can do more things, and that's why I don't like newsreel documentary filming, because you thread the camera and you wait, you wait. It's too long for me.

Documentary is based on a false notion: they think it's the truth because they recognize what they see on the screen as what they see on the street, but what they see on the street isn't truth. It's just the appearance. You have to look beneath that surface for the truth.

Eric Rohmer wrote about one hundred wonderful pages on film's relationship to other arts. It's called "Celluloid and Marble," and he said that all the other arts play some part in film. But the more important, in fact, are actually the less important. For instance, they always say that a shot is like a painting, but a painting is, in fact, one of the less important elements. It doesn't matter if "it looks like a Renoir." Or sometimes they say a film is musical, that the shots follow each other in a kind of musical way, but that, too, is not very important. It's important when inside of you you have a change of mood, something like that; but "it's like a novel"—that's not important or true.

What is important is the architecture. You can't actually see it in a film, but it is there. It is abstract but you must have it. It's a general form, a balance.

·7·

THE PROCESS
Writing, Shooting, and
Editing the Film

*Differences and similarities among the filmmakers that have emerged in
other sections of this book are confirmed and even more apparent here
in the overview each gives of the process of writing, shooting, and editing a film. In terms of style, choice of subject, attitude toward co-workers, as well as toward the prospective viewer, the finished film illustrates
the "politics" of the film; that is, the way in which the filmmaker views
the work process and his role as director, its responsibilities and limitations.*

*A main issue, once more, is that of control: the amount of control
possible over a film during its three major stages; the amount of control
the filmmaker exercises over those who work with him; and, most important, the question of how much control is even desirable; is it preferable
to be, as Chabrol describes it, like a fisherman who waits, follows, and
finally reels in the film?*

*Another element of control deals with how much the film follows or
manipulates the "real" or visible world. Some filmmakers prefer to use
natural locations, natural lighting, to allow the ambient sounds of a
location on the soundtrack without alteration, to permit actors to play
out small actions in "real" time. Others conceive of film as a form in
which artifice is art, guiding firmly the viewer's reading of the film with
pre-planned screenplays and camera work, studio sets, clean soundtracks, elaborate use of artificial lighting, and aggressive editing.*

Where does the film happen? Should the shots be planned on the drawing board rather than improvised on the spot during the shooting period, or should there be a compromise between planning and leaving it to the inspiration generated by the set and the actors? Does the editing actually happen in the post-shoot, editing period, or does one edit as he shoots, controlling the results of the editing by the choice of angles, the length of shots, or lack of choice on the same subject? Robert Altman compares the three stages: "In the beginning, from the initial script or idea, as we start working on it, it becomes entirely different. And by the time you get the film finished, you look back and say, 'Wait a minute, that's very much like what we started out with.'" For Elio Petri, parts of the process call for the director's more rational skills, others for his more poetic faculties, but throughout, the director must deal with economics: "Only the story and dialogue are planned in advance. There is a kind of balance: these things belong more to my rational sphere than the camera movements do. But both are also, consciously or unconsciously, expressions of a compromise with production and distribution." Werner Schroeter addresses one implication of the issue of how much the filmmaker can control in the process, the notion of perfection: "It's very important that you always work with your own mistakes honestly without hiding them, so it means you shouldn't be too narcissistic. What damage does it do if you stumble a little bit and you can't get exactly what you want to say, but somehow still achieve what you have to say anyway. It's less brilliant and it's less virtuoso, but I think virtuosity is without importance anyway. I think the whole definition of aesthetics on that level, and of perfection, is profoundly related to our materialistic society."

Of course, the film does slip away from its makers, and well it should. As Mark Rappaport notes, "Scripts are blueprints. If you gave the scripts of twenty very famous films to people who had never seen the films, could they possibly reconstruct the films from just reading the scripts? A movie like Double Indemnity, *for example, which has a great script, but also has that smoky kind of seedy way it looks and Barbara Stanwyck's platinum hair and Fred MacMurray's dimple in his chin—all that stuff is very important, and you can't get that directness, that gritty feeling of that movie just by the script. It helps, but it's like a Polaroid of someone you love."*

Bertolucci makes the final point regarding the elusiveness of film in noting that the camera is always in front of reality, and "reality is reality. There is always a percentage of vérité, of truth, which you can't change because it's a real moment and the shooting gives reality to it. The Rules of the Game is my number one movie. Once in Los Angeles, I asked Renoir about improvisation and he told me, 'Il faut toujours laisser une porte ouverte sur le set' ['One must always leave a door open on the set'], because someone, something, can suddenly come in." It's exactly what filmmaking is: leaving the door open.

JEAN-LUC GODARD

Anne-Marie Mieville and I have a company and I need her because she's the raw material and I'm the finished product. I'm the director and she feels she's not capable. She says, "I'm worried about the shots, about analysis . . . it's too professional." But as a professional myself, I need a non-professional. We have an agreement and she's fifty percent of *Everyman for Himself*.

I prefer to use a new technology, because the rules are not yet set, but I find myself to be very lonely in this preference. I'm more aware of the whole mechanism now, of how it works, really, and the way you have to be to do something through it.

When I plan a film, the story line is always mine, but then I need to discuss it with people, not to be alone, to communicate, to need critics. I think I follow the screenplay when I shoot, but it depends, because I've done things for television and it was different. This last film was done more like the old way by having it more precise. The editing is the real shooting. I try to take takes, then "to shoot" with the takes. Sometimes I take lots of takes when I'm feeling insecure and I need that security. With video, of course, you can see immediately what you have, but with film you don't know immediately what you're doing sometimes, so you work a different way.

I rehearse before. I know the place, I've thought of it, so when I shoot it's like the army: "Do this, do that." I know the main elements of a shot, but the difficulties of the moment create the unexpected.

Cinematographers are too difficult, too professional, kind of army people, technicians; they know some technical things, like about lights, but not about paintings. There is no discussion possible there. I would say that the photography of a picture has been done by Kodak first, by me second, and by the cinematographer third.

On *Everyman for Himself* I was so afraid to quarrel with the camera personnel, as they were holding onto more classical views of film techniques. We had many arguments about things that one could or couldn't do—about lighting, shooting in the dark, special lighting, etcetera. There were two operators and one of them had made broadcasts with his associates for TV. They helped us a bit to put together the studio in a different way and to relearn technique a little—microphones, etcetera— and to be more up to date. Since this was a French-Swiss co-production, I thought we needed two camera operators, one French and one Swiss, and this also came from the fact that I was a little scared to fight with them, since they came from a more classical technique of making movies. I also thought if there were two operators who were friends, they could fight with each other and not with me.

But they presented themselves as specialists, as scorcerers. The fights came from the fact that instead of becoming sanitary agents they became scorcerers. They couldn't help it. We fought and discussed as if their goal was to say, "Okay, Jean-Luc, if you want to make films, we are going to show you what it is." The fact was, I was reduced to a trick that I hadn't used for twenty years, which I had used for *Breathless,* where I was so scared, where I hated a photographic style that was done a lot in that period in French cinema of quality. I was very un-trusting because that was a period of cinema in which one couldn't put a white shirt against a white wall or things like that. One was very intimidated and it still exists in TV. I was so afraid at times that I was very happy when one of the cam-eramen proposed a guy to work with us simply because he had never made a film. And I think that unconsciously I told my-self, "At least he will not know more than I do, and he will also be as scared as I am." The American reporters were the first ones not to limit themselves by considerations of lighting. They simply used light-sensitive film stock. And I had to do some-what the same: I really didn't want to fight with them. I wanted to discuss lighting a bit, but I became aware that they were technicians and one couldn't light certain things unless they could see a technical reason for doing so. In other words, if I wanted to film a black person in a tunnel at night without any light, they would say, reluctantly, "We will try and see if any-thing can be seen," and I would respond, "You will see *something*. Godard has prepared for this situation." On the other hand, I would film crows in a wheat field and tell them, "Here, take this Polaroid, give me two or three shots, so I can see what interests you. If the wheat is telling you something." This was taken as a very provocative gesture. I would tell them to go experience a day in the sun, stay there and rest peacefully, read, listen to music, bring a friend, when nothing was happening. The production would pay for it. Just see the light change and tell me afterwards in the course of the day, in the full sun, there were four different types of light and I like "that" one. This was not so unthinkable, but their reaction to it was rather violent, they were taken aback.

In the editing, it is as if you have gathered the grain and now you have to make a bread. In the editing you feel you "covered" almost nothing. Everything's wrong and different—that's what you discover. That's what is so different about working with video: in a way you want to see it right away, which you can, but in a way you don't want to see it. It makes some film people uncomfortable being able to see the results immediately. Maybe you want to see it in a day or two, or maybe in a month, but it's here and there is something in that. Both are interesting, but since there have been so many movies, the use of video could be interesting. You see it right away and then you have to do something else because you know it's not working. It's more of a commitment—at least today. Ten years from now, maybe not.

There is a slowed-down motion shot from Marcelle's point of view in *Everyman for Himself*. It is panoramic. When Marcelle comes close, the speed slows down at that moment. At regular speed, one sees nothing. It is the slow-down that I want to see. I want to see the drag on the landscape, like Monet. Effectively, it gives the impression of advancing, it gives what is missing in the script.

As a filmmaker I discover things that I have deprived myself of when I started making movies with my camera on my shoulders. I tried to reconquer grammatical formulas, like someone who has studied occidental, Western poetry. Sometimes I really ask myself questions, such as why are you creating a background or showing a piece of scenery. A script makes you want or leads you to create a particular background. When one wants to talk to other filmmakers it is not enough to knock at the door and say, "Here I am, let's talk." I tell them, "Well, did you bring a scene or a photograph? Talking is not enough. It is too easy."

To communicate is the function of movies. I think that the movies that I try to make, the techniques that I try to domesticate, are not aimed to get "there," because one always gets "there" sooner or later. They are more ambitious. I want to have the time to reflect and to organize the moment or a script or the idea of a script. In other words, I want to have a motive or pattern from which I can make a script that can be sold to TV, which when filmed one can see that the next scene cannot be something that one could have predicted through the writing. But one is chained to the written word because it is written for the production and everything is chained together. There is the writing of the screenwriter but also the writing of the banker. There is the banker's interest and also the cultural interest. And the interest of the banker and of the culture at some point become mixed together. One has to pay a cultural interest or debt. That is my experience. In our production house we pay that cultural debt. One can see when one has a relationship with the Third World. We tell them often that the cultural debt that they pay to the occidental countries is in inverse proportion to the interest paid by the World Bank, where one is loaned money at five-percent interest. The cultural debt that the Third World pays will be eighty-five percent sometimes. So it is better to pay more money and pay less on the cultural debt in order to finance your film.

HENRY JAGLOM

When I was shooting my first picture, *A Safe Place*, I had my hair up in a ponytail, and this crew that had just come off *Love Story* was very unhappy with me. They didn't know what I was doing and every time I had to shoot something, the cinematographer and the grips would say, "It can't cut, it doesn't match, it doesn't work." They were trying to impose their kind of logic even on the process. They were looking for it in the script and I use a script only as a guideline. It drove them crazy and they drove me crazy. I finally asked Orson Welles, "What do I do about this? They're driving me crazy. Every single time I ask for a setup of a shot I have to explain to them that it doesn't *have* to cut, I'm going to use this later as a collage, I'm going to figure out later where this fits into the story." Well, Orson was incredibly valuable for me because he's had this sort of experience all his working life. He said, "Whenever a crew tells you 'It won't cut, it doesn't work, it doesn't make sense, you can't find it in the pages,' you just say to them, 'It's a dream sequence.'" I said, "Really, a dream sequence? Will that work?" And he said, "Yes, they know that dreams don't have to have a normal form of logic, but they think life has to. Somebody told them that life has logic and structure and they know dreams don't have to, so tell them it's a dream sequence." Right after the break at lunch I went back and did the next setup, and sure enough, the cinematographer said, "What's this, what page is this, it's not going to cut." And I said, "It's a dream sequence." "A dream sequence . . . oh." And he was a pussycat for the rest of the movie. He would get on his back with the camera, rolling around, showing me how willing he was to do weird things. Suddenly, he didn't need his rules about what cuts and what's logical and so on. So, you parallel what you're trying to do subjectively *on* film, which is break down those rules for the audience, as well as try to let the audience know that it's all right not to know, just to feel.

I'm not interested, therefore, in giving freedom to the crew. I have not yet found a crew that makes me happy. When I do, I will be very happy to. If I can find somebody who works with the camera the way I would like to if *I* operated a camera, I would probably give them the same freedom, because that would just increase *my* freedom, you know. But since I don't find such people, I have to be very specific and very constrained in what I do with them, and I want to be sure that I get what I want to get from them. It's terribly important for any camera person working with somebody like myself that they not concern themselves ever with the technical things that allow them to stop and prepare. For instance, I never let my actors wear makeup. I don't want lights. I want a minimum of lights because the actors are freer from the process of thinking of themselves as acting if they're less conscious of lights, if they're less conscious of makeup, if the camera is moving with them rather than having to be set up in a precise way.

I don't care about technical perfection that much. I hate the thing being out of focus, because in life you don't see somebody out of focus, so that *is* very disturbing to me. I hate things that look badly lit because you're thinking, "Oh God, they're lit." But if it's dark or if the structure is that it's over "here" and not over "there," who cares? I don't care. I really have never understood why they care so much about it. It has never had anything to do with how I've liked a film or not, unless the film was about visual beauty. *Days of Heaven* has to be technically perfect to be *Days of Heaven*. That's what it's about. That's not what interests me in film.

I have always liked a hand-held feeling and so I like to have a cameraman in a wheelchair moving, which is what I use a lot. Now that the Steadycam exists, I would use that. In *A Safe Place* I had all that stuff, so I played with it, and I had this crane going up and down, and I liked it. But unless you're doing a movie about a battlefield, what's the point of being up there particularly, you know? The couple of times I've wanted to get up there, I've put the camera on a ladder. But that's not what filmmaking is about for me and I think people get too caught up in sets, too caught up in equipment, and structuring all that stuff and decorating and technology and technical perfection.

I want every surprise, every surprise that's possible to happen. It creates new stuff with which to work. I don't want to think of it all myself because then it's going to be my mind, it's *just* going to be my mind, and I want to form the image of the thing through what I understand of the pieces. That's why actors are very happy to work with me. There's a good reason: I cannot get a bad performance because they can do *anything*. They can be brave; they know if it doesn't work, it won't be in the picture. Even if it's a vital scene, I'll just throw it out and there won't be a vital scene in the movie. You can change constantly.

There are three stages for me. First, I write the thing down, very thoroughly, but it's really a structure to start shooting with. I don't do camera shots. I do camera shots in my mind pretty much. But then I never look at the script when I'm shooting the movie. The actors do, but I just never do because I don't want to be stopped by what *I* did in the script. And so it changes constantly while we work, and then I take it all back. I like to shoot as large a ratio, obviously, as I can afford, and I spend a year cutting it. Once again, I don't look at the shooting script. I don't look at what I've shot and how it fits into the original idea. I just look at all the pieces of film over and over again. And, you know, you start creating a new pattern to satisfy what you're trying to feel.

I've never done the same take twice. The only time I've ever done that is with Orson Welles. He required a certain way of working that satisfied his needs. Young actors prefer not to. Why do it again? Then they're acting; you're "acting." I would rather try a new way of expressing the same thing and then a third way and then a fourth way, and then I have the job of cutting together the best pieces of what I get. It's a task, and you've got to figure out how to cut away, but it's nice, I love the task. But frequently it is a task itself, and the results are a new visual form.

The editing is all pretty intuitive and you're sort of putting yourself in the place of the audience and the place of the character, and you're judging how long you're going to hold the shot from the point of view of myself and of my sense of what the character does. But it's emotional. I've watched how long it should go on. It has to do with how it feels, if it's feeling right, rather than by any logical thing.

I do the editing. I'm really my own editor with an assistant, sometimes, filing things away. I'd like to get a good cameraman who would help create a film. I'd like to get a good editor who would contribute ideas, but it's my vision. Film is not, despite what they tell you in Hollywood, a collaborative medium. It's one person's vision, like a painting. Although you can be helped enormously by all kinds of things, the input of many other people, and mainly, as I think I told you, by the actors. Everything else is secondary to me. Technical people are wonderful and valuable but they don't create the film, they create the *look* of the film, which helps sell it. The only people who really help the film are the writer-director and the actors. And the director is the conductor of the orchestra, so to give somebody else the film to let them cut it is insane. I don't understand that. I would like to have a pair of hands that could do a lot of that stuff for me, or somebody who has a similar vision who would come up with ideas for scenes, but since I'm not putting together scenes but rather images and moments, how can another person really do that? And I like doing it also. It's my fun. It's from school when I used to cut out and paste. That's some of my best stuff. You know, I get to sit down in my room and cut and paste.

I always screen during editing but not for anybody, for friends. I did more of it for *Sitting Ducks,* because comedy has a lot to do with how the audience is going to get it, so I was very curious as to how it was going, and I was learning from the audience, in this case, whether certain things that I thought worked, did. Comedy is different because we can't look at it fresh. The scene between Michael and Zack in the bathroom— after that there was a scene where they get knocked unconscious and they are lying naked and unconscious in a room and they wake up dazed and then they run out to look at the car, which has been wrecked. I cut that middle scene out, because everybody thought they were homosexuals. How was I supposed to know that when I shot it? It would never occur to me, but it turned out that almost the whole audience thought, after seeing them naked in the bathtub, then lying on the floor, that it was some sort of homosexual orgy. That threw off so much their sense of what was going on, that I had to take it out. So I let audiences affect me that way.

There's all this technical shit that I wish didn't exist. There's always the fear that something's going to happen, or it will be out of focus, which sometimes happens, or that the sound's no good. But I just know what's going to be good. And there are three processes for me, really. It's writing the superstructure, shooting the movie—making it happen then the second time— and then taking the pieces and cutting it and making it happen then a third time. They're three totally separate processes. Each one is like starting from scratch and each one is new. And the picture goes through three evolutions that way.

JACQUES DEMY

I wrote all my films myself, except the film I did in English, *Pied Piper,* because I know how to write a letter in English but not dialogue. I know how to construct. I'm really proud of that. This is helpful for a screenwriter. Very few people have this these days. It's a virtue that's been lost somewhere. It started about ten years ago in France with people wanting to make long films and they were too long. It's very difficult to make a film over two hours. For years and years, the length of a film has been ninety minutes. There was a reason for that: your attention, your concentration, lasted that long. In a novel, another two hundred pages doesn't matter; in a painting, it can have a large or small frame. But I found it very difficult to sustain strength as I wished it to be for over an hour and a half. A three-hour movie is another experience. You can go out for five minutes and come back. It's a different thing.

The film mainly happens in the shoot. It can happen in the cutting room in many films. That's okay, but I believe much more in the shooting. That's when it happens. Not five minutes before the take, not five minutes after the take. It's when you say "Roll it." It's when you say "Action" that counts, because after, it's too late.

The day before, we say, "Tomorrow we are going to shoot in that room or that spot," and the director of photography, the lighting man, looks with me. So, he has two things to do: as usual, he has to light the walls and the room, which has nothing to do with the action anyway, so he knows the space. And then, the second thing is to finish by lighting the faces of the actors. And during the rehearsals, the lighting man can follow me and see exactly what to do. So, the actors come from Makeup and Costume, and lighting has been done. Outdoors, of course, there's no lighting to do, most of the time. In *Lady Oscar* what I wanted to do with all the outdoor shots was use a crane. I used a crane systematically with every shot, which gives you a feeling of air, of air in between everything. I love that.

As far as improvisation is concerned, in *Pied Piper*, for example, to get a six-minute shot, you have to rehearse, there's no other way. And it's not improvised. But what I do, anyway, is to improvise the shots on the spot. I never do a shooting script. I like to be on the set with the actors and the props, and then I know what to do to get the best out of it. But I cannot think of it abstractly because I think it's wrong if you think about it in your hotel room without the actors and the props and the set. There's no life. There's just an abstract concept. But when you're on the spot with everybody in the room with the real set, the real size, the real things, the emotion you want to get, then you know what it's all about and you start thinking. It's also very dangerous because it depends on your inspiration. If you're in bad shape, you might be in bad trouble. But it's the same for every director. You have to be in good shape at eight in the morning when you come on the set every day for two or three months. I like that way of shooting because it gives more life, more truth. I have no preconceived ideas at all, and I don't want to, except on the whole concept of the film. I have that idea of the whole film, how it's constructed, but in detail. I want to leave it open for freedom. And it's also better for the actors. They feel more comfortable.

GEORGE ROMERO

What I like most is the cutting. I don't feel that I'm making the film until I have all the stuff and I'm in my little room and everybody's gone and I can have a lot of fun.

In fact, when I cut, I cut with a lot of tracks. I don't cut with just picture and voice. Sometimes, if it's really subtle, I'll let it go and work on it separately, but I like to cut with all the tracks. I'll lay in some music. If I don't have the music for the film, I'll go to my soundtrack albums and get something, just so I can put some flavor on it. And then I don't like to look at it. I don't like to work at speed, like on a flatbed or on a Moviola. I just use a table, and I like to just lay all the tracks out. There's a certain tactile thing about that; there's a certain visual quality about seeing the mag and the leader. There's a certain checkerboarding of patterns that I really like. And then I'll go down and mix the track and then I'll look at it when it's mixed out. I like to see what kind of internal momentum it has. When you look at something on a flatbed it's always at speed. You see it backwards, forwards, and you're refining. You know, you make a cut, and immediately you're refining it. And you shouldn't refine that cut you've just made before you look at the whole sequence. And, so, I like to lay it all out and put everything together in a rough cut and look at it and get an impression from it, because then you can feel something about the pace, about what kind of integrity the scenes have to each other, how they juxtapose, where a sound effect comes in. You get an overall impression, and you can say to yourself, "Well, I'm going to lay in this," or "I'm going to mess around with this cut or overlap," or throw it out, or put another shot in. You can't get a sense of that when you're at speed all the time. You're constantly looking at it.

I'm very aware of the rhythms of the cutting. And I did a lot of dialogue cutting, a lot of paring down from my rough cut on *Dawn*, to get it to work.

The scripts for most of my films—*Martin* is the exception—are skeletons. It's all there: if you read the screenplay for *Dawn*, it's very close to the finished film.

SIDNEY LUMET

I look at what the picture needs. What is it about on its internal level, in terms of what is *not* written but what its real point is? I've done pictures in which I've improvised eighty percent of it. I've written scenes or movies when I was in desperate trouble and couldn't get ahold of the writer because he was off on another assignment, and I still wouldn't think of asking for a writing credit or a writing participation. My job is to direct the writers as much as it is to direct the actors and direct the technicians. That's part of my function and to therefore call for a screen credit . . . I even object to "so and so's" film or "production of" as a billing thing.

I'm not a writer and so I've never written my own screenplays. I think the two talents are different. I know very few writer-directors who are as good in each. Almost all of them are stronger in one or the other. But I do a lot of work on the screenplay and you can improvise on the piece. Again, it varies according to the piece. When you're doing a script by Chayefsky or Jay Presson Allen, you cannot improvise. The rhythm of the language is as vital as the rhythm of the editing. The selection of the words is as important as the selection of a frame. Other instances, you want total freedom. On *Dog Day Afternoon*, well over sixty percent of the movie was improvised in language and shooting. There were three cameras and I let them go to it. Usually what I do is use more than one camera so that I've got my freedom for the one scene: a wide one and two close-ups, so I can go in and go out whenever I want. Also, if I'm going to improvise, I never let the improvisation exist for just the take. I will have improvised it during rehearsal first.

I still wouldn't call it "my production." It's not. It's gone so crazy. I mean, the lack of confidence this country has in whatever itself created, so that they keep having to pick up dopey ideas from the French all the time. I'm obviously talking about the whole *auteur* nonsense. How much of an *auteur* are you if you're dependent on whether or not the clouds are over the sun? And you're at the mercy of anything. It's ridiculous. Not to mention human personality, whether you got laid the night before, whether your fried egg was good or not. It's so amateurs-in-search-of-a-theory that I find the whole thing dismissive. My job is very simple, and I think that every director, unless he's crazy or egotistic, knows that his job is to get the best out of everybody working. That's my job and that's a reflection of me, and that's where the personal statement lies.

BENOIT JACQUOT

I try at all the stages of the filmmaking process—writing, shooting, editing, even when it opens, the publicity, the press—to keep the film as close as possible to the original idea that I envisioned at the start, knowing all the time that the film never stopped escaping and separating from me. Fundamentally, my life consists of keeping that which I have created as close as possible to me, and to try to keep it from moving away from me, but obviously, it keeps moving away further, like a fork in the road.

First I write the screenplay like a novel: just the story, with dialogue, characters, descriptions of all that happens, but as if it was something to be read. After, I break it down into scenes, shot-by-shot, very precisely. The script is capital for me, really very important. It's fundamental. The first thing is that the script proceeds as I want it to, but it would be a nice effect if, for example, the dog barking offscreen overlaps a part of the text without my expecting it, without my knowledge. That can create a strong effect of reality. I don't write scenarios for themselves, but as a function of the film to be made. Sometimes, paradoxically, I do write in such a way that they could be published and read, I might add, because they are quite sufficient in themselves.

I see the locations as a function of the screenplay that I write. I look for the decors that most closely resemble that which I wrote. The idea is to come as close as possible to the original idea that I had imagined. That's why I say reality is nothing but smoke, because I never stop trying to manipulate and transform everything in such a way that it conforms to my ideas.

What counts most is the rapport between the script and the *mise-en-scène*. That should be like a contract between the director and himself. The directing is the realization of the contract. The director might be a pervert who tries to play with this law that the contract is, or he could be a Straub, who follows the contract, point-by-point.

So, for me, the shoot and the edit are two stages of the same operation. To edit, to cut from an image, that is the *mise-en-scène*. And the organization of a frame during a shoot, that is already editing. Since I write the screenplay like a story, but broken down scene-by-scene, very carefully and precisely, the editing is implicit in the writing. The editor has only to take out the slates.

The surprises, the improvisations, are my invention. I determine them. I am always surprised by the things that can happen during the shooting—an actor who doesn't quite do what he's told, all the little mistakes, slips. The shoot is a cloth woven with mistakes, and all these little slips are a surprise for me. But the surprises that the film puts into play, they are my invention and I try to direct them.

I control the actors very much. Before shooting I rehearse the script with them to find the exact rhythm I want them to say the lines in. There is no question of improvisation. I want the script to be repeated word-for-word as written. I don't want the actor to be the inventor of the text but rather the carrier of it. I don't want the actor to invent, but rather to get as deeply as possible into the script that he reads. I don't want him to start to move it away from where it is. I want him to dig deeper until he finds something with the greatest possible force.

I rehearse, always in a room off to the side, never on the set. I start rehearsals off-set without giving them any indication of camera angles or placement or decor. After, when they really know the rhythm and rhyme of the text, they go on the set, and there we do the blocking, the looks, the camera, etcetera.

All of that for me is part of the same process. The slightest tilt of a head, the least little look, the smallest blink of an eye— each is a gesture I have directed, and each little thing is an important part of the filmmaking process. Everything is controlled, everything is precisely scored. Nothing is left to chance.

ERMANNO OLMI

Beauty, emotions, must be revealed by indications that most resemble reality, not by artificial ones. This is precisely so that the viewer's approach to the screen isn't protected and deceived by devices, but that he or she succeeds in discovering alone its values, certain atmospheres, certain states of mind, through indications that are more those of life than those of theatricality, in the sense of spectacle.

I use artificial illumination because it's necessary for the effects of the film stock; sometimes the light doesn't reach the film. But I also do it respecting natural atmospheres as much as possible. As for filters, I never use special filters to alter or in some way modify the tonalities of the natural atmosphere. For example, when I shoot a close-up of the female lead in a romantic situation, I don't use those filters that normally a script would call for to make her seem like a commercial. To give you a technical example from shooting, when I shoot in a certain place, I don't frame and then, on the basis of the framing, establish the lighting. I set up the kind of lighting that will allow me to shoot anywhere in the location.

Since I do the camerawork, I know exactly what I shot, so much so that often I don't even look at the developed film. I call the developer and if they say the negative is okay, it's fine for me.

I work a great deal at the Moviola. For *Tree of Wooden Clogs* I was there for a year. The editing is the moment when all these emotions, these liberations felt at the moment when I begin to think about the film, to organize it, to choose locations, faces—these things—come together. The editing is the moment when I "add up the bill" of all these things, when I work out this choice and this synthesis, which is the "emotion of the emotion." And it's not an administrative work in the sense that you look at the screenplay and say, "Okay, such and such a cut at such and such a scene. Now the close-up, where's the close-up?" It's a new creative moment, an extraordinary moment. I rarely write organized scripts, but lots and lots of notes. When I'm shooting, I arrive on the set with all these notes, a little piece of paper filled with scribblings, and there, on the set, I begin again in a critical-creative phase, not critical-executive, to think about the shots.

I write the indication of a subject, a story, then they are divided into many chapters, many moments, like the movements of a concerto. And everything that comes into my mind regarding one of these chapters, at any moment, when I'm scouting locations, etcetera, I write down on pieces of paper and throw them into the chapter. Then, when I have to shoot, I organize that fraction of story I have to shoot in the most definite way possible. But when I'm there, shooting, I'm often, let's not say ready to change everything, but to add, to subtract. That's why I never have a script. It's like how I shoot, how I frame the shots. These notes are indications of dialogue, of atmosphere, of a face.

When I'm at the Moviola, I don't look at all at this written stuff again. It's a new event that is happening. So, creation, like the act of love, is always in the becoming, is always in motion, there aren't any stops. When there are stops, one doesn't make love.

DUŠAN MAKAVEJEV

At the beginning of the process I have no idea of what I will do. I just have a kind of very strong feeling. Sometimes you *feel* there is a movie. So, then you move there and then the movie starts happening. Sometimes you have a very good day, a good scene to do, a good location, and you still don't know how to approach it. Then you move about. I like to move with the cameraman. So, we move around, and I also like him to propose things. It's difficult for me to say, "I want *this.*" If I have two or three choices, then I can not only choose but I can find the right one and correct it. In correcting I can find the solution. But if the cameraman asks me, "Do you want movement or a static shot?" I'm just paralyzed.

I work with the same people most of the time, but not always. As far as editing is concerned, I'm there practically all the time. There's a constant feedback going back and forth and we change things from day to day many times. In *Sweet Movie* I had a crew of young French kids—very energetic; they loved to work. But they absolutely learned to work in the manner where you edit the film, and as soon as you have it, it's okay. And for me, the first edit, the first draft, is just the beginning; but they believed it was finished. So, we did something else and they were pleased, but then we did something else again. After the third screening, they said, "You know, this is fantastic, how it changed from the first version to this. It is incredible, we didn't believe we could reach this." They were talking about this third version as if it were a finished film, and the movie still had far to go. "But," I said, "we have several things left to do." They said, "You can't do anything. It's finished." So, we did another re-edit, and for the next two weeks they were constantly surprised because almost every day there was another film. During one period we had two screenings, one in the morning and another in the evening after we'd changed things, because it was like juggling scenes from the beginning to the end of the film and we were changing the story all the time. They were obviously never exposed to a situation in which a director was allowed or allowed himself to change the story. See, it was a great surprise for me because I always believed that's how everyone should work.

For example, in *Sweet Movie* it was difficult. In the scene where they make love in the sugar and she kills him in the sugar, chronologically you have the boat, you see the sailor, and then they slowly make love, he gets killed, and the children appear. When the children come in, he's already a corpse in the sugar. But when I got this in chronological order, it was so strong that everything else was anticlimactic. After this scene you couldn't watch for another ten or fifteen minutes. The scene was killing everything after it. And then we knew that this scene had to be somewhere towards the end. So, I moved it towards the end. And, at some point, you like to try different places: somewhere there's a point where it fits, there's a point where you can see it without being troubled.

Sometimes you can make three very good takes of the same shot, and if they're really good, they all stay in the film. They go different places. For example, you might have two very good long movements. So, you use, let's say, three quarters of one and this you interrupt with something else. And then, instead of continuing with the rest of the shot, you get the last three quarters of the second take, so instead of having one take, you actually have a take and a half. People don't see you did this overlapping. I was a little surprised to learn that Bergman did this in *Persona*. When Liv Ullman watches the guy burn himself—this shot is used twice. Her face is intercut, but the next shot does not continue the previous shot; it starts a little earlier, so you get the same guy running towards the camera. So, obviously, he used more than one take. He was stretching time, which we do all the time in movies, like stretching chewing gum. It's never realistic. It's a great pleasure to find the "real" time, the time people need. It's strange. Sometimes we have to cut out a lot of time; often you can stretch it easily.

Most important, you look to see how the film breathes, how it moves, because if you disturb people too early, then you lose them at some point. Sometimes you have a beautiful sequence that goes unnoticed because it's sandwiched between something. So, good sequences have to be sandwiched between boring stuff. And boring stuff has to be kept as a rest, as a platform for the audience. A good scene can be placed by anything boring because people don't need to have the film go on. You have the film going on, but they still are digesting, they chew. For example, in *Sweet Movie* that's why from time to time you have a boat. The boat is just beauty, but it serves also to give you time to think about some things twice, to get ready for something else. And maybe to whisper something if you're with someone. It's important.

JEAN ROUCH

Last night there was a meeting in the theater room here at Cinématèque Française to see an homage to Margaret Mead, and I had made a film of Margaret when I was in New York one and a half months ago in the Museum of Natural History with my friend John Marshall as soundman. I was interviewing Margaret with the camera, speaking to her as I was shooting. And the result is very interesting because she is speaking to the camera. Of course, she calls me "Jean," she does not say "Mr. Camera," but there is a contact and the contact is with the camera. And what she said was said because there was a camera. The camera was provoking something: a new relationship between people.

One problem, then, with using Super 8 is that you have this wide angle which distorts, so you have to be at a distance that is really too much for the contact. You have to be close to some people, and then you are really sharing the experiment, the experience. For me, the solution lies in being able to get close with Super 8; and if you can do that, you can make a fiction film in this way. Cassavetes tried to do the same thing some years ago with *Shadows,* only he was using professional actors.

But the problem in the States is very different than the situation here in Europe. For example, you could not make a film like the Maysles's *Salesman,* a beautiful film, because when you come to the door with a camera and the people were to see a camera with the Bible salesman, they would say, "No, we don't want to speak." In the States, people are easier with the camera and with filmmakers. In France it's very difficult, which means you have to be very close, emotionally, to the people you are filming, or you can make the film if it's a special event or public ritual. You can make a film like that, but to follow a man through his day is very difficult in our mind.

When I'm making anthropological films, on a ritual or a hunting party, the only thing I have to do is be like a newsreel cameraman and try to write a report with the camera: record it with sight and sound. It was easier when we were shooting silent films and putting sound on later. With single system sound you are always a slave to the sound: people start to speak and then you must film them. That's why a lot of these *cinéma vérité* type films are so boring. You think it is very important to stay with a person who is talking. Of course, I'm not sure of that. I have to be trained more. Maybe in ten years I can give you an answer. I think you can cut a sentence in the middle. You cut the frame often in the middle of a movement. But we are not yet there. Now you can't cut like that. I think we'll learn a lot from the Super 8 single system, because you have to edit that film a lot. Right now the difficulty with Super 8 is that it is very difficult to transfer to 16mm, but I've some students who are studying at the University of Nanterre who are preparing their Ph.D.s in film and they are working in Super 8 in a really avant-garde way: the filmmaking of tomorrow.

For example, to use my own case, I shoot alone with just a soundman: we are two, using the single system, which means that we have to be very well acquainted with one another to know not to put the mike in the middle of the frame, etcetera, because when you're following a movement sometimes it's very embarrassing. You're shooting with one eye and with the other looking to see where the mike is, telling the soundman to move closer. We experimented in Super 8 with putting the mike on top of the camera. It's very good because you have the sound of what you are shooting, but if somebody is speaking off-frame, it's not very good. But now we are shooting in stereo. I've been using both small tracks on the film to record sound and some projectors are double system now.

What we've learned is that if you are alone, you are a one-man team with an automatic sound system, automatic focus, and you can really make a film where the camera is a pencil. It is no longer a pen, it's a pencil. The filmmakers in Super 8 are showing the way. And now the men who are making the new cameras, for example, J. P. Beauviola, who built one of the best 16mm cameras we have, is trying to have the same gadget in Super 8, and it would change everything. If you are alone, then there is something different. Even with my soundman in Africa, we are a group, we are the filmmakers. And we are strong, we have this big machine, and so on, we are strong in front of the people we are filming. If you are alone, you are feeble, and you have to share your experiment with the people you are filming. Then my improvisation proceeds in this way, then we can see what is the reaction of the people. When I am making a documentary, I am following the subject, I have to follow it. I have to be at the best place to shoot what's happening. And I try to make long sequence shots, at least ten-minute takes. I now need one half-hour's worth of film in my magazine; that would be a good thing. Then you can do a film in one shot.

When we are editing, we change the order of the shots, or sometimes we suppress some sequences, but the majority of the films were shot exactly in order of the story. I'm speaking of the fiction film. We are telling a story, and when, for various reasons, we have to do a flashback or something not following a chronological order, really that's very difficult with an amateur actor. To say to them, "Well, it was one year ago or one week ago or it's tomorrow," that's difficult. You can do it if you are doing some shots after you have screened the first batch you've shot, but very often I make films in Africa, films like *Jaguar,* which was made during one and a half years in Africa. And I never saw a meter of rushes. I sent my stock back to Paris and some friends told me if it was okay, in focus, properly exposed, and nothing more. They didn't know the story or anything else about the film.

Now I try to shoot part of the film and come back with film edited, see it with the people I'm working with. And then we decide what to do and go on. But it's not very easy. When I was shooting in France, for example, and you could see the rushes every two, three days, the amateur actors were doing their work over all the time. They were acting just like actors. I remember when I was shooting *Chronicle of a Summer* in 1960 with real people playing their own parts; we were showing them the rushes. In this film there was a girl who was crying, and the other girl in the film said, "I want to do a dramatic scene," because she wanted to cry on screen, too, which is very strange. It's what we call in French *cabotinage. Cabot* means "small dog" and we use that word to describe an actor who is acting like an actor, to be more like an "actor." He's showing everyone that he's an actor. So, it's better just to make the film in long sequences and then show it later on. That's been my experience with amateurs. I don't know about professional actors.

When the film is finished, the first spectator of my film is myself through the viewfinder. The second is the editor, who is always someone who was never on the spot when I was shooting. When I did make films with an editor who was on the set during the shoot, the film was badly edited. The editor has to see what is on the screen, but not what is off-screen, only what I am showing. If not, he can remember the climate and everything else, and the film is not that. On the screen you can see only what's on the screen, nothing more. Then the editor discovers another truth, which is the truth of the film that is only on the screen.

But, of course, I am working with her or him and there is a lot of discussion. But I'll give you an example from a film that I did some thirty years ago, about hippopotamus hunting on the river. We followed hippopotamus hunters for months and months, and sometimes the group of hunters were on the right side of the river and sometimes on the left side. For me, it was very important whether they were on the left or right side because it means something in Africa. This notion is very important. But, in fact, on the screen you cannot tell what is the left or right side because there was no current in the river, the sun was absolutely vertical, and it was impossible to know which was west, east, and so on. You see only the subject and that they are on the bank of the river. And I remember I was absolutely angry at my editor, who said, "I can put these two shots one after another." And I said, "No! They have to cross the river between the two shots because one was on the right bank and the other was on the left bank." She said, "Well, Jean, I regret I don't see any difference between the two." And, in fact, there was no difference on the screen. There was no reason to preserve it. It was not important at this time with the subject. They were hunting hippopotamus and they didn't care if it was on the right or the left bank. It was not the crossing of the Rhine

River during the war, where you have the German army on one side and the Allied army on the other. That's quite different. But, you see, that's the truth. The real truth of the film was on the screen.

Another thing that is very important for me and which, fortunately, happens to me often when I'm making a film with people, is to allow them to shoot the film themselves. I've trained maybe five African filmmakers—not many, but now they're making films. They are using the same process. You do not have to be trained to read or write to see a film or to write with a film, that is, to shoot a film. We did that in Mozambique; we trained some people in Super 8, and they are making films, expressing themselves. That's important. It means to me that filmmaking is no longer a job, it's an activity. I don't know what it means to be a professional filmmaker. Maybe you have only one film in you to make, but you can write with the camera. You can make two or three films, then do something else, and maybe do another film twenty years later. But that's not Hollywood, that's not being a member of MGM. That is a new cinema which is just coming.

AL MAYSLES

In each of our films, if I showed you the first day's rushes, you could see important moments found in the final films. Even the very first instance of filming is as valid as the last day's shooting, and sometimes better. Think of your own relationships with people: sometimes you know each other best the first day. The first day's the best. You can't beat it. But it's also characteristic of what I would call the photographic process. In so many films I don't see the photography at all, because that aspect of it, of not knowing what's coming up next, cannot be characteristic of a Hollywood film that's been worked on, labored on, sometimes for years before the shooting day. And the director of photography who is the lighting man isn't even looking through the camera to see the unexpected, which isn't going to happen anyway because he's trying to get the lighting set up.

When we first started out, we were given all kinds of admonitions that we'd never get anywhere because we didn't have a point of view, that we could never film things like a killing, or we could never get the intimacy that you can in a fiction film. We were told that, sure, you might film somebody famous because they know, they're sophisticated enough to react properly in the presence of a camera, but somebody who's never seen a camera before would be thrown off by it. Then we were also told the opposite, but we filmed sophisticates and nonsophisticates alike. I'm not prepared to think that there's anything that can't be filmed in this fashion. Maybe you can't film a dream, but then, in one way or another you do. I had an incredible dream about my father two nights ago, and as I related it to my wife, it was as if on film, so that even dreams can be filmed that way.

I think you can gain access to any person. It's a two-way thing. Whether it's Brando or somebody who's never seen a movie camera, it doesn't make much difference as long as you've the capability to make a connection with them. And part of that capability rests on your confidence that they have certain needs to gain access to the screen in order to communicate with other people by being filmed.

But then there is this other thing that tends to contradict that trust, where people feel that if you're going to make a movie there's money behind it somewhere and there's some dark, cynical force behind it all, so that you can't trust anybody with a movie camera. And I can't begin to tell you all the various forms of which that's a part of our culture. Somebody said to me, "Why are you so surprised about this? You know that the philosophy of the West is cynicism. That's our philosophy. That's what we believe in."

We've been so jaded by film and other influences in our lives that when we see someone getting attention we think of it as spurious, but it can be the kind of attention that is spoken of in *Death of a Salesman*, where the wife says, "Attention must be paid." That's the sort of attention we're trying to do. We're trying to pay attention to people for that kind of compulsion, for that kind of reason. That's why the Beales did *Grey Gardens*. They received the kind of attention where you're interested in them for what they intrinsically have, what they are. I don't view communication with people we film as anything more than the way anyone would approach a stranger in an attempt to get to know him. The camera and tape recorder are not intruders or impediments. I see them as devices to get you that much closer.

EMILE DE ANTONIO

First of all, I have to be moved by something, and I don't mean divine inspiration. Usually it's anger and it has to settle in. For instance, in the case of *Year of the Pig*, it was an accident in a way. I was thinking and had been thinking about Vietnam for a long time, and two people who knew nothing about film, two academics, came to me about making a film about Vietnam. I said, "You're right. Why don't you guys produce it, raise the money, and I'll make the film." So they diddled with it for a few months and they raised nothing. So, I'm very good at raising money; I've raised over one million dollars to make left-wing films, and I said, "Okay, you drop it. I'll give you associate producer credits and one percent of the picture or something, and I'll raise the money," which I did. And that's the beginning of the process, obviously.

But the beginning of the process while all that's going on, if you're making a film like *Milhouse* or *In the Year of the Pig* or even a film about McCarthy, you have to know everything. That's the difference between a network project and mine. Even just looking at faces. I knew whose faces they were, so they were identifiable on film. You have to know your subject, you have to do your homework, to be able to do your research. I do a lot of that stuff myself. Frankly, the problem with most documentary films is that the people who make them don't have the intellectual substance to make them. None of the people who worked for me were prepared to deal with a subject like the history of Vietnam, or the history of painters, or Nixon. They simply hadn't done their homework, but they learned it on the job.

In the case of *Milhouse,* as the 1968 presidential election approached, I got more and more pissed at what was happening. I wasn't a supporter of HHH, but I thought it would be an interesting corrective if everyone asked, "Is this the real Nixon?" Nixon changed, so I thought it would be interesting to see the "real" Nixon, as he was in the 1952 Checkers Speech with the frozen face, the Frankenstein gestures, the wife literally white and frozen who never moved except on cue, like the Bride of Frankenstein and Frankenstein.

I did my best to get ahold of that thing because I thought it would be interesting for my distributor, Dan Talbot, who then owned a theater. So I called NBC, where they knew me, and asked to borrow a print. They said, "Sure, d', we'll have it delivered by messenger tomorrow." Tomorrow came and a guy with an abashed voice called and said, "Listen, we can't give it to you. The guy who has the copyright has to give it to you." I said, "Who's that?" He said, "The Republican National Committee." So I called them and spoke to a drunken-voiced PR man who said, "Naw, we don't have it. Mr. Nixon has the copyright." So I called and was immediately wired into a smart woman lawyer whose job it was, I think, to take care of the hard parts of Nixon's past. "Certainly, Mr. de Antonio, I loved your film *Point of Order.* I'll call you in two weeks." Two weeks passed, so I called—no answer. I called John Oakes, then editorial director of *The New York Times,* and said, "Don't you think this thing should be published? It's kind of outrageous. This thing belongs to the American people." He said, "Not interested." I just couldn't get anywhere with anyone. So I called the *East Village Other* and they did a lovely piece: a page and a half with a picture of Checkers, the dog, and Pat and their kids, and they ran my introduction, which I've just told you, and used chunks of the Checkers Speech. That was in '68.

Two years later, I was working on *Painters Painting* and I was in the MovieLab Building, where I had some cutting rooms, and the phone rang, and a guy said, "We've got all the Nixon material—the whole morgue, including 'Checkers.' Do you want it? You've got ten minutes, cause this is very hot stuff." So, I said, "Okay, give me ten minutes, call me back." So, we'd finished shooting *Painters Painting*, and Mary Lampson, I, and Cinda Firestone were cutting it. There were five or six people around and I thought, "Jesus, this is going to very hairy," but I really hated what Nixon stood for, so I said, "Okay". And they called and I said, "I never want to see you. I'll leave word with the superintendent at Movielab and you deliver it at midnight." They did deliver it and it was more film than I've ever seen at one time. It was literally six-by-ten-by-ten feet of 16mm cans. I went through it all. There was a lot of stuff I could never use, like the Native American takeover of Alcatraz, and I put all that aside and gave it to the Cubans. I told Mary what the danger was, but she agreed to work on it with me, so that's how *Milhouse* and *Checkers* began. And then I took *Checkers* separately while I was working on *Milhouse* and sold it to Dan Talbot as my property and tried to copyright it and sent a print down with all those copyright forms. The copyright people sent it back—REFUSED, which I find amusing. Dan, to this day, still sells the thing. He sells it for six hundred dollars a print. It's thirty minutes long and, of course, the networks are also selling it, because as soon as we put it on the market, everyone realized that no one owned the damned thing.

When I work on a film I have a big space; I used to know a guy from Great Neck who owned a box factory and he gave me corrugated paper, which I would unroll and put on a wall and then start writing. I would relate ideas I wanted with a chronological view of what happened with how I thought it should go filmically, and with the Steenbeck over here and a couple of editors, we'd start playing with stuff and shaping it.

When you're looking for footage, you not only look for what's appropriate, you look for a single metaphor that can stand for the whole experience. For instance, there's a sequence in *In the Year of the Pig* where Frenchmen are being carried in rickshaws. Yuck! That's the whole thing. Now that's Paramount stock footage, nobody even took that out;

thousands of people saw it, but I saw it as standing for five thousand pages of writing about the history of the colonial experience. It's all there. Then, when I found the Foreign Legion footage, I taped music, the *Light Cavalry Overture,* and I mixed it all up electronically, so that it has a different mock-heroic feeling rather than the other feeling it had. So you create a whole thing. In *Milhouse,* I very clearly wanted to begin with my usual self-indulgent signature, a collage signature, Nixon being made at Madame Toussaud's, the wax dummy, because everyone always asks if this is the real Nixon. That *was* the real Nixon, but then I wanted to begin at the bottom, in 1962, when his career was washed up and he was done, and then to go back, using not a clear narrative line, but a broken line, the way life is lived: the end, from nowhere, to go on to become the president. And that's really what the film is: going all the way back to the early political days of his youth, his childhood, everything. It's the Horatio Alger myth gone sour.

So all that's going on throughout the film: pasting up transcript, sticking in the image, sometimes even a piece of film or a drawing of a description, and then moving it all around. You get tremendous ideas that way. I would come in at six A.M. and start working with that stuff alone, running it through the Moviola, originally, then the Steenbeck. Then the editors would take over. I don't actually cut the film; I've never learned that. I have no interest in doing that and it's not snobbery of any kind. Most of the people I hire are very young; one woman had never worked on a long film before. She's just finished *Hair* as supervising editor. I always hired young, inexperienced people because as long as they could splice, I had the ideas and that was all that mattered, and they really learned more that way because there was a continuous give-and-take between them and me. I'm not an autocrat about listening to people. I had horrendous arguments with Mary Lampson, with Lynzee Klingman, with all kinds of people who worked with me. I didn't even win them all either, because film is a social art and there has to be a lot of give-and-take. But the give-and-take takes place, in my films, under the general umbrella of who I am, the subjects I've chosen, and the direction of those subjects.

One of the hardest things for me is when I think a film is over, it's finished. Then I run it a lot. Editors go crazy. They don't know how I can do it. I run the whole thing through and look at it again and again and make changes in it. It's a curious judgment because during the shoot, as well, at the time when you know you have a lot, is when you have much more than you need to begin with. And it's not just a question of covering yourself, because you see in your head, you have a sensibility of what's going on. With *Point of Order* my idea was to make a twelve-hour version and I longed to do that because I like long things and I like the idea of being hard on an audience because audiences are treated softly. But it was at about twelve hours that I knew I had enough and the other one hundred and seventy-six hours could be chucked.

But there are no rules of thumb. It's how it plays. I'm more or less content with my films as they stand. I think in *Pig* there are seven minutes on negotiations—it's not that the negotiations became trivial and unimportant; it's because I was struggling to make a point that I did not make successfully. I could cut it out now so that all future prints would be without it, but I would hate myself for that because I made the film that way and that's the way it is. It doesn't get changed. You don't rewrite your own work.

But there's a lot in the process that's sheer luck and inspiration. I had no end for *Pig*. I'm very hard on people when things aren't going well. My way of working is not regular hours. If things are going badly, I'll say, "Why don't you go to the movies and I'll sit here and think about it." But I had an editor working on that and a young millionaire Marxist guy. I kept him up all night and we were into the next day and there was still no ending. I had an ending I hated: some North Vietnamese footage of a bridge running north with fields along the side and the camera moves slowly along the road and suddenly the fields move and it's people with guns. It's cornball, but I couldn't think of anything. And, then, a whole bunch of things

fell into my mind about ten or eleven in the morning, having
been working the day before and up all night, and that is the
current ending. I finally said, "That's not the point. The point
is that Americans are dying there." It's not that I feel that senti-
mental about Americans dying, but the Vietnamese are going
to win. That's the point I really wanted to make and so we
started trying it out. It takes a whole day just to fiddle around
with that stuff. But it all came to me. I could see it all in that
place. But it still took a day to pull the footage, to try the sound
and everything else. When we were done, the woman who was
working on it, who was a terrific person, was hysterical and
crying from exhaustion. But it's a pretty good ending I think.

R. W. FASSBINDER

I've made some films following a perfectly thought-out
screenplay where I didn't make any important changes. And,
then, I've also made films that, in a way, I worked out with the
actors and for the actors. There are no principles involved in
this; it has also happened that I have a completely written
screenplay that I change totally while I am shooting. Even that
happens.

It's important to have the possibility to work with a big
crew—you need that experience, and it's as important as knowing how to work with a small crew. But I don't think one
should specialize in one way or the other of making films. It
might happen that you make a film with lots of money and
then there might be no money at all. And then you sit there,
screwed. There is a difference in motivating fifty-five or five
people. Of course, it's easier to motivate five people. But the
difference between working with large and small crews is interesting and it is also interesting to learn how to do it. The more
people you have, the more reasons exist for making a film. For
some, it just means to make some money; others are interested
in the film. But you also have to make the people who just want
to make money become interested in the film, otherwise it de-

stroys the atmosphere. Then you have to work against the crew, which is not good.

On the matter of the shoot, I am not for natural lighting at all. Every shot has different lighting. I don't care if there are special reasons for certain lights. Each shot is done separately, and I use the light that the shot requires. I don't care if the shot is realistic or not. All I care about is the shot at that moment.

Mostly the editing is done while I am shooting. The task of editing is to cut what you can't cut exactly with the camera. In the old days you could only shoot, stop, and shoot again. Then the film was finished. It was not possible to cut. But nowadays we can do it. The important thing when you edit is that you find exactly the moment when you *have* to cut. But, generally, the editing is done with the camera. I only shoot the possibilities that are given. If I have a ninety-minute film, then I shoot the ninety minutes. Other directors can make two or three films out of what they have been shooting. I don't do that. I want to find the right moment. It is not simple. Mostly it requires hard work. Sometimes it is easier to choose the right thing or the right moments if you have a lot of material than if you have only a little.

If the editor and I work together the credits will say so. Editors have a name and it appears in the credits, and if the editor has worked alone it says so, as well. But even if he works alone he discusses it with me. When I made my first film my name appeared too often in the credits, so that's why I used different names after that.

I have always said that if you are making films, let us say like a worker, you work all year except for the five to six weeks' vacation. Then you make more than one film a year, you make two or three. I often wonder what other filmmakers are doing between films.

MICHAEL POWELL

Of course, writing and directing a film would be ideal, but it's too big a responsibility, in my opinion. I don't like to do it, but I've had to do it occasionally. Either I couldn't afford a writer or I couldn't convince a writer of what I wanted. But the responsibility is really too big for somebody, particularly in Europe, where you don't have such a strong team or a producer to lean on; you have to make your own decisions.

But it's a very rare writer that really can almost hear a film. Very few writers have big cinematic ideas. A director's mind is not like a writer. A writer's mind is preoccupied immensely with human beings and human emotions. And if he's any good as a dramatist too, he'll know exactly where you need a twist in the plot or to spring a surprise. And I don't think directors are so good at that. It's not their job so much as writing. Their job is more as interpreters, and, of course, to find ingenious ways of doing what the writer has thought out. But the writer supports the director with the constant preoccupation with the human development of the characters and also the twists and turns of the plot.

A film is improvisation. There's no good in one telling you, "Oh, it's all worked out and designers have done this." It is still improvised. Every morning you come to the studio, not really knowing what's going to happen with the first shot. You've planned it out and you've even discussed it with the actors and still you don't know. And when you see it, when you see what you want, you've got to grab it quick and get on to the next shot, not hang around thinking how clever you are. So, that's a big responsibility. And directors who want to do everything are not crazy, they're just wrong, in my opinion. What could be more delightful than to work with a writer whom you can trust, as I did with Emeric Pressburger. But nobody collaborates with the director on taking the sole responsibility for every shot that's he's actually got on the screen in that part of the story.

When I prepare a film, we're all there for about four weeks before we shoot. We're there every day with all sorts of questions and things that have to be prepared and solutions for doing new things. Usually we don't have any rehearsals. We might have sort of brief discussions and in the intervals we talk about coming sequences and scenes. But when it comes to the actual moment when you've got to do it, you say, "Good morning and how about this, photographing it this way?" And we walk through it that way with the script girl. And the actor would say, "That seems all right with me"—this is all before he goes to Makeup—or else he'd say, "Well, how about this? Maybe I could do that?" And it's up to me to react, to maybe suggest something different, or decide if it's better or worse, or scrap the whole thing and try something else. But usually when we've got it right, he would then go off and get made up and dressed and we would line up the scene with stand-ins.

You don't want it to be too strenuous. When you're really getting into the shooting of a big scene there's quite enough suspense, I can assure you. For example, that last scene in *Peeping Tom* ran about seven minutes non-stop, with sound effects and lights popping off and everything set with check wires. We all knew what we wanted. We had discussed it with the art director first, of course, and naturally they needed to know that I was going to shoot it all in one big take. And then they had everything ready. It worked very well as a scene. We had one master camera and another camera picking up various things. We shot some close-ups of the exploding bulbs and things afterwards.

I'm not jealous about the camera at all. A film can be vastly improved in the editing, mainly on questions of tempo and speed, because where you might need speed in the action and there weren't enough shots, a good editor will come to me and say, "You undershot the scene at the break into the shop. Do you mind if I take the camera and shoot a half a dozen close shots?" And I say, "Fine, go ahead." It was undershot and he would know better than anybody what was wanted.

JEAN-MARIE STRAUB

What doesn't change in a film is a certain abstraction that exists before you have found the people and the places. The abstraction must be something "iron," as Fritz Lang said. Once the abstraction is planned, you can and must improvise to the limit. You can have a peasant come unexpectedly into your shot with two beasts pulling a cart into the frame, while others are saying the dialogue, only on the condition that the situation and the framing of the planned idea—the abstraction—is strong enough. You can, you must, film by chance. If a leaf falls through your very precise frame, you must keep it in. But the thing that happens by chance must be in contradiction to something that is the opposite of chance. If, from the start, it is all chance upon chance, it's of no interest. What's interesting is the contradiction of chance by something that precedes it and which in the sound and image is opposed to chance. A film is a life of contradictions. The more abstract and predetermined at the start, the more interesting it is when chance enters. Chance is only interesting when it comes in opposition to the iron-clad, firm idea you had at the start. That's what makes it more interesting to shoot outside. One has supplementary contradictions and surprises in the light and in the air that moves.

You can recover your original idea in the editing and only in the editing, but only if you had an idea in the first place. If not, you discover nothing in the editing.

I think that to make a film is besides everything else an act of love. Brecht defined love as the possibility to work with the capacities and abilities of others. If you make a film where you need a soundman, a cameraman, and an actor, you must naturally give each person the greatest possibility to realize his fullest capacities. It has nothing to do with manipulation, nor does it mean you let them do whatever they want. You must ask them what they need to do the job: if the actor needs half a day to get a good take or if the soundman needs two hours to find the best position for the mike—and often it's difficult if there's a lot of wind. It's not only the cameraman who always gets his two hours to light and the others have no time to work. No, you must give each one the possibility, even your friends who are working as production assistants, stopping traffic so there will be less noise on the track. You must give them time to arrive at the spot where they are going and you must have the patience to wait.

MILOS FORMAN

I feel it's a great asset for the director to be involved at some point in the development of the screenplay, because finally, things have to be done by him. The director is the one on the set who is going to tell everybody, starting with the set designer, what to build, how to arrange the space in front of the camera, through to the costume designer, choreographer, if you're doing a musical, and then to tell the actors what to do and how to say things. And everybody who is writing is somehow visualizing what he's writing. This is absolutely normal. It's an essential part of writing and of reading. When you read, you also visualize what you are reading. Now, everybody visualizes differently and very often writers write things because they echo their own visualizations, their own images, and they're dependent on their own image—for example, the dialogue or the way the scene is developing physically. If you as a director didn't have the same echo, didn't visualize the same things, then you can make a very bad mistake, because you are interpreting something in a way that will not connect with the rest. So, I think it's a great asset if a director can join the writer, at least for the final script, and go through it from the very beginning, word-for-word, so that he is sure and I am sure that I am visualizing it in a way that will work for me, for the screen, and, hopefully, for the audience.

This is, of course, all individual. I started to be a writer and I made my living for a few years as a writer. But I never liked to work by myself for one simple reason: I just can't find inside myself enough provocation. I can't mobilize enough energy myself for myself. I need a partner to fight with, to argue with, until the juices are provoked to a boiling temperature. One of the rules is that the moment you can't go any further in the idea you're developing, even if it's a small idea for one scene or for a dialogue, the moment you feel "This is it, I can't go any further," in that moment you have to start to doubt it, to doubt everything you did. And only when it survives the doubts do I feel comfortable to go ahead, to continue. And it helps me if somebody else is playing this kind of Ping-Pong of doubts and approvals.

When I am filming I look at the rushes every day, of course. Sometimes, especially when we are studying new decor, new sets, we even look the next morning—since the lab develops them overnight—just to see if it looks right, before we continue in the new set. But you don't really let yourself be influenced too much when it comes to overall structure, or overall vision of the film, because you have to follow your instincts from the beginning as you set your style while working on the script and preparing the film. To judge from bits and pieces can be very dangerous. I remember that some films everybody was absolutely ecstatic about from the rushes had very disappointing final results. And I remember films that were made with a lot of doubt and skepticism based on seeing the rushes, and the final results turned out wonderfully.

I really don't know why this is. I remember, for example, making films in Czechoslovakia when I was much more interested in photographing human behavior than I was in story or spectacular scenes. I had to encourage myself on the set because we were shooting and the people were doing what I wanted them to do, but it looked as if *nothing* was happening in front of the camera. It looked so dull and boring that I had to pump my own self-confidence up. It looked like, "Jesus Christ, I should be doing something. Look. The electricians are beginning to fall asleep, the script girl is sitting there like a zombie, looking at it with sad eyes. Maybe I should ask them to do somersaults or something." But then, you really have to hold desperately to your own self-confidence: "I am sure this is the way this should be done and treated. Let's just stick to it." And thank God I did, because in the editing, suddenly things came out differently. It's not that the action is so small or that there's a big screen, it's due to the nature of photography.

During the shooting, I assemble little pieces, not really rough editing, but I like to begin to put it together about three, four, five days after I start shooting, to spend one day in the editing room just to be sure it will splice together the way I thought it should. Then I don't cut anymore unless I feel that I might have made a bad mistake and I might be in trouble, so I'll go back and try to edit the sequences. I am there all the time in the editing room, but, of course, it's not me who dictates or the supervising editor or the other two editors. It's a cooperative thing.

MARK RAPPAPORT

Every time you create something, it's sort of a compilation, a synthesis of everything you've done and thought and known, so, in that sense, I don't think that anything is unconscious. For example, it's surprising to discover that Bresson actually improvises. He goes out and shoots: he gets on location and he improvises. But I can't imagine what his idea of improvising is. I assume that he means he doesn't have a storyboard and he'll use the locations for whatever is there, but one doesn't think of those films as improvisational since the whole film is so clearly structured in his head. Well, if you come to a fresh location and the film is in your head anyway, you're sort of improvising from "here" to "there." It's not like exploring a totally new continent. So, in that sense, it might as well not be improvised. In terms of what the viewer sees, it's very tight and controlled. I think there's an example in Hitchcock, who always made very storyboarded, accurate, planned shots in his films. There's one scene in *The Birds,* the first attack on the house, and for a reason that I don't remember, he couldn't shoot it the way he wanted to, so he improvised. It's a great scene, it's as good as anything that he's ever done, but when you've been living with a project for a year and a half, can that really be called improvising because you hadn't planned to put your camera "there"?

MARTIN SCORSESE

I might come up with an idea and get someone else to work it out for me in structure and then go back and work on it with somebody closely associated with the film, with an actor or a writer.

As far as casting is concerned, the actors read what's there in the script and very often they shouldn't feel obliged to read *exactly* what's there. If they read and they're good but don't jump off into an improvisation, I may ask them to open up a little more to see if they're good at that. Not necessarily that I'm going to use the improvisation, but it's really just a matter of seeing if they could relate to the other person and maybe believe what they're saying. You've got to believe what they're saying, that's all. Or how they move; I've got to believe how they move. Very often an actor will be saying something to me in character and I believe that they're telling me something for real. That's good.

During the shooting of *Raging Bull* everything was in control, very tight control, but as far as the equipment is concerned, it was difficult to do what I wanted to do with the equipment that's being used. I might as well have used the old Mitchell instead of using the Panaflex or Arriflex or whatever we use today. Not that the Arriflex or Panaflex are bad cameras and the Mitchell is a bad camera—they are all marvelous cameras. But the point is that everything seemed harder. When we got to New York and shot some of the dramatic scenes, everything seemed to move a little quicker except for the problem of being in one little room with two big cameras. But in Hollywood everything seemed a little harder: for example, getting a crane in to make certain shots. As you get older, you get bigger equipment and different things and then they bring out the old dinosaurs and in a way, you're getting more tired too. So you can hardly fight it and you say, "Okay, I'll wait the hour. I'll wait the forty-five minutes. I'll wait. The shot's important. It's got to be done right."

I drew every shot for the fight scenes in *Raging Bull;* I drew only a few of the dramatic scenes. I drew the fight scenes when they choreographed the punching, and I tried to work it out on paper, but, of course, those pictures changed a great deal during the shooting of the picture. You wouldn't recognize it sometimes. So, there's improvisation, but with total control because you do have those drawings and you know the effects you want. Even *The Last Waltz* was all storyboarded, except for the concert footage, and that was all planned—two hundred pages of it planned. The lighting effects were all written down as were the camera moves, though, of course, the camera was improvising on the concert sequences. The things we did on the soundstage took a week and a half. They were all shot from drawn pictures. I work those out by myself and then with the director of photography later, either the day before, or the week before if there's a special kind of shot I want, or even a month before. But in my older days, when I used to do films more quickly, I used to draw every shot. Now, of course, it's a little simpler in the sense that you realize that the camera doesn't have to move all the time. You don't have to show off all the time. So, in a way, it's merely a matter of finding the right angle. Sometimes a static shot can go on for twelve minutes. If it's the right angle, it works for you. So, if you walk into a place the week before or the night before or even the moment before, even if you just have a minute to take a look around and work with the actors, you can decide where they and the camera are going to be. I work it out so that they do have some room to breathe, so they should not stick rigidly to marks, but they should know when they're going to be out of frame. So, if they do something interesting, I can open it up for them. I do it that way, but you have to be very careful about using two cameras, because if you're using the second camera to pick up improvisation, the second camera won't be that controlled. But if you have two cameras—one for the master shot, and one to pick up one or two close-ups at the same time—they *both* should be controlled, not just panning and dodging and winging it—no. Some people think we do that, even close friends of mine think we do. I remember one guy saying to me, "You know, I used to be like you—put the camera in front of the actors and let them improvise."

There's no such thing, no way, never. So maybe there's an extra camera that's controlled up to a certain point, because when you put that second or third camera there, you are always, always compromising lighting and composition. Always. So you have to make a value judgment in terms of what you want. I want performance, particularly in *Raging Bull*, where I worked with a lot of non-actors. You have to have control, otherwise forget about it, it's absurd. So I pretty much know what I have after I've shot it, unless it's got a lot of special effects, like a violent scene such as the one where Bobby De Niro is beaten up and bloody. That took eight days to shoot and it lasts less than a minute on film, but we had to keep doing it over and over again to get it right. In the fight scenes, I focus on the face: there aren't very many audience reaction shots where they're saying, "Go get him!" None of that stuff. Before that there are some reaction shots to characters, but during the fight, the camera sticks to the fighters. I drew forty-five drawings for those scenes and there were actually more setups than that when we shot it.

In general, when you have less money, etcetera, you have to plan, draw all the setups. Now I don't have to draw all the scenes but definitely ones like the fight scenes in *Raging Bull*. Violence has to be drawn. Certain dance scenes, musical scenes, and some dramatic scenes also have to be drawn, but even if they aren't, the angle has to be certain, as do any specific moves.

I have ideas about lighting, but I don't know technically how to get them. I trust my director of photography and our relationships have always been very good. Laszlo Kovacs was good with me. Michael Chapman worked on a number of films with me and he knows what I want. I tell him what it looks like to me, I might have an idea about something that was in another film, and he knows a lot of movies and knows what I'm referring to. Or I'll draw a picture with a kind of shade effect: "Can we get that? What about the shot that preceded it? Are we going to have to change the lighting in that?" On exteriors it's different; if it happens to rain, if it doesn't affect the scene before, or the one after, sure, why not? Let it rain.

I usually work with one editor. In *Taxi Driver* and *New York, New York* I worked with about four or five editors, but Marcia Lucas was in charge. We had to finish by a certain time, so we needed more people. *Alice Doesn't Live Here Anymore* was edited by Marcia Lucas. On *Raging Bull* Thelma Schoonmacher is the editor. She was the editor of my first picture, *Who's That Knocking on My Door?* I do what I want but listen to the people. What's the sense of having those people there if I don't listen to them, don't trust them?

The thing is I'm not a "director." I don't know what the hell I am. I don't know what you want to call it—filmmaker? I don't know. That's all dead. It's all gone. Hitchcock died today [April 29, 1980]. Mario Bava died yesterday in Rome. They were both eighty years old, and they were flip sides of the same coin: Mario Bava made horror films, more or less, but he was a genius at what he did, the style and his movement and his color— it was like comic books—it was amazing, basically film comic books. In a sense, Hitchcock did too, but higher, different. He was a master. Mario did low-budget stuff. He started out as a cinematographer. I got to meet him a few months ago. I would've loved to work with him. So, Hitchcock is dead, Ford is dead, John Wayne is dead. It's all over. We don't make pictures like these guys did. As they say, "They don't make pictures like they used to." I say the same thing. I don't go to the movies. I watch Home Box Office, I watch other things. They don't make them like they used to, and *I'm* making them. So, there's no fucking rules. You can do whatever the hell you want. As long as you get what you want, as long as you really believe in what you're doing, and you can get up in the morning and you can go there. And you know what you're doing and you like the people you're working with. You don't have to love them, just like them. And if you've put your name on the picture, you've put your head on the line, and that's it. That's all there is to it. I don't know about going forty, fifty million dollars in budget for a three-hour film—I don't know anything about that. A twelve-hour film, maybe. It may happen. You can't help the cost. But I'm not interested; I'll go see them, but my work is a different thing. So if I work with an actor on a script, I work with an actor. If I want to work with what they call a producer—that can be anything, too—I'll work with the producer on a script. Basically, it's got to be an idea from me or from a writer that I like. There's no way I would just pick up someone's script and do it. I may have to, God forbid, in the future, just to keep alive. *Raging Bull* comes out in November—who knows what's going to happen. I may be wrong, but eventually, why not make pictures like writing books, like writing short stories? Cable TV can help us with that, tape can help us with that. Filmmakers can be a little freer. Now, people are afraid to make a move—it's going to cost you your entire career or it's going to cost you a million dollars: "Which do you want?" "Okay, a million dollars." So, you're safe for a while in your career. It's crazy, it's a way of killing off the filmmaker, of killing off the talent.

·8·

THE VIEWER

The role of the viewer in the experience of a film is becoming more of a concern to both filmmakers and film theorists. At one extreme, the viewer is seen as passive, a subject in the filmmaker's experiment. His responses to a film are carefully predicted and painstakingly measured. At the other end of the spectrum are filmmakers who consider the viewer to be the real maker of the film, the final collaborator responsible for giving the film its final form. The movie house is the place where the film's life begins, where the viewer's and filmmaker's dreams meet, merge, and then glance off each other, like bubbles from a child's toy, from where each viewer leaves having shared an experience while spinning his own fantasy. The film, then, has at least as many separate identities as it has viewers sitting in the quiet dark.

To what extent should the filmmaker consider the "collaborator-viewer?" How much information does that viewer need? Does he pay to be hypnotized, as people commonly did before the advent of motion pictures; does he want to be entertained or seduced or fascinated or challenged, or even tested? Does he willingly offer himself up for a few hours to whatever experience the film promises, no matter how disturbing, or does he go to the movie house asking only to be narcotized by the rites of the Western, the horror movie, the love story, soothed somewhere in his consciousness that this dream will end satisfactorily when the movie is over?

It is clear that the central issues are whether or not the film is a roller coaster ride of the filmmaker's design; whether the entire art form is manipulative by definition; and whether or not there is a point where that manipulation of the viewer is no longer an artful technique but an unjustified offense, an intrusion into his active participation in creating the film.

ERMANNO OLMI

Everything is manipulated in this sense, everything: the economy, not only the cinema, religion, anything, any of man's activities can be corrupting or saving. It really depends on the moral basis on which you do these things, both in producing the things and in consuming them. Even the car can be corrupting or saving. If we use it to pass others, to give us an idea of power through the engine's horsepower instead of through the horsepower of our participation, creativity, etcetera, it can be negative. For example, even neorealism degenerated at a certain moment because it became a fad, a slickness, a fashion, and it was enough that you had a certain type, shot a certain way, like the New Wave where if you didn't make the shot jiggle in shooting the subject, it didn't seem real. But it isn't making the image jiggle that is real; it's real if *you* are real in front of what you are shooting, if the things you're shooting have this authenticity. If not, you may as well work in the theater, which has its own reason and aesthetic.

So unmasking the illusion is fine, in everything one does, in everything one reproposes. Clearly, resemblance to reality is not reality. It's obvious. However, sometimes, even in Brecht's theater, this attempt to "disenchant" the spectator, to remind him or her it is theater, sometimes this in itself reinforces the magic component of theater. When the grandmother tells her grandson a fairy tale, the story of Little Red Riding Hood with all these great emotions for the child—the woods, Little Red Riding Hood, the grandmother, the wolf—the grandmother's face continually reminds the grandson that between the reality of the fairy tale and himself there is his grandmother's face. But sometimes the grandmother increases the fairy tale's power of suggestion. So this attempt to mediate between the magic of theatricality and reality, to disenchant, is reinforcing, instead of the opposite. However, in my opinion, neither takes away from nor adds very much to the need man has to live both the problems of fear at a child's level and the problems of existence, at an adult level, through the fairy tale. This is because we all share the problematic situation of not risking ourselves, of not being in direct contact with the event, but in the comforting arms of Grandmother or in the armchair at the cinema, or in our living rooms in front of the television set, which protects us, guarantees us. We protect ourselves to the point that sometimes the same authentic reality—news film on television, for example—in the safety of our homes is transformed into a fairy tale, by which we see real happenings removed far from our consciences, from our responsibility. We see them again in a fairy tale atmosphere, so that they won't touch us, not only physically, but also not touch our painful sense of participation and responsibility. Certainly the thing "enchants" us, but we want to see the thing within this enchantment. In fact, it's even better to enjoy the fact that yes, theater and cinema remind us of reality, but even more of the fairy tale. This is why we can watch people fighting and killing on television and, at the same time, stir our coffee.

These are things you can't establish with a classification. What does Brecht try to do? To disenchant us so that our critical faculty is always active. Thus he says, "Don't be taken in by this. Be careful, I'm acting, watch carefully so that you won't be taken in." I understand this critical distance. The spectator in the cinema or the theater feels this fear I was talking about earlier. He tells himself it's not real so he can feel defended and then he returns back into his fear. This critical distancing is like Grandmother's face; it's Grandmother who is telling me the story, but then I go back into the emotion. So this suggestion is important for the viewer. But what happens? He doesn't always, in fact he rarely, achieves the result that Brecht or others sought. Why? Because if the result is only emotional and not critical, it reinforces the emotion. If, on the other hand, you come with your own abilities to critically participate in the event, sometimes this helps you, sometimes it disturbs you. The spectator is already able to critically participate, to analyze. It's like life when people let themselves be swept away by the emotion of a crowded piazza and everybody shouts, *"Viva il Duce"* together, while other people, instead, within this emotion, have this critical distance and succeed in judging.

There are different levels of reading. One person takes in

only the exterior aspect of an event. If there are certain scenes, he feels moved if the characters kiss or if horses run. Within his own structure he is not yet able to enter into a critical relationship with events. Participation in an event is many-sided, and in a complex sense, critical. One participates in the emotion, but, at the same time, there occur a series of postponements one doesn't see only with the eyes. It's like a camera, behind which are the presuppositions of the reading. The same camera in the hands of ten different people shooting the same thing will certainly take ten different pictures.

DUŠAN MAKAVEJEV

It is the nature of really good movies that they create this bridge between the spectator and the screen and you have this glue—that's really good linking. Good cinema is recognizable by this. Sometimes you have good camerawork or good movement—you just know that it's good. But then there is this kind of glue between you and the film, and you don't know who is where, because you are "here" and this, the film, is "here." There is no difference between you and what is on the screen. This is very "hot." But movies are made to be kind of half-cold, so we are not accustomed to it. Movies are like a cold buffet; you're not supposed to get really excited. You're supposed to participate in movies with a superficial part of yourself. You're not supposed to be disturbed on a level that's going to question your own sense of your own life. You're allowed in classically commercial movies to be disturbed only to the point, "Is he going to be killed now?" This kind of banal level. But real movies do something quite deep.

What real movies do directly, primarily, is unique: they really relate to our dream world and our understanding of ourselves on a gut level. So movies relate to much deeper parts of ourselves than we're aware. That's why we're attracted to it, because there's this incredible quality of unknown ingredients. For some people movies can be a house of prostitution, for others a religious paradise, for others just their secret life, for some a flying machine. Films give private meanings to people. So, speaking psychologically, movies are good for voyeurs, but they're also good for people who have interesting taste because you can get oral gratification from watching movies. For a lot of people movies are very sexual; they're a place of erotic gratification. And for many people it's a sense of balance and a kinesthetic sense. So there are all kinds of sensual gratifications in movies plus secret life transformations of all kinds.

Actually, movies are always subversive operations. What happens between people and film? What happens between filmmakers and the film? A lot of "illegal" things happen—illegal things, psychologically speaking, things people would never confess. But what I do illegally, what I smuggle into my films, does not necessarily have to be what you smuggle out of the film for yourself. There are all kinds of shifting; sometimes it's direct, a film reaches people on the same level. For example, all these catastrophe films work with this post-1968 angst, before everything became ordered and reactionary. There was this great disturbance that happened and there were these earthquakes in the new position of the ethnic minorities. And people felt it—the new position of political forces—and there were all these films of burning houses, of earthquakes, sharks eating people. It was like a collective bad dream, nightmares people wanted to go through. Unfortunately, they wanted to go to a safe place where dreams are extinguished. But the whole period of these corny catastrophe films was very good, Jungian.

And coincidences between films and life happen all the time. Take, for example, the Jonestown Massacre. It's like the ending of Coppola's *Apocalypse Now*. He was always hesitating to finish the film for some reason, but he always had some sort of suicidal action planned for the end, of people being lost in the jungle. Now, suddenly, the Jonestown Massacre obviously makes his ending not unusual and strange. Suddenly, you have something you didn't produce in a movie. But that sort of thing is happening all the time.

For the audience, watching a movie is like before you go to sleep. There's still some light but already you're closing your eyes. So this theater is basically a twilight zone, twilight space, and recently they've learned that the fetus can see through the mother's belly before it's born; there's some sort of murky shadow perception. They know because the fetus responds with eye movement. So maybe movies are projected in the same kind of light situation we already lived through in, say, the first seven months of our aware life—growing up before being born. You have this total undefined light and in theaters there is not only undefined light but undefined space because one of the conditions of watching movies is to forget where you are. So you forget you're in a theater, and then one of the conditions of watching films becomes *not* seeing what is there. You're not supposed to see the screen. You're not supposed to see reality. So, practically, you're supposed to be kind of blind. Not seeing well, blindness, is a condition of enjoying movies, of "seeing" the story.

But people like to know where they are. People are unhappy if they don't know which genre they're following. So they can allow great gestures to opera people; they can allow funny movement to Charlie Chaplin. Each genre has its own pace. I just find it a great pleasure to make it more visible, this specificity, this untruthfulness of the situation, because this stylistic unity of each of the different genres serves the illusion. There's great pleasure not only in breaking the illusion, but in breaking the illusion you don't send it away, you just amplify it. That's something that Godard always knew and people still don't understand about him. He was never concerned about truth. He was concerned about cinema.

So, since movies are based on seeing what isn't allowed, since they are working basically with a taboo field, since the structure of movies is always a system of alibis to get on the screen some things that are not allowed to be shown, since this dirty little game is part of watching movies, why not be aware of it?

BERNARDO BERTOLUCCI

The question of audience involvement is interesting because this is the point of departure and the point where I am now. In 1968 I made a movie called *Partner,* and it was very successful. It was based on an idea very sixties, very Brechtian: the audience must keep their distance from the movie so they can judge without being involved in the emotion. I said it was the point of departure because it was a kind of misunderstanding of Brecht, because if you see a Brecht play, it is absolutely involving, like Shakespeare. You don't have any distance and you're completely involved. I think you have to find the way to give a certain amount of information about things, about humans, but you have to do it through emotions. There is no other way. At a certain moment at the end of *Partner,* the lead character looks into the camera, into the eyes of the audience, and says, "There is no rest. You know you are sitting in a theater, this is a movie, and remember American imperialism, blah, blah." It was strange because my nature is to make a very narrative kind of emotion, and now I hate to be forced to think and I love to be passionate, drawn into a thought but seduced through feelings.

But the sixties notion of filmmaking was very beautiful, I think. It was very important because it changed cinema. It was the first filmmaking of its kind, and so it was beautiful also just because it was the first. So it is when you hear a sound or a word for the first time. It's very moving. I think that in the moment it was valid, and I think today we are progressing.

WERNER SCHROETER

Film is more or less telling a story so people can learn by seeing that story. You know, you shouldn't be too masterly or professorlike. You should always leave the possibility of the public to find out for itself what is going on and what you want to tell. I am not a friend of Brecht, by the way. I hate Brechtian theater. I like not to have to learn but just to see and to listen to things. I am not one to tell you that you have to look *there*.

I don't like this "finger pointing" cinema. The spectator should have the chance to understand everything in his own way, which means that if you don't want to be only provocative on your aesthetic level, if you want to get the meaning through what you are saying, you have to use what is left of sense and sensitivity and openness from the spectator after fifty or sixty years of cinema. Which means you have to follow a certain system, otherwise you can't get it through, only with very sophisticated people who may understand everything. You have to make it clear, but you don't have to point out with your finger, "Look!" Only if you have a really strong political subject like *La Hora de los Hornos*, which is really a film of *agitacion*. I really liked it a lot because it is exactly as strong as it should be to get the people out of their seats to thrust down the houses of the rich. It's a very simple but important subject. But look what came out of all that. What is left of South America? It's a little political colony of the C.I.A. So, not even Solanas was strong enough with his movies to cause a direct impact anyway. It must have been extremely difficult for him to get through what he did with this movie.

To me it doesn't matter if someone is realizing intellectually, "Aha, here he is doing this and there he is using that effect." That doesn't matter to me. I think it should be simply the whole organization of ideas and images and sounds that has one single impact. It should all serve to get a new view or a new idea through all this. I think it's about an impulse of some people who know cinema and who know how it works. It doesn't matter to me. Most people don't realize it anyway. They look at the screen and listen to the sound and there is one impact and if you ask them two days later, "What did you see?" they tell you the exact story of the movie as if they had lived in the film with the people of the film, because to go to the cinema is like buying a cucumber in the supermarket. It's no different. It's part of our lives.

So Godard's late films and his ideology, for example, are very important as an intellectual pushing other filmmakers and intellectuals, but for the public there is no interest, because his public is so limited by now. He is important as a motor and an engine for other filmmakers, for intellectuals, and for people who are trying to find out if there's a better way of cinema, but the public wouldn't esteem it compared to the success he had with his early films. It's very limited, but, as a matter of fact, it is very important stuff he's doing.

I think the position of Godard is one of the most important ones. He never did stuff to make people different than they are. But he even thought what he was doing was too corrupt to be honest. This is really extremely important. He is like the Holy Ghost of Cinema.

PERRY HENZEL

At the opening of *The Harder They Come*, fifty thousand people surrounded the theater, and they beat the doors in. When there were four thousand people in a theater for one thousand five hundred, we ran the film. When the bus leaned over in the first sequence, they began to scream and they never stopped screaming for two hours. If they hadn't liked the film, they would have destroyed the theater. How passive is *that*?

Interaction, if any, goes on between the audience and the screen. I see it like a tennis or a Ping-Pong ball, a bouncing of radar back and forth. The audience is sitting there looking at the screen. When it sees something that reflects its mood, the mood is heightened in the audience. When that happens, it is as if you have given the audience something to which it responds, "Yes, that's true." That's the only moment that's worth a damn. Now, people say that can't happen in the cinema; they say it can only happen in the theater. But then they're talking from the point of view of the actor. They're not talking from the point of view of the director.

When I'm thinking about a film I constantly think about how the audience is going to react. I want to be able to know. You know that thing in California where they have people wired up and they read on a graph what the audience reacts to. It's not totally ridiculous, but the way I look at it is this: I should have that knowledge of the audience in my head when I'm shooting the film. I should know exactly the level of the pulse of the audience for any particular moment. I should be able, on any page in a script, to say, "What's that on a scale of ten?" I should be able to say, "Eight or six or five or four." That is your job as director. If you don't know that, you're not supposed to be a director in films.

I'll tell you where I learned it for a particular audience—by being a movie reviewer. I was a critic for five years for a paper in Kingston, Jamaica. So three times a week I sat in a movie house and I knew all the time how the audience was going to react. I knew where it would laugh, I knew that because I was there. My ear was practiced to it. I'd seen an incredible variety of films and I know the way the audience reacts. That's why you still have to go to movies and get the feel of the crowd in order to constantly be aware of the audience.

If I ran a studio in Hollywood, if I found anybody viewing a finished film on the lot, I'd fire their ass off the lot. So far as I'm concerned, no matter how great I was, if I was buying a film, I'd want to see it in an audience. I'd want to know the audience reaction. This business of people sitting in isolation, away from the audience and second-guessing each other as to what the audience is thinking is absolute bullshit. Do you know the number of people who are buying films from me and never taking the trouble to go to a theater with the audience? No, you send the film to their private screening room. Okay, that's the way they do business, but what I'm saying is that if anybody was working for me, they would have to go and sit in the audience and tell me what the audience is thinking, not what *they're* thinking. I don't want to know what they're thinking.

I have two rules, perhaps simplistic, but . . . One is, Nobody needs advice, and the other is, Everybody needs information. I don't want to know what people think. I want to know what they *know,* and I assume they feel the same way about me. I don't think anybody is going to watch a film because I'm going to tell them what I think. I think somebody will watch a film because I've gone out and found out something.

If you want to be manipulative, you might have to use certain techniques. But if you want to tell the truth, you might have to use those techniques, as well, to get to the point. Truth is a question of intent, not of technique. Obviously, the ultimate manipulation is with commercials. Commercials are exciting the audience with the talent of artists who are then selling products. But it's also the place where you can learn to put across an idea very quickly, so it can give you tremendous advantages in skill. So why not use those techniques to really tell the truth? I made four hundred commercials and one of the things I would love to do with the technique is make short films with the impact of commercials, just giving information about things that people should know. I'm reading a book at the moment called *Food First,* and apparently there is no food shortage in the world. It's a bureaucratic fuckup. I'd like to make a commercial every week saying, "Mr. So and So of the United Nations Food Department is a fuckup. He just damaged sixty thousand tons of grain." Convey information that people need to know.

EMILE DE ANTONIO

To me the great unknown theme of *Point of Order* is that McCarthy himself is the triumph of technique. He used his technical ability. He had no content, he didn't know a communist from his ass. But what he did understand was how to manipulate the media, and this was one of the things I was trying to say: that ours is a technique-ridden, sick country and we stress technique over everything.

I think that's why human beings have such a hard time, because so many aspects of human relationships are technical in a sense, instead of being open and free and willing to be wrong, which is reflective of what we're talking about. Nobody shoots film better than it's shot in Hollywood, and they are empty. When I think of the films of the fifties during which the McCarthy hearings took place . . . They were done very beautifully and there's where you had a separation of form and content. This was the horrendous weakness of those films.

Art is never an abstraction in a person's head. It is always an experience between two people, generally among many people. It's very nature is different. I think maybe a poet could be on an island and get up in the morning and recite poetry to himself, but a filmmaker can't. Film is essentially a social art; it's involved with people. The whole enterprise is a human enterprise. I want to see films made by people. It's tempting to do all those other things. Godard's position is understandable. When he made *British Sounds*—nobody saw it, maybe about ten thousand people—and yet, that opening sequence of the assembly line, that jarring noise, is genuine, tremendous. When Paul Schrader does it in *Blue Collar,* not a bad film at all, it's so much more muted and controlled and glamorized. It still works though. And Godard was almost killed going down to that factory making the film. People were outraged: "We don't look like that! What have you done to us?" That's a step that's going to take place in some society in the future. What people want to see now is escape. They want to see what's on television.

I had an idea during the Vietnam War. Dellinger asked me to cover a demonstration and I said, "No, I'm not a newsreel cameraperson. I'd do a lousy job. I have a better idea. Do you have any money? Why don't you get about five hundred of those thirty-dollar Fujica Super 8 cameras and let somebody give a day course in how to use them and give them to the demonstrators and have everyone shooting from within the demonstration from different sides, and maybe something will happen with it. It would be much more interesting." In every art there is a distance, a spatial distance between "I" who made it and "you" who looks at it. That distance is always there and we're always aware of it and to pretend that we're not aware of it is to be ridiculous. And there, I think, the pure commercial guy is more realistic than the semi-artist, the half-assed artist type of filmmaker, because the pure commercial guy who's giving you an armpit deodorant has got one clear, simple thing to do: to take that relatively useless package and get millions of people to buy it. So he's looking for a rapport that I would disdain to find and maybe that's my weakness.

Ultimately I make my films for myself. In the early days of the Russian Revolution they were talking about film for the masses. But then they realized, "Who are we? We are not the masses. We're educated, we're artists." So, what is film for the masses? That is the hardest question, a very difficult question for a Marxist. I finally got hung on that dilemma and made the decision: films that suit me first and I hope they find an audience, because I didn't want to pretend I was making films for some mythical audience that I couldn't see. And there's no doubt that, like most people who aren't working class, including Chris Marker who belonged to the Left, including Godard when he was still Left, all of us are stuck because the films we make, if anything, are more intellectual than the films made by the man from the Right or reactionaries or any different social point of view. My films were never meant for masses of people, except in funny countries like Sweden.

HENRY JAGLOM

The audience has a conditioned expectancy to see things from the outside of a person's behavior. Traditionally, what audiences are given is a safe barrier between themselves and their emotional experiences. So they can watch something that somebody is doing but they know more than the character on the screen knows, and therefore they really are a little bit on top of the situation. I wanted to avoid that. It seemed to me very important in *A Safe Place* to experience what this young woman, the Tuesday Weld character, is going through, and that *has* to be experienced through her mind, not through us looking at the outside of her. And in the same way in *Tracks*, to know what the soldier is going through, it has to be experienced through his mind. In both cases there are breakdowns.

It all really has to do with aiming at subjectivity. Because the requirement is totally different. If I'm really going to try to get the audience to identify their experience with what a character is going through, and if it's a breakdown that the character is going through in both these films, people resist going through breakdowns because it's unpleasant, it's emotional, it's difficult, and they're not used to having to do that. They want to *watch* breakdowns, but not to go through them. If I'm going to make them feel the experience they are resisting, I have to find new techniques that support that. I certainly have to allow the actors to bring everything that they can give me to help. And I have to use music in every way conceivable and use anything else that is also going to trigger that. If I go through that crying experience, I've got to assume there are people out there in the audience who will feel it, and if I use it again and again, it'll connect that way. I can make it work for the audience that way. Tuesday Weld is me in *A Safe Place* like Dennis Hopper is me in *Tracks*.

Many people have told me that when they see my films, there's a sense of a childhood loss and they don't think about the character necessarily. They start drifting into their own life. I love that. I think that if you point the way toward it, it becomes a universal experience, and it shouldn't be just about the characters you've created, because it should be about you, the spectator seeing a film, having his own feelings, his own memories, his own life triggered.

If I think that the viewer is half-watching a movie and half-daydreaming, I feel I have done my work best. If I'm tricking him into rigid attention to my images, I feel that I'm denying him a huge part of the meeting where that process should be. And that's what makes it different again from the theater. You can do that in film. It's all about memories, it's all about creating memories. It's a huge range of feelings and they're all constantly operating. So it seems to me that they should be operating in my films. I didn't think that out. It just works that way. Who is it who said, "Life is a comedy for those who think, a tragedy for those who feel"? Well, that's life. I haven't heard anything better yet.

AL MAYSLES

So much money is required to make a movie that the people who pay for them want to be sure to get their money back, and so they tend to rely on substitutes. They tend to rely on action and frivolity and titillation. It's the difference between the *New York Daily News* and the *Christian Science Monitor*. I think it's always been the *Daily News*.

I think that all the great film directors have this one flaw—they are directors. When you take the word *director* and you think of it that way, what does it mean? That they are determining what's going to happen. I think that's a terrible limitation. Just as suddenly we're discovering that men have been limited by conceiving women in a limited role, so I see that filmmakers are limited by conceiving their subjects in a limited role. Men conceive of women as not having the ability to do this or that, and the filmmakers haven't seen their subjects as having the ability to do anything but follow the director or follow the script. But there's something much bigger and more important than the idea of the director or what's in the script and that bigger thing is real people, but they all think "I got this great idea." When we had this idea about salesmen we thought it was only a beginning because then we would let the salesmen, the people, go wherever they go—the people would take over.

There have been reviews occasionally claiming certain scenes were on instruction by us. That was "obvious" to them because that's the way things are normally done. But the fact of the matter is that it did actually happen that way—spontaneously. Like in *Grey Gardens* there's a moment when Edie comes out onto the porch and weighs herself. It's a very funny moment because it's so human. She looks at the scale and she says, "Oh, my God, I'm so fat." And people have said, "Obviously you set up the scale because you knew you'd get that kind of reaction in the film." But knowing anything about this woman means knowing that at some point, wherever that scale is, if she's near it, she's going to step on it, and she's going to reveal something about her feelings about being overweight. So when she's near it, you get near it and wait.

I think Hollywood is where we were before women's liberation, and this style is where we will be when both men and women are liberated, because it encompasses a very democratic attitude towards people. In fact, you place every bit of your reliance on the people you're filming, whose capabilities you cannot really know ahead of time, but you base it on faith in them, as much on them as on your own ability to extract it from them. So that when a film like *Grey Gardens* is made, these people are under their own direction. If it turns out well, as it did, and if it encounters a resistance from the public, it's the subjects who can be proud of the film, and you are in a position to want to defend it.

People don't expect to find something of such power and integrity on the screen, so when they see it, they think they're being fooled, or it is of such power that it tends to strike a nerve that is sensitive, a nerve that is in an area of human experience which traditional film has never touched because of the fear that they might lose a customer. For example, one speaks in theater and fiction film of an actor's vulnerability, but still there is always the protective buffer of fiction. So, traditionally, we always look at a movie and say, "Well, it's only a movie, not anything to worry about." Viewers are not truly disturbed by it, but when they're looking at the lives of real people they can't say it's only a movie. They may attempt to deny the reality, claiming it's the presence of the camera that is the reality, which is difficult to prove one way or the other, but which I would say most of the time is the protective device of some viewers from seeing something new and bold on the screen.

LINA WERTMULLER

In the period I made *Love and Anarchy*, for example, there were many little acts of terrorism. The most fashionable was skyjacking. And there were many young Arabs dying in these things and causing catastrophes. I was impressed by the fact that people never asked themselves why these madmen did these things. They all approached it with their wonderful love of justice; they never asked themselves why. And that's how the audience is: it stops after a first reading of the film and doesn't get what's really behind it. It's a danger in my films too. When the man killed himself in *Seven Beauties* by jumping into the shit, an intellectual I know, a professor, didn't understand that he was saying "No."

You have to say things at least three times: the first time for the viewers, the second time for the viewers who sneezed when you said it the first time, and the third time for the critics because they are idiots.

The audience is used to having one point of view, but life is everything combined together. The grotesque, irony, humor is more difficult and so rarer, and therefore more precious. There are no comics left. During the war many people like Charlie Chaplin worked on tragedy with laughter in a humorous way. Most difficult of all, I think, is mixing tragedy and the grotesque. I think it's possible to combine different genres because the division into comic, tragic, ironic genres is only a division we make out of convenience. The newspaper classifies a film as tragedy, comedy, science fiction, detective film. They pretend every film is one thing; I think everything can be together. Why is it so difficult today to make a really ironic movie?

JEAN-MARIE STRAUB

Godard unwound the illusion very well, but it doesn't interest me. His films interest me, but it doesn't interest me to do it. I think people are quite aware that a film is made with certain techniques and there is no reason to further impose this on them. It's so evident. When Godard did it, it was sometimes very interesting and diverting, but since he did it so well, I wonder why I should do it.

Films should be made these days to divide people, not to unite them. The idea of the masses is an invention of the producers, of the cultural industry. It's a totalitarian dream. The masses are themselves divided into classes and film is a form of revelation to them so that the identity of the classes can appear. I think a film should be made so that people can leave the room. Films that pretend to be made for the masses are really made to keep them in their place, to violate them or to fascinate them. Consequently, these films are made in such a way that they don't give people the liberty to get up and leave. Our films are made so people can leave if they want. We are not happy when people leave the room during our films, but it is clearly a risk, for those who leave might have been moved if they had seen more.

CLAUDE CHABROL

When anyone goes into a moviehouse, well, the problem isn't for him to understand the world. For me, the audience is always ready to be bored. They sit there, poor people. So the lesson is, when the audience doesn't want to think, they just want to be interested. They deserve that, we should give them that, too. If they want to think, okay, but if not, they deserve to be entertained. It's okay. Why not? So, even though I hate plots, we must give them a plot. Anyway, I think the plot doesn't matter.

The problem with Godard was different because he felt the simple fact of directing actors and giving them something to say was a kind of fiction, and the audience must know it's a trickery. That's why he used so many tricks like that, but I'm not sure he's right because you cannot assume the truth by yourself and try to say *the* truth.

It's exactly the same thing with the actors. Some are very

professional and very concentrated people, and they show you
that: they are very professional and very concentrated before
the shooting, during the shooting, after the shooting. But if
you are a very elegant actor or actress, you are very professional and concentrated, but you don't *show* it, it's for you
alone. You are absolutely inside the part but no one knows
that.

So I'd rather give entertainment instead of showing tricks.

ELIO PETRI

The only way to take account of the viewer in the cinema in
the intellectually correct manner is to look at the scene from
the eye of the viewer, which is something I've always done instinctively. But then, it's always a lie in the sense that in the end
it's always me who's looking.

The public is a very vague sociological notion. You don't
know what it is. The public is a projection of ourselves, perhaps. In reality it isn't. In reality it's something else. It's a mixture of many people, many different cultures, different
generations. Maybe it's best to think of the public as a projection of ourselves. If you see the public this way, then in some
way you do know you're at the cinema, you're there watching a
film, but at the same time in some way involved in the story.
The problem is to succeed without dazing it. At least, I believe
so. The structures of communication are always easily visible,
clear, and yet the audience is emotionally involved. This is what
I try to do.

But it isn't necessary for this to be completely simultaneous,
second by second. There can be sequences that suddenly clarify
for the audience that they're at a film, others in which the audience can forget they're there and think they're elsewhere. It's
a little like a dialogue with themselves.

It's political in the sense that the audience isn't seen merely
as the servant of the spectacle. But neither is it seen as the sole
protagonist. So, in a way, you have to approach the audience

today exactly as you would approach yourself, and so you can also refuse the emotional level of the communication. It's very intellectualist to think a film should be totally alienating. There's no sphere of art in which the sentiments aren't also involved. The problem is to balance the sphere of reason, of ideas, and that of the feelings. This, I think, is a political idea in the sense that you can't consider the spectator inferior and his feelings as contemptible, and that you try to put in motion between the spectator and the spectacle a dialectical process, authoritarian neither from the point of view of the author nor from the point of view of the spectator. There's a lot of talk about the authoritarianism of the work, but not the authoritarianism of the spectator.

So I'm not afraid of manipulating the spectator. That's too Calvinistic. Art is, of course, manipulation. What did Rembrandt do? He was a great manipulator. I love the great manipulators. I like Stroheim much more than Flaherty. I like Stroheim and I don't like Flaherty. I don't like documentaries; they make me laugh. They're the maximum of manipulation because they pretend to document what isn't documentable. I like baroque; I like everything that is spectacle. Just choosing a point of view out of the points of view there are in this room we're in and framing it is already a manipulation. I think the greatest form for representation is literature because it can simultaneously give a thousand different points of view without seeming to be documentaristic. One can only give a document of oneself, nothing else.

CHANTAL AKERMAN

If you see a movie, you know that you are in a movie theater, but from time to time you do forget you are in a theater. In fact, you are feeling the story and, to some extent, you are believing it. But it's not so simple. You are believing that you know that you are in a movie. So, it's the two things together. It means that you know that it's not true. So, it's the fact of illusion: you know you are going to be tricked though you know it's not true. The theater is the same thing, as are movies, opera, ballet: you deny the illusion to some extent, but you still know you are in it. So you don't have to walk into the middle of that illusion, in the middle of the movie. It's much more complex than the people who say, "Oh, you forget that you are in a movie and you identify." It's that double thing all the time.

Unfortunately, almost all films are manipulative. It's seen in many things; it's the plot, the way it's done. Everything, in fact, is done to manipulate feelings, and you are not free to feel what you'd normally feel in that kind of situation because you are very deeply manipulated. But when I see a movie that is false and I'm being manipulated, I just don't feel it. I see that immediately and it doesn't work on me.

SIDNEY LUMET

I don't deal with that at all, because I don't know what an audience does. They're a constant surprise to me. Sometimes I go see a movie of mine with an audience there, and I find they're hopelessly behind. They don't understand the point, and I keep thinking, "Why don't they understand it? We said it, we showed it four times already." Other times they're so far ahead of me, I could kick myself for not taking it back to the editing room and cutting out the next three references to it because they caught it before I even said it.

They're a constant surprise, like all people are. And, therefore, there is no specific relationship: in certain pieces, I want them to do a lot of work. In other pieces, "Lay back and let me take you, baby." The sexual references are quite correct because that's what it is about. It can be participation; it can be "I'm going to take care of myself," or "I'm going to take care of you completely." And every variation in between. Again, it's indeterminable, so in the making of the movie I never pay attention to it, except in comedy; then I'll look at it. The first time Peter Finch says, "Bullshit," in *Network,* if that didn't get a laugh, if that was a shock instead, we were in terrible trouble. Because in a drama you get another chance. If a scene doesn't quite work, the next scene can grab you and you're off and running. If a point is being made through laughter, and the laughter doesn't happen, it takes you much longer to recover. You're back to not just square one; you're back to minus ten, because you've punctured a belief, you've punctured a reality that you've set for them. Reality is whatever we choose to make it in a movie, and that's why titles are important. We tell you, "Hey, you're *here* for this kind of story." So what makes you really sweat on a comedy, as I say, is if the reaction to "Bullshit" had been shock. Then, we'd be in trouble.

The toughest yet is mixing comedy and tragedy, because there your control has to be masterful and it's one of the things that Paddy and I are so proud of in *Network*. The audience went where we wanted them to go. One of the biggest laughs of the movie had to be cut off like that because it came just before that marvelous scene between Betty Straight and Bill Holden, the breakup scene. I knew how to stop the laugh: the laugh just cut to her staring. And they saw her face, and the laugh was cut with a knife. And it was interesting, because the first time I cut the scene, I didn't want to start with a close-up on Betty. I started it over her with a shot of Bill looking very sheepish and guilty, and the laughter continued because the audience knew the breakup scene was coming since they knew he was having an affair with Faye Dunaway. And I thought, "Uh-huh, I can't let that laughter overlap even into the beginning of the scene." I had to cut it off like a knife. The solution was very simple: cut to her first.

I don't want anything to break the audience's concentration until they're halfway home. I want them to stay with the picture. The nicest things to have ever happened to me in theaters are all kinds of different movies. A nice, good caper movie like *The Anderson Tapes,* when that kid—Chris Walken—came busting out of the big van in the little van and you cheer. I love that, it's fun. When Al Pacino was doing the "Attica, Attica" thing in *Dog Day* and the audience became the people on the street in the movie—it was incredible. The audience reactions on *The Wiz*—the numbers of times I went to see that in the theater and four numbers never got finished, they'd be screaming so. So that kind of total involvement is what it's about.

ROBERT ALTMAN

I think ultimately the real, efficient use of the medium, which is moving pictures, is to have an audience not understand what they've seen, but have an emotional response to it. The ideal response to a film would be not to be able to articulate what they have just seen, but to be able to say, "It really felt good." It's like being able to describe any emotional feeling: that sense that everything in your head, everything in your body, works out.

It'll eventually seep up to the intellect because you bring it up there. It doesn't touch your body, your skin, so you're doing all the work by yourself, you're absorbing the images through two senses, your eyes and your ears. It's triggering computered information, experiences you have in your head, whether they're fears, desires—things that are in your mind, which is, in fact, a computer that stores information. And the film is triggering those things and it's withdrawing responses. Those are intellectual responses even though you can't actually say, "The reason Sherlock Holmes figured out so and so is because so and so." Those kind of films are terrific. There's no reason you can't have linear stories, psychodramas, straight dramas, melodramas. All of those things can exist on film but all film should not be alike. I mean, Kubrick's films should not be any more like my films than S. S. Van Dyne books should be like Proust. There's room for all these things. The one thing that we should strive for is artists working who are excellent at what they do and are not doing it simply for the money.

JEAN-LUC GODARD

It's certain I'm becoming more aware of the viewer in the sense that when you make a movie, you are cut off from the audience. In the beginning the only one who is aware of the movie is its creator or the so-called creator. He is interested in the picture in a too-limited but truthful way. So you are separated from the audience; you pretend you respect the audience but it's because you work for a big company or a small company, for bankers who respect the movie, but from a very narrow point of view. But if you don't have that commercial success, you come to think "Why me?" You don't feel as bad about what people say, and since you don't want to do movies exactly like the commercials on television, you begin to think of the public as another self which is invisible and often doesn't appreciate some of the things you do when they are good and when they are not good.

When you are working with a small video camera and small video screen, you are better off in a sense. Then you begin to wonder who your audience is. If you have a big audience, you can't really say you respect them—it's like saying you respect the people on the street—you don't really know who they are. But if you only have ten people for your audience, only ten people come to see your film, you begin to wonder who they are. You become interested to know them at least, because they have taken time, spent money to see your film. Ten people have a reality; a medium has no reality.

Think of the relation of the spectator and those who make TV films. Even if he doesn't say it, the director thinks that he belongs on the viewer's side. One tells the viewer, as in my film, that he is part of the production and that he participated in the financing of the film, even if it's only the money he paid to enter the theater. So the spectator is a part of the production, and the film is made by the spectator. Today three-quarters of films—the editing, the music, the news—are made by the spectator, and what they take for a relaxation is of cultural interest. But bad films exhaust them a lot more than they think, and the next day at work they arrive even more tired and tense. If a film is bad, it is the spectator who has to do the work, and, further, it is the spectator who pays.

·9·

FILM AND SOCIETY

From the beginning, film has been a "vulgar" art form. For some, "vulgar" weighs heavily with negative connotations: pitching the film to the lowest common denominator in the audience so it performs well as a product, working only in reductive genres that propogate, even create, our fondest, most deluded myths about ourselves. But a film's tie to the parent culture can be valuable even when it is pandering to a lying myth because some truth, whether of beauty or of ugliness, always manages to sneak in. No matter how deliberately a film may lie, enough details of real life insinuate themselves, sparking in the mind of the viewer a desire to fill in a picture of the total context, the surrounding culture that gave the film its birth. Every film, no matter how poor, tells us something real about the time and place in which it occurs—that is, the time and place in which it is made, *not necessarily the historical period it may be describing. No film can be controlled totally by the artist, nor can the filmmaker escape entirely his own acculturation. So the culture always intrudes. It may be expressed only as background— cars and buildings glimpsed around the edges of the frame or passing deep within its recesses—but these brief and seemingly insignificant details are relics that fix a film definitively within a specific world. Even a totally fabricated set on a studio backlot will reveal in its aesthetics the sensibility of a particular time and place.*

The relationship between film and culture is not, however, one-sided, with movies merely reflecting what is simply there. Movie myths are also self-fulfilling prophesies. The larger-than-life images they project are injected with our most potent cultural and personal placebos, fantasies that maintain the cultural condition, for better or for worse.

If film is tied to the culture that gives it birth, what effect does this child have on the political life of the parent? Can films effect socio-political changes in the world, or do they merely reflect current conditions, allowing at the most for a few idle grumblings or fantasies of what could *be?*

Most of the filmmakers feel films don't change the world, only people do. Film's influence is subtle and indirect, not traceable as a direct cause of any specific political event. While a film can have a powerful effect on individuals, only when there are other elements operating as a totality toward the same ends can enough people mass together to produce some significant change. Others feel that film has the potential to be an effective political tool, but thus far it has either been relatively unused or misused. Some dismiss the whole notion of film's healing or transforming powers; film is just one of countless events experienced by the individual. Film's special gifts seem to lie more in the direction of stretching our imaginations beyond the limited spheres of our own experience toward understanding the experience of the Other. In that sense, in the more expansive meaning of "political," film encourages tolerance and thereby improves the general political condition.

Once more, the question arises of what are, if any, the responsibilities of the filmmaker toward the viewer—in this case considered on a mass scale. And, if he is responsible to society, what can the filmmaker do? Despite what film could *do, one can hardly deny the fact of Renoir's masterful* Grand Illusion, *perhaps the most compelling of all antiwar films. It was released in 1939, but did nothing to prevent the onset of the Second World War. Perhaps Chabrol is right, at least thus far: "Film is a way to do nothing. Film is not a gun."*

Perhaps film can be an agent for change, but on a more personal, individual level serving as a vehicle for getting out of psychological traps. On the other hand, perhaps film only stirs people as a kind of cathartic agent, and, in that sense, is capable of serving as an avoidance mechanism, a resistance to change. Or even worse, films may serve as narcotics, deadening us with their endless clichés: we willingly give up our vital selves in order to lose our psychic hobgoblins.

AL MAYSLES

Film can give us all kinds of information, information that's peculiar to the kind you can get only on film. It's incredible that it's only in the last few years that we have come to know a regular family at all on film. The series on the Loud family wasn't particularly well done, but that and others that were better, have been done. But we still haven't filmed war in anything but a Hollywood style, in a fragmented way. I'm convinced that the Vietnam War would have come to a close much sooner had there been one film that in some length truthfully showed us what was going on, even the simplest story, like the *Life* magazine story of the man who went over there to look for his brother missing in action and crossed both lines. The power of film is in its ability to give us an understanding of how things are, and it's so strong. Yet we neglect to use it to inform us that way. There still hasn't been a film of a psychoanalysis. Isn't that incredible? Sixty years later there still hasn't been a film of it. What are we afraid of? We are afraid of granting the camera the power to give us certain kinds of information. I don't know if there's been a film of—well, almost anything that's been handled by Hollywood has been done the other way. What I'm trying to say is that just for the camera to record how things are, where we are at this moment, what is happening, what life is like here, there, everywhere, what life is like to this woman next door, would broaden my own vision. Just seeing one film that would show me in an hour and a half the separate lives of a dozen interesting people living in this building where I live isolated from them. I'm not even talking about Harlem or other parts of the city or the world, but just my immediate neighbors. That's a film. Yet that sort of film isn't being made.

JEAN ROUCH

I think film is really the avant-garde of politics. It tells us that we don't have the answers and nobody has the answer. If you are a Christian, Socialist, Maoist, Marxist, and so on, maybe it's good in its place, but why? Is it good elsewhere? You have to see the difference. You can say it's "myself and the other" that film shows, and that the other is different from you so you can try to understand why you are different. That's the new anthropology, which we call sharing anthropology. I can ask you about your ideas on life after death and you can ask me about mine. That is the way: you have to reverse roles. You have to get rid of the old idea that we just have to give access to the rest of the world to the American or European way of life. That's really imperialism. And film can help combat that.

I'll give you an example connecting us to Utopia. I make anthropological films and people ask, "What does it mean to make anthropological films nowadays with all these ways of life disappearing and so on?" Well, what I now know is you have these kinds of films more and more, and people are more and more interested. For example, three years ago there was a film shot in Amazonia among the Indians of Amazonia called *Wahari*. It is a very strange film, one hundred and ten minutes, and it was shown in theaters. There was absolutely no translation, no subtitles, no explanation, and there was a public for it. The people were interested and they could understand something. Maybe it was their own explanation, but who cares? They were just following something and they were discovering that different ways of life exist.

I think with this kind of film you can change all of humanity and discover that the world we have to create will be a world of different cultures, not of one culture, and it's happening now. And I think that in this way film is very important. When you are making a film about a so-called primitive tribe, you are giving to this tribe dignity in acknowledging that it exists. That's the power of film.

I made a film called *Les Maîtres fous,* which is about trance dancing in the old Gold Coast. It was just before the independence of Ghana. And it was a very tough film, where the people were in trance and dancing and killing and eating a dog. It was a very difficult film. When the film was shown for the first time here in the Musée de l'Homme, it was in 1955. My professor of anthropology said, "You have to destroy this film. It's a shame to show that." And some young Africans said the same. And now this film is a classic in Africa because there was something in this film and it was their culture. Anyway, it's better to kill a dog than your grandmother or your baby or to kill people in Vietnam or in concentration camps, or to put some people in jail. Then, you see, in a film you can have this kind of message. If this message is not understood when the film is made, maybe the message will be understood in one or two centuries. That is very important.

The real truth is to be honest yourself before the truth, and to show in a film what you *think* to be the truth even if you don't understand it. If you see some people killing a dog, well, they are killing a dog. Then you can try to understand why, what does it mean, why are they doing that? Then you begin to discover a lot of connections to our very old Dionysiac background, all of which was at the beginning of creativity, of theater, and so on. If done this way, film can show such things.

WERNER SCHROETER

It is very strange. As a matter of fact, in the nineteenth century, there are two cases of direct influence, and those were authorized. For example, there was an opera by François Aubert that caused a revolution in Brussels, because it dealt with a subject that was very close to the oppression at that time in Belgium. Another case was *Il Trovatore* by Giuseppe Verdi, which caused a revolution in Venice. The people took over the revolutionary idea in that melodrama for their own identity in order to beat off the Austrians. But nowadays I couldn't think of an example where a film caused such direct action.

But cinema always transports ideology. All those films of the American cinema of the thirties, forties, fifties, transported the average American ideology. People are really manipulated and they have a tradition of ideology in the American cinema, so it must be very difficult to get through to destroy those images in order to get out a new message. It must be very difficult to use the cliché of the American cinema but to put some new meaning in it. Because as soon as a woman doesn't look like an American woman should—I mean, I'm not talking about intellectuals, I am talking about the so-called silent majority—as soon as a person doesn't look like that image that's been built up for decades and decades, people won't listen to the different message. But if you are following the image absolutely, you can't have a different message. It's always the same, like a Doris Day kind of film or the top intelligent woman, Katharine Hepburn, or the fragile, erotic child like Marilyn Monroe. You have done them all in cliché, and somehow everything has to follow the cliché line, otherwise people reject the image. And you have a very limited audience that already knows everything that you know, so it's the kind of act of *reconnaissance,* recognition, but it's nothing new for them. You should put out that kind of stuff to people who are not used to seeing something that gives a new idea. And that is an aesthetic problem: how to have a big audience, a rather big audience, without falling into that cliché image that absolutely destroys your possibility of saying something more progressive. It's very difficult.

There is no time for playing around anymore at the moment. It's not the time. You know, in the late sixties, it was different, or in the so-called *Wirtshaftswunder* time in Germany in the fifties and early sixties, which was when the student revolutions started. But now, you should concentrate on the more concrete reality because you can't escape the consciousness of what is going on and you have to add something positive to the discussion about our world. So cinema becomes more direct and primitive. It has to become a political means. And the reason I decided that my more or less artistic films of the late sixties and early seventies became useless by now is because while there is a kind of artistic revolution in the image, they don't transport more than a vague anarchism in what I consider should be the position of people in politics and in social life. But what I wanted to express I always got. It was what my eye saw, and what was inside of me was expressed in the way I wanted to have it on the screen.

EMILE DE ANTONIO

As a people we're very sick. The media—film, particularly television—is endemic, pervasive, destructive. It makes us all insane because it's the one genuine experience of our culture since it cuts across class lines. The president of General Motors looks at the same piece of garbage as the janitor in his building. It's morally and visually bankrupt. For instance, how could they make all those shitty TV movies if they didn't have helicopters? Everyone has the same shot chasing the cars down the road from a helicopter. We know how cheap that is. You know the technology was developed about nine, ten years ago to plant the camera gyroscopically in the helicopter so it's just as smooth as if you did it in a studio on a dolly. It only costs about one thousand dollars a day to rent a helicopter and stick a person in it. It's not like Hollywood, where they're glad to get two, three minutes of screen time in one day. And you can shoot all that scenery, cars rushing by. You can fill it up—cheap, cheap, cheap.

The illusion of freedom is the greatest will-o'-the-wisp our culture knows. When *Year of the Pig* opened commercially in L.A., people broke into the theater in the middle of the night and took heavy tar and put a "hammer and sickle = traitor" on the screen. That's very effective: other theaters cancelled their bookings. They don't want you to fuck around with their screens. They don't want trouble. What most people forget is that the essence of film is, obviously, the moviehouse, and the moviehouse is a real estate operation. You've got so many seats that you've got to fill at so many bucks per hour, and if you don't do it, you go out of business. So they don't want trouble. They don't want ideas. They don't want problems. They want people to be soothed, to eat a lot of popcorn, and to look at *Star Wars* or encourage the specious kind of phony mysticism that comes out of *Close Encounters*. When you think of all the poor people who have spent four bucks to see that movie about people from outer space who don't exist so that they won't have to think about riding home on the subway afraid and about eating improper food and having lousy schools and supporting an idiot Pentagon, then *Close Encounters* has done its job.

It's very hard in our culture because the pressures from Hollywood are surely to make more and more enormously profitable films, to make genuinely pig films, and it's hard to get out of that. There are a lot of gifted people trapped in that. Power goes with the money, and that's a fairly rough thing to resist. You want to do that, you know, within the limits of one's own work; one wants to reach as many people as possible without turning oneself into a second-rate hooker. And this is the real trouble with a guy as gifted as Francis Ford Coppola. There are sequences in the two *Godfather* films that are really good, and the idea of *The Conversation* is brilliant. But he wants American Zoetrope, he wants to be involved with Lucas, and that whole thing. Haskell Wexler and Coppola were involved in *American Graffitti,* which was one of the "greatest" films in the history of Hollywood because the budget was so tiny and it grossed over fifty million dollars. But Andy Warhol is much more interesting. I've known Andy since he was a commercial artist. The significance of Andy is that he duplicated the whole history of film as he started making films. His first film: a person on a couch, not moving much. Then he used some motion. Then he introduced some sound, which is very crude.

The film *Painters Painting,* which I finished in 1972, is a film that I've never talked about too much. It's a film that basically had to do with the incongruities and the problems I had with my own life and my own work. In other words, here I am from this upper middle class background and my friends are making the painting that I put in that film, which is the painting I like, but it's a painting that belongs to a minuscule world, a world of rich collectors, slippery, brilliant dealers, crummy museum curators. It's a world of five thousand people in a country of two hundred and ten million. Yet, that's where I am. What is art? What should it be? What should film be? I began by giving you my answer: it should be social reorganization of experience, and yet I question myself now and I always question myself. I have no absolute on the truth, no hold on it.

It's very hard for me to judge the effect of my films. I'm not going to pretend that people see my films the way they see *The Godfather*. But time is with me; I own time and history because people keep wanting to see my films and things happen. There's a guy from the Museum of Modern Art, a film curator, and he wrote me a letter saying, "I just cared about film. I didn't know anything about the war in Vietnam. Then I saw *Year of the Pig* and joined a peace group and demonstrated." If you do that to just a few people, you've changed them in one way that some other medium or other film didn't change them.

KRZYSZTOF ZANUSSI

Film is a bastard, a newborn and illegitimate art, still. Many people would agree that this is not art at all, which for me is very painful and embarrassing. But I realize that is a pack of lies. These people believe that all other disciplines are dignified, and film is not. But somehow I would say it corresponds to the lifestyle and to the sensitivity of people of our times: people who read less, people who live in an industrial environment, and so on. This is the social trend all over the world, and film is a product of this trend, as well. I'm a reader myself, but I understand that film is getting a more and more important position in the cultural and social life because of this evolution of people's sensibilities, and this position of film is evolving slowly but definitely. Also, there are many other elements of this evolution, and some are very sad to me. People are losing a lot of their power of concentration and are being overloaded with stimuli. That makes people immune to art. We don't listen that carefully anymore. We don't notice strange voices and strange noises that surround us as we did years ago. Whenever my grandfather was taking a stroll in old Warsaw and he heard music, he stopped, because this was very unusual. It was unusual at that time to hear music.

Film is a matter of communication. If there's no communication, there's no film. I would say the special value of art in general—because it's true of all disciplines of art, though film is the most complex—is that art has the power to convey these vibrations, which is a name for something I can't define, which cannot be rationally perceived. And, of course, some common experience of living together with people may be a substitute for art, or the opposite: art may be a substitute for the experience of communication in real life. It's not that we just talk but that we go through some experience together, and then we still observe each other because our own perceptions of our experiences are not the same as other people's perceptions of their experiences.

Film develops the imagination, and imagination has crucial value in our world. We cannot be tolerant if we are not imaginative, if we cannot put ourselves into different situations than we really are in. And that's what society's missing, this power of imagination. People cannot understand that other people have different experiences and different backgrounds, and this is a most painful gap which art can cover to a certain extent. All we understand of Japan is through Japanese art. There is a lot that philosophers or social writers told about this country, but still it is so hard to relate to another culture or another mentality without having a personal experience, and film helps us to stretch our imaginations and gain some understanding.

PERRY HENZEL

I have a theory about culture. Culture is not the same thing at all as cultural energy. Cultural energy occurs when there is a *need* for culture, but no established culture exists to fill that need. Jamaica is the most obvious example. You know, very often an established culture doesn't create cultural energy. It does just the opposite. Established culture is like a weight on the shoulder of the artist in Europe and the Slavic countries. It's a heavy weight.

In Jamaica we have no cultural tradition, but we have tremendous need for culture because it's a brand new nation, brand new breed of people, and so on. So, it isn't a vacuum;

there is an incredible energy filling the need. And that cultural energy is best carried by film and music. Cultural energy is a flow of ideas and emotions from one source to another. Again, taking Jamaica as an example, you have two cultural polarities: Africa and America. On one side you have Africa and on the other you have America, and Jamaica is in the middle. Africa has no common language but it has a deep cultural tradition and cultural emotion. America not only has a common language, but a language that better than any other carries a message of freedom.

Jamaica is an island that has two million Africans who have drifted four thousand miles, who listen to Miami radio and speak English. It is *the* strongest connection. It's the switch through which that energy flows. Everybody else in the Third World doesn't speak English or is too far away to pick up American radio. That's where reggae comes from, of course. So the language and the culture meet in Jamaica and if you use sync sound, you've got it on film.

I think there is an enormous crunch coming to this degree: man has the ability to blow up the world, and there's nothing to guarantee that having been given this power, he won't misuse it. Obviously, there's going to come an incredible race between the "goodies" and the "badies." The "badies" have the guns, but the hope is that the skill of the singer, the skill of the person in communications, will create a drastic change in mass consciousness. It is a matter of political urgency that communication be used to effect this change. From that point of view I'm ashamed to be a filmmaker. I'm not proud of being in the film business when I think of what singers are doing to bring love to the world and to calm, to cool, people out, and when I think of what filmmkakers are doing. For the most part, singers are doing good and films are spreading visual pollution. But there are more and more filmmakers who are doing good. I think that when the need for that tremendously high level of communication is felt, to fill that need we will have a generation of children who will have learned the grammar of communication in their cribs from watching TV. They will know things instinctively that we now have to think about. They will be able to communicate very quickly and very effectively when the time comes.

BERNARDO BERTOLUCCI

Politics is very important in movies. It's the kind of element that is always present, directly or indirectly. But when I say that, even after making a political movie like *1900*, the effects are very limited. That's why when you asked me earlier about film's ability to reflect or transform reality, I asked if you wanted to know the effects aesthetically or politically.

I was at the Moscow Film Festival once, and a journalist from *Pravda* asked me if I thought *1900* could transform reality. I said, "Of course, I would like that everybody who comes out of the theater runs to a party of the Left around the corner, and says, 'Oh, I want to be a member,' but I know that this is not true, and I know that the movie cannot change society as we once thought in 1968, in Europe. For one year everyone thought movies were going to change everything, but it cannot change society in itself. It is, however, part of a cultural process which is much bigger." Then *Pravda* cut the second part of my statement, and they only quoted, "Yes, I would like everybody to be a member of the party." They didn't include the part of my statement that said that it won't happen.

The culture itself in a sense transforms reality, and cinema is a part of the culture. But, of course, there is an interaction between the vulgar expression and the languages of cinema, and so, too, there is an interaction between cinema and theater. There is an exchange that goes on. But to me making a movie means that for ten, fifteen weeks you are in the town you are shooting. And the great difference that I couldn't accept when I made my first film was that I was used to writing poetry, which means to be alone with pen and paper, and so I could not accept that cinema was a collective art. For the first two or three movies I made, I tried to conserve my loneliness, loneliness in a sense that I tried to be alone in the middle of a group. Also, it was a period when we talked a lot about *cinéma d'auteur,* the author of the film. Finally, I had to accept something that is the opposite. I think now that cinema is a very collective art. I know that it is very evident to everybody, but, to me, it was impossible at the beginning because my previous experience was different. Finally, the movie is made by everybody who is on the set, even the people who are not really involved, who are simply in that town where you are filming, because film is very sensitive. It just picks up a feeling, a vibration.

Here, too, is a contradiction, because I think that my movies express totally my feelings. But at the same time I think that my movies are very *cinéma d'auteur,* I know that they are made by a lot of people who are with me.

LINA WERTMULLER

"Political" is an overused word in America. Everything is political. It's a word with many different meanings. "Political" is very near to us if we mean by this word the organization of men with other men. The structure of social life is a very difficult problem. In our century we have seen many "falls," many ruptures, breaks, crises, in many ideologies. It's a very interesting century. Italy is one of the more interesting places in the world from this point of view: all of society's contradictions, industrial and socialist society, explode here. It's a beautiful country, so full of problems of bad administration, but, in any case, what happens is always very interesting, because the contradictions explode everything around us. We export labor and capital and there are contradictions between the Left and the Right. We are a little country but very sensitive to these contradictions. The great crisis of ideology and of socialism—these two currents come together here.

My film, *Love and Anarchy,* gives a sense of what Italy was like as an agricultural country, a poor country that the fascists tried to change into another thing. It's full of feeling. Afterwards, anarchy became terrorism, right action was deformed into mass murder. The film has become very contemporary today. It was meant as a warning about all this passion for justice. I began as an anarchist. Then I became a communist and then a socialist. But only because the sphere of socialism is one of experiment, research, not an ideological sphere. The danger came from ideology.

It was totally different to work in America, in another culture. It's not easy to express yourself in another language. I think it's impossible. It's impossible for me to represent another part of the world. It's possible through conventional films, when you make a deal to do a police story in New York or a Western, but when you go near to life, near to the problem, it's difficult.

In our filmmaking we express our culture, as does the States, but in a different way because the industry there is so powerful that movies become a way to distract. Somebody like Woody Allen feels the need to confront things. He is a real speaker of the habits and mores of America in his pictures. He shoots America well. He is a good "antibody." But now he works in a private sphere: neurosis. The followers of Bergman and Antonioni are people like that, working in their private spheres. It was much more difficult for Woody Allen to work as he worked in his previous films, before *Interiors*. I hope he will not abandon what he did, that he won't end up led astray by art with a capital *A*. He's much more important, more engaged, committed, political when he does his own things than when he enters the world of Bergman or Strindberg. When I made *A Night Full of Rain*, I was so filled with anguish at the things around me, it felt like the end of the world; we felt the end of *a* world, for, in effect, that's what the crisis is. It's very human for an author to feel what's happening around him and to return this anguish to his work. Clearly, even Woody had a crisis, but I tell myself that it's very important to work through laughter. It's more difficult.

I'm afraid of a society that is afraid to laugh, because self-criticism, self-irony, and the ability to laugh at yourself are the life of civilization. When Italy was fascist, when there was Nazism and McCarthyism, nobody laughed. In Russia they don't laugh. The first artist to be forced to kill himself in tyranny is the comic.

ERMANNO OLMI

When, as a child, I went to the cinema, I felt good and I felt especially good when I started seeing the differences between Hollywood cinema—*all* Hollywood cinema, not just the American—and a certain cinema of Italian neorealism, the first films of Rossellini. I was fifteen, sixteen, seventeen, and in those years I passed from my grandmother's arms, who affectionately told me wonderful fairy tales, to the bitterness of my father, who began to introduce me to life. I was torn away from the suggestion of the fairy tale to come closer to the complicated problematics of life, to live in direct contact rather than in grandmother's embrace. The films of Rossellini had this effect on me: I remember leaving *Paisan*—there were only seven or eight of us in the audience although the cinemas were always packed when they showed *Girls of Madness* and similar titles of American films. I went to *Paisan* probably because I had seen all the other movies around. And strangely enough, I realized it was time to tear myself away from grandmother and mother. Leaving the film, I continued to experience the same emotions I felt in the cinema, because it was life that was there. I took the same relation to life, the same perspective, the same participation that Rossellini had. The cinema began to fascinate me because of this: this idea of making films around a table together, not just to live, to eat, but to look into each other's eyes. So film, for me, is a way of being together with others, both when I make films and when my film is in some way with others, the viewers.

I loved Hollywood films very much, but if today my grandmother came back and wanted to take me on her knees and tell me the story of Little Red Riding Hood, to smile at me in such and such a way, I wouldn't like it. It's what people call becoming an adult viewer.

I think film has great value when they turn off their televisions. If it weren't for the cinema, contemporary society would be very disorganized. It's a kind of comfort, a false mirror like Snow White's stepmother's. We want the cinema, the representation of ourselves to somehow say to us that we are fine and good, even when it represents the negative aspect of life. But we are the winners, we are somehow saved by this mirror that deceives us continually. This, it seems to me, is society's attitude towards the representation of itself. As far as I'm concerned I could live without cinema if they took it away from me, but I couldn't live without my friends, my wife and children—people, especially those dear to me. It's the infantile question: "Would you prefer that the family and friends or cinema was taken away from you?" Then I'd say, "Cinema."

MARTIN SCORSESE

I went to Rhode Island yesterday with my parents for Italian-American Day, because the government decided to give me a citation of some sort. It turns out that Rhode Island has the most Italian-Americans in the country and so I went and got some idea of what the group was like.

I realize more and more that Italian-Americans are neither Italian nor are they American. They are Italian-Americans, and I think it's important to preserve that culture. Even recipes. That's why the recipe at the end of *Italian-American* is not a joke; it's funny, everybody says "cute," but it's not a joke. It's important that the recipe is *written down*, not that you're meant to cook it. It's important, for men too, and I mentioned that in Rhode Island when I received the award. I was going to donate *Italian-American* to them, but then I received another award from the governor, and I said to myself, "Okay, they should realize one thing: they shouldn't get hung up on aspiring to this petit bourgeois kind of situation, so I'm going to donate *Italian-American,* but *also* I'm going to donate *Mean Streets.*" One is the counterpart of the other. They seemed very pleased because they know the film, but while *Italian-American* is often very easy to like, *Mean Streets* and the new film, *Raging Bull,* are harder to like, but they are also an accurate image of what the semi-culture, the subculture, is, which I see slowly, slowly being disintegrated. Even if we're not Italian and we're not American—in the sense of white-bread American—we are a subculture that exists and has to be preserved. This country is very young and assimilation is very good—it's the beauty of the country—but not dissolution. There's a big difference. So, whether they like it or not, they got the copy of *Mean Streets* too. I'll go anywhere the group's really interested. That's the first time I've done that and I wanted to make sure that they're really on the line and really interested in what's happening in terms of their own selves. And that could be for Polish-Americans, Jewish-Americans, everything, because it's very important that one keep one's own identity, one's own subculture, the roots of it, and not become too assimilated. The country's very young, and if in another hundred years, it would be so mixed that you can't tell one from the other, my God, it would be disastrous. Now, you can hear and see different cultures, and it's great to see the different people, especially in New York— that's what makes New York great. The lesson is to be learned from the Jews who have been able to preserve culture for thousands of years. It's very important, but they have to accept the bad and the good.

So, film *is* culture, isn't it. It reflects something about the people who make it, about the country it comes from. And what sells this or that film represents part of what the culture of the country has become. Look at this ridiculous screen [a huge video projection screen]. This is nothing. Wait until you see what's going to happen in another couple of years. I've already seen some of those things to come in Japan.

·10·

MOVIE BUSINESS
Production, Distribution, and Exhibition

"A friend of mine, a Brazilian director, told me once that a movie director is the person who finds the money to make a movie. It sounds cynical but I think it's very real. To make a movie, first of all, maybe even before the idea of the movie, you need money. You need money because it's an expensive language."

—Bernardo Bertolucci

Film may be an art, but within the context of the prevailing economic system, it is first and last a product, a profit-making enterprise. As the Marxist filmmaker Elio Petri notes, this affects all aspects of the film process, "from the number of days you have to shoot to the fact that the actors have to be known, the type of films you have to use, the hours the film can last. You can make the list yourself."

Every second of film time represents a tremendous financial investment. It is not surprising to know that since films are usually made to realize a profit for the men who put up that money, that is to say, the bankers, many a "creative" decision, such as eliminating ten pages of "unnecessary" script, is made by the production auditor after a look at the books tells him the film is over schedule and therefore overbudget.

Within this framework, success in terms of communication with the viewer is measured by box-office figures and by the faith in one's money-

making ability as it is expressed by the amount investors are willing to gamble on one's projects. But no one really knows what will succeed at the box office. The audience was called "headless" by Charlie Chaplin; they don't know beforehand where the film will take them, but one could easily say the same thing about the Hollywood executives who seem to have no bases for their decisions to "go with" a film or to drop it, other than how closely it is patterned after the latest success. As Sidney Lumet, who has managed to enjoy a prolific and immensely successful career in New York City, puts it, "Hollywood is no place for a grown-up to work."

American filmmakers may be in a more difficult position than some Europeans because commercial considerations seem to weigh heavier here. Despite the well-founded complaints along those lines made by the European filmmakers, they can still find the patron of the arts: the man or woman of means who is interested for their own personal satisfaction in supporting an artistic enterprise. How is it that Mark Rappaport, a New York independent feature filmmaker with a definitely non-commercial style, has been able to make so many low-budget fiction films? Usually through European money, European distribution, and European exhibition. There is a place for him, but it may not be here.

At the time of interviewing and writing this book, financing a low-budget feature-length film aimed at theatrical distribution is almost impossible: the unknown filmmaker has to convince the studios (the banks) that they will get a return on their investment, and the whole process is so mired down in our beloved legal mazes that Phil Messina, a New York independent who finally went West to play those stakes, says, "You make the deal, you shoot the deal, you edit the deal, and you release the deal." It's no longer a movie, and you forget why you wanted to make films in the first place.

There is hope, however, a new twist that may totally change the situation: the explosion of the home market for video product. The very medium that was originally perceived as a threat to the film industry may now be its savior. With the advent of video discs and tapes there has already been a demonstrated increase in interest in producing low-budget films and videotapes aimed exclusively at the home video consumer. Many American filmmakers see this as a way to gain financing and distribution for films they can make the way they want to. Altman compares the accessibility of films on video discs to paperback editions of novels. Scorsese, tired of the cumbersome mechanics of big-budget, big-equipment, big-crew filmmaking, says he may be looking to the home video market as his only outlet, where he can bypass the censoring arm of the studios and deal directly with his public.

The more optimistic filmmakers look to this happier relationship between "Cain and Abel" as the way to free film from its obligation to entertain on a mass level, as an escape from the confines of genre, formula-ridden filmmaking. On the other hand, many others feel television style has hooked the filmgoer on a steady diet of medium shot-close shot and endless clones of the same neatly resolved melodramas and sitcoms, neatly sandwiched between commercials.

The hope is, of course, that the tremendous growth in home video entertainment systems—pay cable, local free cable—as well as the advances in video technology and means of delivery, may serve to clarify the different spheres of television and theatrical films as the two media divide the audience territory. It might be that news coverage, special events programming, stock genre movies, and sports are the tube's métier, while film can continue to develop itself in areas where instant replay is irrelevant. Film may be able to mature and stretch its limits, measuring its success not by box-office figures but by the level of its intentions and its ability to realize them.

It is clear there is no "resting place," no "I'm finally there" for the filmmaker, even for those who bow to the formula of the moment. One of the most striking lessons is to discover how many projects were taken away from people like Robert Altman and Michael Powell, to name only two. They are generally considered masters of their art, but they are not masters of the marketplace, nor is that their goal. Until what Jean-Marie Straub terms the "barbaric notion of profit" disappears from this planet, many filmmakers would agree with Elio Petri, whose father was a shoemaker: When a filmmaker finds himself on the losing side of the tug-of-war between art and commerce, "Maybe it's better to make shoes."

EMILE DE ANTONIO

Since film is a social art, it costs money, and I've found that from the beginning until now, I've had great luck. First of all, I had a kind of class advantage in knowing people from the beginning. With the first film I made, *Point of Order,* one guy I knew, as soon as I told him I was thinking of making it, offered me one hundred thousand dollars. I've always known people who had money and they were liberals. I would say liberals provided half the money for the civil rights movement, the antiwar movement—for all those causes that once seemed so important and so real. And for most of those people, although they didn't approve of radicals like me, it was good for their consciences to help somebody who was a little far out for them. I also found that not being shy about it was very helpful. I felt that my work should be made and I was always very capable of making a good case for that. I know it's harder now because we live in a different kind of society and I think that I would have a very hard time were I to be making some of these films now. But I've come to a different point where I'm going to be looking for much more money. I'm going to be making a union fiction film, which means I'm going to have to raise twice as much money as I ever had to raise before for one project; for fiction it's not so hard because of the glamour of it. There are all kinds of people who are willing to get involved with that.

I think money-raising is a duty. If you're generally independent, you have to raise your own money or someone who is part of your life should raise your own money, not just somebody who is working in a film with you. Let's face it. In this culture, money is independence. Unless you can actually raise the bread somebody else is controlling the picture. That's the whole nature of the exercise. That's why I've never applied for grants. I can't see those people judging me. First of all, I wouldn't want to do that. In the second place, and more importantly, I can't see them saying, "Sure, d', we'll give you two hundred thousand dollars for a film on Nixon while he's still in the White House." No way. It's a fantastic way to siphon off a lot of social filmic energy by giving people grants because you know they have to conform to certain preconceptions. You write it down and present it and you feel the hard edge that says "No," and the next time you go to bat, you make it a little smoother and more palatable.

And there are all sorts of things investors can get. They get paid back, and in every one of my films, one person who puts in a lot of money gets a huge tax thing. Because when I'm done with a film, I have acquired the biggest library of material on that subject that exists. So then I give that material to that person and say this is a sort of inducement for investing in the film, and then he donates it and it's valued at ninety-five to one hundred thousand dollars. So that's a tremendous tax thing.

I would never put my own money into a film because I feel I have to convince other people that the film should be made and one way of doing that is to get them to put money into it. I put five thousand dollars into the film on the Weather Underground because I couldn't tell anybody about the film. I was meeting with those people and the F.B.I. was looking for them, and I would've broken security. So I put in the first five thousand and Haskell Wexler, who shot it, put in the other five thousand, and we raised the rest. But that first ten thousand dollars—there was no other way I could've asked anybody for that money except on the basis of "I'm making a film I can't tell you about. Give me some money."

It's incumbent upon me to get money from other people. That shows the project isn't just tied up in my own head. That gives it credibility outside of me. I want to control it, but there are other people who have to believe in it. I'm open for criticism: I won't let people look at the film when I'm making it; but I will when it's done, before I mix it, so it's not an idle gesture.

ELIO PETRI

I don't think television has influenced cinema. If anything, the discovery of television has been a positive thing for film, within certain limits. It has, in practice, given cinema back the possibility of being like the theater, a more autonomous means of expression, because a large part of the genres that appeared in film—the Western, the detective film—in practice have been taken over by television. The cinema is in some way more faced with itself, simpler. Many commercial film genres have been practically killed or absorbed by television. Cinema as a nickelodeon doesn't exist anymore. Television is the nickelodeon now. This, too, is a very complicated question of a sociological nature: television, in absorbing film, changes, somehow mystifies it, betrays it. However, this is just film's crisis today. Once again everyone is under the law of profit, authors included, not only the producers, because the authors share the profits. So that there is no longer the possibility to start once again at point zero, something that is indispensable for television.

So, in a certain sense, television has brought cinema back to its original problem: its expressivity. It's clear, though, that the producers are the same, the principles that control distribution and production are the same, and the artist's role is always the same. The problem of expressiveness, of the nakedness of art without compromise, hasn't even been confronted. There's a refusal on the part of all the corporations, the people who make films, to consider this, because things are going all right for them the way they are. But things aren't going well with the public. That's the problem.

Everything is affected by the commercial nature of films: from the number of days you have to shoot to the fact that the actors have to be known. This is a separate story, because often the well-known actors are the best, but the principle is this: You have to have a certain type of film and the film can last only a certain number of hours, etcetera, etcetera. You can make the list yourself. Every minute of film costs money, and the producer wants to spend little and asks that you invest all of yourself into the goal of profit. With us here in Italy cinema is made with the absolute idea of profit-making. All of this, even at the level of the greatest authors, such as Fellini, Antonioni, is unavoidable. You can use the example of the Antonioni film, *Il Grido,* with an American actor, Steve Cochran, as the main character. There was a reason he was cast. *Satyricon* was shot in English—it makes the chickens laugh, as we say. Fellini can give himself airs, but he, too, bows to commercial law. His great outlet is shooting an insane number of weeks, but it doesn't mean anything. On the contrary, it shows how tied he is to the question of time. He unconsciously contests the production by prolonging the shooting. Perhaps von Stroheim was the only director in the world to have ever honestly recognized this dependence. He didn't like the system and he stopped.

Then you also have to look at the positive side of the thing, if you take profit as a symbol, a prize. But I really don't see profit as a prize. I see that profit rewards aggressivity, possessiveness, egoism. So, I personally hold profit as a negative goal of human life. But I say that if a film is rewarded with profit because it has succeeded in honestly communicating things, then at least profit in this case is a positive symptom, a proof that there has been communication. I don't see many other positive things about it.

Even if a director produces his own films, it's very complicated. You end up being more of an exploiter than the others. You pretend you want to protect your art but you only want to get rich. Maybe I'll produce films, but I'll do it to get rich, not to protect the art of film. I don't believe in it, it's all hypocrisy, because the conditions of the market remain the same. If you wanted to "protect your art," you'd have to buy a cinema in Rome, Milan, Florence, Palermo, Bologna, and then show the film only in those cinemas. And it would be horrible if the film turned out to be ugly. I don't believe in defending one's art; people are really defending their patrimony. Sure, if it's for your own amusement, your sense of adventure, great, but then you're producing cinema, you're not defending art. However, it's interesting to see a director producing his own films. It's not always a negative thing. When you make films for a salary, you are a dependent. It's possible I'll produce my next film, but I don't delude myself. I pay myself a salary, but then, if the film makes money, so do I. This is something you have to recognize and not say, "I'm Don Quixote." Going against the current is the only way to fight routine, to fight profit. Being a producer is also being a worker. Producing *Jaws* is like producing shoes; he gets rich. Maybe it's better to make shoes.

GEORGE ROMERO

On the distribution level it all comes down to deal making. We [Laurel Film Group] have rejected a lot of situations because they didn't seem like they were going to do anything. When you're operating outside the mainstream, you have to have a very strong film to come in with it finished and say, "Handle this film." You're fighting a lot of things. First of all, they have so much money tied up in something like *Superman* that you're the poor relative coming in. And to work with them from the jump on something is tough because it will take a year and a half to get the script approved. It's just no fun.

But making films is fun. It's all we ever wanted to do. Making movies should be fun. That's also what I mean about the business of making movies in this country. You get these people who want "to handle" your career. It's not exciting that way. It's a whole other thing: "We'll get you two million dollars for a feature, then a four-million-dollar one, then six million dollars." And if you fuck up along the way, forget it. And what does that mean?

I think the real revolution, which is my hope, is coming with the video disc. In fact, if those disc players catch on, forget it. It's directly analogous to the record industry. First of all, it's familiar, it's not intimidating like the tape decks. There's no piracy factor. They're just players. The audio is impeccable. The stuff comes in a sleeve, it's ten to fifteen bucks—you can buy *Jaws* for fifteen dollars. I think that's going to open things, it's going to blow the roof off, if in five or six years everyone has those players. And then, for the first time, the artist will be put in direct contact with the audience. There is no such thing today. You either have to have a network or you have to go to PBS or you have to go to one of these theatrical distributors; so if you make a film, there's maybe forty people you can go to. You've got to sell one of those forty before you can get to anyone else. And this will be the first time where if I have a film I want to make, I'll make it and I'll go somewhere and press a master disc and then press one hundred thousand discs. You can shoot either film or tape and press it onto one of those discs. And somehow I'll sell them. People say it's frightening, and it is in a certain sense because *National Geographic* will be coming out on disc rather than on paper, and people aren't reading enough as it is, but aside from that, it's really going to blow the roof off if it clicks. So I have really high hopes, just in terms of being able to do things.

MARTIN SCORSESE

We're not as free as we used to be in the early sixties in Hollywood. It's kind of regressed, actually. I think that some of us who came up in the early sixties got ourselves saddled with "big" movies, at times, and that can be the *métier* of some of the guys, that's what they want to do, that's what they're going to do, and that's fine, but, myself, when I found myself saddled with that on *Raging Bull*, I got nervous, and felt I was regressing. Because it was "We can make the shot, but the crane . . . which crane can we bring in?" It takes hours to bring in the crane and it went on and on like that. Finally, I felt I was dealing with dinosaurs, until we left California and came to New York. But when we hit New York, of course, we had other problems. We had union problems and police problems: the police department wasn't very helpful. *Taxi Driver* was fine, but that was 1975. Our names weren't very well-known then, and everybody was very nice to us, everybody was great. Now, with *Raging Bull*, all of a sudden, we couldn't turn around without it costing us millions. But that will come out later when I open the film. We just can't do that anymore. You can't consider the cost; you have to consider the aesthetics. When I started choosing locations for this film, which was shot in black-and-white, I found it was much more difficult, because nobody knew how to process black-and-white film anymore. The same thing happened to Woody Allen, so that whole technology has to come back. It's a shame; we have to get back to a sense of freedom of movement. And I don't mean a hand-held, shaking camera, although I may do that next—I don't know. But I mean just being able to use black-and-white film, to be able just to move, making things easier. Basically, if I choose a location that is the size of a fairly small bedroom—a lot of scenes in my movies take place in bathrooms, real bathrooms—I'll use one camera, maybe even two, with a small lens on it. So I chose locations for *Raging Bull* the way I used to: small room, small this, small that, and I found that we got in there with two cameras and the lenses are even bigger than the camera, and we are limited in that space. But why should we be limited? It seems to me that the use of technology is slipping behind in filmmaking, and, in a way, people on the crew are added because you're no longer independent. The technology, which is getting lazy, means you can't use a small location because it's too small to contain the cameras, the lenses, and the crew members. So I have to choose a location which is not as real as I want it, and we refurbish it to make it look real. So I decided "No." I wanted to use the small places where I used to be able to shoot, but when we went in with two cameras, it was a nightmare. There is lighter-weight equipment but nobody is using it: it's bigger cameras, bigger lenses, more people, more people, and more people: "Please, quiet on the set, please get everybody out." It gets to the point where you can't even fucking turn. So from now on I'm going to do other things, and whatever they're going to be, they're going to be. I don't know. We're trying everything. With all this aggravation, we also realize that the films aren't going to last, because the color stock is made to fade: a print has a life expectancy of six years. A negative has nine, ten years. That's sad, a horror, and I feel we are being sold out. They don't even put it on their film cans: "This film will fade." This is Eastman Kodak who's doing this. There's got to be some research to find a new way of insuring that color stock will last. The American filmmakers, the cinematographers, even the actors—because if they think their performances are going to be preserved on film, I have news for them—are going to have to get together. Even when you transfer to videotape it isn't effective because you can't see the image—it's faded away.

We have sent out seven hundred and fifty letters and what we really have to go for is a revolution. If we have to use other stock, we will, or we'll go to videotape. Everyone who cares should do something, and eventually it'll reach the public because the snapshots they're taking fade in about a year and a half or two. And then archival pictures with anthropological interest, pictures one hundred and fifty years old, should be preserved, but what will you transfer them to? I'm not a chemist or a physicist—that's the problem, I don't know the process, but I have to make the movie and it's going to fade and I'm angry. The filmmakers should get crazy about this, and then we need the people with the cool heads to come in and tell us what can be done and what can't. Then we can make our decision. But it's got to come from us, because the film comes from us. That's the way it should be. Naturally, some aren't going to do it. But we shouldn't have to go to Germany or Japan for a product; it should be here in America. Film is *the* American art form. Why should Eastman Kodak do this to themselves? It's crazy. It is, of course, a big problem because the machinery is revolving around a certain way of doing things and what we're suggesting is another way. Maybe in ten years it can be switched over. We'll all work together on it. But I *can* get angry about it and I *am* angry about it, because they don't care. We're going up to Rochester soon—they're being very open about it—but nobody even knows what the possibilities are with video and how it can relieve this and other problems.

I had to go to Kansas City to show a product reel of *Raging Bull*, a fourteen-minute trailer. I didn't even know Kansas City was in Missouri, but I was there for a day and a half. And I went there because there was a meeting of theater owners called "Showarama." I'm very glad I went there. United Artists was showing all their product and the longest product reel was ours. It was interesting to see such an ethnic kind of film, black and white, certainly very strange: it's a rude film at times, very funny but very rude. I would like to see more of these exhibitors because these are the people who show the films in their theaters. On the other hand, they have to remember that something else is happening, that films are being made directly for cable and cassette and this will increase. If they don't want to promote my films and put money into them, maybe I'll work with smaller budgets and make films only for cable, maybe there will be more people watching on cable. There will be a whole other way, because some of the things I'm planning may possibly be too disturbing or the language might be too much or whatever else. Then that kind of film can be made for video systems and another kind for theaters. We should all work together, but everybody has to realize the possibilities, and we can all do what we want. But the main thing is if everyone works together, not against each other. The exhibitors shouldn't be threatened by cable and television—it will actually give them more product.

On the best video systems right now, you get eight channels with fine reception if you're far away enough from the set, and when I play three-quarter-inch tapes of my movies, they look fantastic. But imagine if we ever get the Italian, or French, or the English systems, with their great image; we could work it all together. Of course, the whole television situation here is run on a system, and imagine changing the entire system. But we're working on it and there may be another way: shoot a film on their system and transfer it to film. There's a laser-beam technique I saw in Japan to make the transfer—tape to laser to film—and if you shoot on an English system and transfer to film, you'd probably be cutting your production costs. That's what I'm interested in. There's so many possibilities that the next ten years are going to be extraordinary. These projection television screens are being bought right now by people for their offices, and the ones I saw in Japan are bigger, the size of the wall and more, and in about five, six years, everybody will have screens this size at least; whether the quality will be good or not, I don't know. And, of course, it depends on reception. This will open up the market for more filmmakers, as they will need product, especially with the cassette market opening. Ma-

jor companies in Hollywood are not only making films but picking up twelve, fifteen films a year just for distribution—films that wouldn't have been picked up years ago, and I mean only three years ago.

ERMANNO OLMI

Since ours is a society that strains to reach certain objectives, of which profit towers above all others, it's obvious that cinema as a means of communication, as a mass medium, is strongly, intensely, utilized to this end: profit, which is not solely economic—it could be ideological profit. But I believe that any event produces certain negative effects that were meant to be produced by betraying certain ideas, but at the same time, inevitably, there is a revolt against these exploiters both on the part of those who produce and those who consume. Talking about economics: in the name of work for all and the growth of well-being, etcetera, the economy initiates its own strategies of profit, by which there are periods when man, within this design constructed by a few, falls into a trap. There comes the time when this same economy revolts and turns against its own little protagonists—the worker who is forced to be in the factory. At the end they raise this revolt and succeed in involving the organizers of profit. So one arrives at a taking of account. So it is in cinema. The suggestive ability of the cinematographic machine, so exploited by these profit sharks, doesn't just go along corrupting its suggestion. At the beginning, when the audience saw a train on the screen rushing towards them, they hid under the seats. They were afraid, owing to the power of suggestion of the film. Today, to give a little suggestion, they have to stab people in the stomach, things like that. They're paying a very high price. It's not that I'm an optimist at all costs, but I believe in the will to survive of life itself, and that when we have come to the end of our cunning and cleverness to trick the earth, to make it produce more, it will revolt against us. It's not just a discussion that involves film, because film goes ahead in the

general noise of all the rest. That's why film *auteurs* today, those who have the talent to make quality films, are strongly influenced by this anxiety for economic success. For example, if their film doesn't make millions, many directors feel inferior to their fellow director whose film made more. Cinema is within this logic of exaggerated profit. The moment will come when we will be so pained by the choices we have made that we will go back to looking at ourselves, to looking into each other's eyes more sincerely.

CHANTAL AKERMAN

Unfortunately you have to concern yourself after a while with the economic realities of film as a mass medium, because here I am now in Paris, and I know exactly when my film is in a theater and how much it's making. And I know that if my next film is going to get financed, I have to be concerned. I have to find the right things to do at the right moment—not to be in advance, to reach just the right point. It's very hard because, let's say, you're writing now and it's taking six months or whatever, then it's finished. Then you will have to find the money. It takes six months to a year, two years or more; then you are going to make it, and, after four years, maybe your subject is not accurate anymore. So you have to be very quick and feel the right moment.

Every subject is interesting, you know. You just have to make it the right way. If you want to make a love story, it could be fascinating. You don't have to refuse it because others have made conventional love stories. The point is that it's also the style that matters. My style is difficult, but still I must reach the public in my next movie in order to keep going. It's an odd period right now; we can't afford to make films without money. It was not like that five years ago. I'm very susprised because all the people who were leftists and who wanted to see art movies don't go so much now. It's getting into very strange things, like it's immoral now not to make money. You have made a movie

and if it doesn't make money, it's immoral. It would have been possible to tell your story and not be *just* right, but, for the moment, you cannot afford to do that. It's very difficult.

My films are distributed, but they are too difficult for some. For me, however, they're too simple. I don't know, it's like the fifties now. People want to cry, to be afraid, to laugh—things like that. It was not like that three, four years ago. And look at all the movies that make money about the fifties. We are going backwards. We'll see what happens in the U.S., and we are going to follow that here in France. So we will have to keep alive for the next ten years. It's a question of life and death. It's certain that they think they don't need us, the filmmakers. They do need us, in fact, if you consider time, but for the moment they don't need us. They want really to destroy everything that is not productive in what they think is the right way, because it's such a big prize and next year it will be more and more.

JACQUES DEMY

I wrote five screenplays in four years, but I hadn't worked for five years before this new film, *Lady Oscar*. I was writing musicals, one with Yves Montand, mainly about his life; he's a great performer, a fantastic singer. I loved it, and Montand was so enthusiastic he said, "I don't want to be paid. I'll put my salary into the production to be part of it." But we couldn't find anyone interested. I also wrote a screenplay about a strike in France. It's a true love story about my father, and I wanted to make a sort of opera about it. I worked on it for two years and then it was put to music from beginning to end. It's a beautiful piece of work, but I never found anybody interested in that either, and it's a low-budget film. I could've made it in France for five hundred thousand dollars, and that's pretty cheap for a musical. I saw everybody in the business in Paris, and nobody wanted to do it. They were scared, scared of the subject matter, scared of the singing, which was pop, scared of the new sort of product that it was going to be. And they said, "You've done that in *Umbrellas of Cherbourg*, why do you bother to do it again?" I said, "Look at people who wrote operas or operettas or musicals. They have been doing that all their lives, not only once or twice, but ten, twenty times, and that's what I want to do." But we couldn't find anyone interested: "The French don't like musicals." That's what the distributors and the producers said, and then comes *Saturday Night Fever* or *Grease* and they are smash hits! I said, "What are you telling me? What are you talking about? I made two musicals and they were successful all over the world, and you're telling me musicals don't work!"

So, after five years, I decided to quit the movie business altogether. Period. I said, "This is enough!" In February it would be five years, and I would quit: "Fuck you, I don't care about that anymore." I cannot write and write and write screenplays which have no value as long as they stay screenplays. You write a novel, it can be published, but a screenplay is nothing. I sat down and started to write novels and to paint, and I was starving to learn piano. I thought that would be a good life, a good way to express myself, since there is no way left for me in the movie business any longer. And then in late January, I got a call from the Japanese to do *Lady Oscar*. It sounded so nice, so crazy, so weird, that I said yes right away. And I felt somehow that the movie was for me. After the five-year nightmare it was a fairy tale; I haven't seen any of my friends in the movie business have such luck, such a dream.

So I don't know what to say now. I was ready to give up, but there's always hope coming from somewhere. So don't be in despair. Learn how to "play the piano" and then something will come up.

MICHAEL POWELL

With the exceptions of Hecht and MacArthur and maybe one or two others, I don't think there has ever been a team of director-writer-producer like Emeric Pressburger and myself who have turned out so many films. We probably made about sixteen or seventeen films together, and the majority were from original ideas.

I was a struggling director, very ambitious and impatient, and I couldn't understand why I wasn't given enormous pictures to do when I was very young. When I got the first chance from Alexander Korda, I was ready to grab anything that came along. At that time Emeric was under contract to Korda as a writer and he had made his reputation with Ufer in Germany—at one point he was their highest-priced writer. He and Anatole Litvak and Billy Wilder were all there at the same time and Emeric was certainly the top screenwriter. He never expected to be anything but a writer. I remember when Korda introduced us we started right away rewriting the script of *U-Boat* with the two stars, and this established a way of working together with the actors and with ourselves, with me as the director and him as the writer.

Then we did another film. This time I said to him, "Why don't you write an original thriller about the blackout in London because nobody knows anything about it?" So we did, and it was my leadership, really, as I was the producer-director and he was the writer. But we were still working together in the same way: we would exchange ideas and we would talk it over with the lead actor, Conrad Veidt, and the actress, Valerie Hobson. By now everyone knew me as a hard-working young director, and they also realized that there was a menace, a portent, around the corner, so the government said they were going to have a policy of making films on the war. They didn't want the film business to vanish just because the Americans had to go home. So I brought Emeric into *The Invaders* as the writer. Again, I was the director-producer; in other words, nobody could contradict me except my writer, and by this time we realized we were working together like a beautiful engine. We would suggest ideas to each other, Emeric would develop them, I would improve them—that way. And so Emeric said to me, "Why don't we form a company and just make films together?" We didn't discuss credit. I said, "Fine, it's a good idea. I'd like to do that." So, when my agent said to me, "Well, how do you see this company?" I said, "Oh well, we'll split the whole thing fifty-fifty down the middle: fifty-fifty credits and fifty-fifty profits, if there are any. And fees the same way." He was quite shocked: "You're a producer-director and he's only a writer!" I said, "I don't agree that he's *only* a writer. He's a first-rate writer and they're very hard to find, and, anyway, we work together like that and it's fifty-fifty from now on." And that's how it started. And we decided to just have one title, "written, produced, and directed by Michael Powell and Emeric Pressburger." But, of course, I was always the director.

We called ourselves "The Archers," and we had a target with an arrow and it got very popular as a screen logo. You saw the target and you heard the sound and then the arrow hit the target. At first, we didn't have it hit the center of the target, and then the second film we made was in color and somebody said to us, "Why the hell don't you hit the center of the target?" We said, "Well, we thought it was being a bit, you know, too cocky." And he said, "Oh the hell with that, hit the center."

But I have ten complete scripts that never got done, and two shelves of books that I would have liked to have done but never have. I can tell you that because whenever there was something that I wanted to do and nobody would listen, I'd put it on a special shelf, and there are now two shelves.

In the case of *The Tempest*, I tried first of all to get people interested, and I wrote it with James Mason in mind as Prospero from the very beginning. We had two or three complete casts at different times, because you can't keep such a distinguished group of actors as you want for a thing like that together for very long. But it really worked marvelously as a project. I had quite a good idea of how to tell the story of *The Tempest*. Half a dozen Mediterranean countries were crazy to have it done there. I particularly liked Egypt. You could have a couple small pyramids in it and Caliban could be sitting on the top of a very small one. But I don't think the businessmen ever read it or could read it. I think they thought it would be like the stage *Tempest* on film. They couldn't visualize it. You have to sit down and read it, after all, and no distributor or financier can read. They really can't. They wouldn't know the difference between *Othello* and *The Tempest*. They just lump them together as Shakespeare. And so, unless they trust you—and I'm regarded as highly unpredictable—it might be absolutely wonderful, they think, or it might be one of the biggest disasters ever. So, although I could raise money abroad, I should have come here really. I couldn't raise money in England. And the people abroad got wind of it and they said, "Well, why won't the British put up the money? It's a British subject. Shakespeare, it seems to us, was a British poet." So that's the way it works, you see. I wasted four years on that. Full of enthusiasm and I thought it would really come off but it didn't.

ROBERT ALTMAN

It comes down to the filthy lucre. If you could get all the high profit out of film, you would be left with people who love it. And the rest of the guys would go out and say, "Let's open a shoe factory," or "Let's open a disco and sell coke." And that's why you probably have better filmmakers amongst the ones who have not made it commercially—or potentially better filmmakers—in Europe, because they just don't make that kind of money. I'm not going to talk names, but ninety percent of the American directors are concerned with "What's my fee?" and "Where's my ascot, where's my chair?" "Give me the money and I'll do the film."

Rossellini is an exception, but it's a much shorter life span for a filmmaker than for a novelist or a painter. It's because filmmakers have to show all their work. They're not allowed to destroy any of it or hide it or put it aside and bring it out ten years later when they may be highly successful. And they're under the gun all the time. Also, as they succeed, they receive such adulation: people say, "Oh, you're the greatest filmmaker in the world, I'd like to come work for you for free. I'll polish your shoes and bring you coffee," and all of this stuff, and you can't ignore that. You have to kind of go, "Oh, well, I'm not really that good, kid." And eventually that rubs off on you. And then you get to where people who work with you don't disagree with you. No matter what you say, they say, "Oh, that's a terrific idea." And you say, "Yeah, that's fine, have another hit and let's talk more story." And the next thing you know, it's too much too soon too fast. And the work diminishes. The other thing is that the process of film itself changes very quickly. Television has taught audiences a great deal about how to view images. Commercials particularly—they tell a story in twenty seconds and do it well. So somebody like Billy Wilder, William Wyler, Hawks, these filmmakers who did just great, marvelous work, they can't make that shift. In fact, I couldn't make that shift to do something that I don't do. I try to keep myself open, but I know that eventually it's going to be impossible, and if we had this same interview five or six years from now, it would be *"When* you *were* one of the leading filmmakers . . . what do you think happened?"* But it's going to happen and it's going to happen to everybody unless they're extraordinarily lucky or they contain some kind of genius that allows them to ignore that.

Right now my process is to work on several films at the same time. I have several scripts being done; I have planning being done. It's like cooking *pommes soufflées*: the first one that pops to the top is the first one ready. It's not necessarily the first one you put in the pot.

I have a lot of hardware and people who are on the payroll all the time and have to be fed and so we have to keep everybody pretty active. And the best way to do it is to make films, and it's also the happiest time of my life—when I'm working with creative people. The unhappiest time of my life is like right now, on *Popeye,* when I'm dealing with all the foolish business things you have to go through, the waste of egos and time. But maybe it's necessary, maybe you need that to look back on.

Probably the closest film to get going that was aborted was *The Yag Epoxy* with Peter Falk for Warner Brothers. We actually had started the set and were in the process of casting. And then the studio started putting too much control on it, to change it, and put too many elements in it that I felt didn't belong. So I just passed on it. That was the closest to getting started. *Ragtime* I worked on for about a year. That was when we first went to Malta, to see about doing *Ragtime* there. We were thinking about building New York City there, because the one place you can't build New York City is here in New York City. But I lost that. *North Dallas Forty*—I had that one for a while. When *Buffalo Bill* failed, I had three projects with Dino De Laurentiis and we're in a court of law over this because he just took them away and refused to pay.

It's like gambling: if you win the first race, you get to bet more in the second. All filmmakers feel their film should succeed and the studios and distributors did it badly, but that's not true. There are some films of mine—and I'll speak only of my films—that I think no matter what, they would not have succeeded with the public. There are other films, however, that I feel would've definitely succeeded had they been handled in a different manner, and there are some that I think are toss-ups.

You've got to be half salesman, half con artist and a hustler. But I'm at the point now where I'm not going to starve to death. I don't have any money amassed but I don't have any need for it. I can go speak at colleges and pick up enough money and keep myself busy for a while, and I'm old enough where I don't really give a shit. I'll always try to keep making films. I think that if *Popeye* is a success, that will give me five more movies. I'd almost rather be in that position. I think it helps to keep you active. Anything that helps keep your arrogance at a tolerable level is important, and I think you've got to be in a little bit of jeopardy all the time. It's absurd but that's the problem when you're dealing with a so-called art form that requires so much cash money to realize it. In other words, to make a movie—I don't care how cheap you go—it's still very, very expensive.

I don't know how this system could be changed. I haven't the slightest idea. But in the first place I don't think cinemas should be put in shopping centers. I think drive-ins should be blown up. I don't think films should be shown on airplanes. I don't think films should be shown on television. I think theaters should be placed better; they should be more attractive. I think their equipment should be brought up to date. They should be more pleasant places to go and they should be special places, the way they originally were. As far as distribution is concerned, we [Lion's Gate] have distributed by ourselves. We distributed *Welcome to L.A., Remember My Name.* And we're always looking for a deal with an independent film with independent money in order to get a new way of distribution. But the exhibitors have you: you know, you have to be able to get so many play dates to get some money out of it. You've got to be able to play the shopping center in Houston, Texas, where the lady and her daughter have an hour: "Oh, let's stop in and see an hour of this movie."

Video discs are something Lion's Gate is going to do very heavily, very seriously. We made a deal with the Shuberts and with ABC, which we will announce next week some time. And we're going to start stacking plays that could not have been made into films, but we're not going to photograph them as plays. We may really abstract them. None of these are plays we have the rights to, but plays like *Wings, Colored Girls,* the Sylvia Plath, *Letters Home,* plays that didn't succeed or wouldn't be bought to make a movie out of, like *Lone Star,* although something like *Lone Star* probably could be made into a film. Doing things and then stacking them requires somebody with a lot of money and a lot of guts, but eventually that's going to open up into a very big thing. I think it will happen in five years and that means three. I think the most optimistic approach is it will be faster. You're selling to an elite audience. It's like publishing: the hard cover luxury volume as opposed to paperbacks. You put it in your library and you don't have to use them, but you can. We plan to expand from theater into music, like records. There's a big problem of structure: you have to get into royalties, rights, copyrights, and who owns what. It's going to be a legal mess, but I think it's going to be it. And, then, you can also do things in your own time frame; they don't have to be one hour and fifty minutes long. I don't happen to own any of my own films, so I can't make them into video discs; the distributors can burn them if they want. I let go of a film when it opens. It's like the bar mitzvah or the kid who goes to college: "See ya. Call me if you need help, but up to a point. If you need too much help, don't call."

I've been very very lucky. I think I've been the luckiest of all the people I know that are dealing in film. It's certainly not by intelligence. It's by timing and by luck.

PHILIP MESSINA

The biggest problem with the art form right now is the fact that it is totally controlled by banks, which now take the form of several companies: MGM, United Artists, Warner Brothers, Paramount, and so on. And these companies are interested in a certain kind of commodity that's going to realize an enormous zillion dollars. The whole system tends to move upwards in dollars constantly, so that realm is way out of the grasp of the young filmmaker, a kid coming out of film school. It's ridiculous. The only real possibility for movies, I think, is low-budget 16mm pictures. It is absolutely astounding that in this economy, at a time when the major studios only produce about twenty, thirty pictures a year total, there isn't a thriving low-budget industry of B movies and melodramas and all kinds of things. You would think there'd be a natural gravitation for investment in that area. TV needs it tremendously, and I've been involved in that area. I've been involved in trying to raise money to do three- or four-hundred-thousand-dollar movies, working with non-union crews and actor friends, and it's extremely difficult to do. The reason is really basic: most Americans who have money don't want to know from art. They're not interested. They want to know if I'm realizing a profit, and it doesn't matter if you're talking about a twenty-five-million-dollar picture that's being directed by Stephen Spielberg or a three-hundred-thousand-dollar picture that's being directed by Joe Schmo. The investors are going to read the script, and they're going to say, "What the hell is this? What the hell is this thing? It's got no story, it's got no plot, there's no action, nobody gets killed, it's not funny," or whatever they think. It's happening to me with my screenplay, *Overtime:* "I think it's a terrific script but it doesn't seem commercial to me"—whatever that means. So the problem still exists that you have to convince money, whether it's two hundred thousand or two hundred million or twenty billion, that it's going to realize itself in a tremendous amount more. So what happens is the people who get money are the salesmen, are the sellers, are the hustlers, which has always been the case anyway. And much more so in this country than in Europe because there people are much more receptive to the artistic. In Europe it's conceivable to sit down and talk to a man who's got a few dollars, an intellectual, and he'll consider backing a hundred-thousand-dollar feature about so and so. In this country it's just much more difficult.

If you want to raise three hundred thousand dollars, the first thing any investor is going to do is call the nearest investment broker and say, "Who do you know in the movie business?" and the first advice he's going to get is, "Ask the kid if he's got a distribution deal," meaning does he have some distributor who is willing to commit to distributing the picture. And if you're an unknown and you've got a good script but you don't have a star, you don't have a bankable director, you are not going to get a distribution deal. So it's a self-fulfilling prophesy. So what do you do? You say, "Well, this is just ridiculous. I can't do this. I'm going to get me a star." So the first thing you do, like I did, is start soliciting knowns and get a couple of known actors. Then the whole ball game changes and the budget goes way up, because they want more money. Their agents aren't going to let them do a low-budget New York picture: "What are you crazy? That's like slitting your own throat! Who is this guy from New York that's got this nice script? What studio's doing it? What are you going to get?" They scare the shit out of their own stars. Stars are scared. They don't want to lose whatever power they've got. So if they really like it, if it's a really big star, the big star will say, "Well, we love the script but you can't direct it. You're not a known director."

The whole problem of bankability is what kills everybody. As soon as you get a real star involved, the ante goes way up. They cannot work non-union, so the budget goes way up. Now, in order to get two or three million dollars, you're dealing in another league. And you need a producer, you need a lot of other things.

The studios are not interested in cultivating all the talent because they have a monopoly, a stranglehold on the available material. Why should they produce six or seven independent one- or two-million-dollar pictures with relative unknowns when they can pay that same six million dollars that they would have spent for six pictures and pump it into Stephen Spielberg and Richard Dreyfuss with a fairly commercial glitzy product and have one bonanza picture that takes the place of all six? So what they do is create a complete scarcity in the market so everybody's dying to go to a movie. The only thing to see is the one movie they've made, so you go and see it.

There's no lively, accessible industry outside that system, and the problem, the truth of the matter is, that most filmmakers, by the time they ever get a picture made, are so frustrated from struggling and killing themselves that their managers rush to the nearest studio to get a nice, cushy development deal, a nice, cushy directing deal. They want it. Look, first and foremost they are all artists, they want to make their art. And anybody who has made an independent film knows what kind of struggle it is. It's really hard. It takes years and years of your life. I couldn't do it. I mean, I did it with documentaries, I did a few shorts, but to do a feature film requires a certain kind of push, energy, and dedication. It's very, very hard to sustain, especially after you've spent three years writing the script, rewriting, and writing, and rewriting, and being pushed around by this producer and hung on a string by this one and that one and so on, so that unless you're independently wealthy, the odds against you ever getting any money are just tremendous.

The only light that I see is that the technology is continually getting simpler and more accessible, and even the video cassettes and the disc technology is really going to make people realize that there is a market for pictures that are not necessarily blockbusters but, like *Girlfriends*, which cost three, four hundred thousand dollars, or a 16mm blow-up like *Outrageous*, will make a profit. The record industry can accommodate jazz musicians who only sell one hundred thousand records; that's all they are ever expected to sell to make a profit. If you'd keep the cost down, you could make a profit from low-budget movies.

The thing that amazes me is that most of what filmmakers do is dealmaking: waiting for a deal, negotiating a writing script, waiting for some studio to agree or not agree. Filmmakers end up becoming like a strange kind of artist without his art. And this is an area that is completely ignored, never dealt with at large. I don't even know any filmmakers who are twenty-five; the average feature-maker can be thirty-five, forty years old before they ever make a film.

I mean, it's incredible that after a while you start talking about a million and a half dollars like it's a little bit of money. Five million is medium-budget, fifteen million is larger. You can build six houses for two million dollars. And we're in that league, so we're dealing with businessmen, with brokerage houses, with depletion bonds, with stars, with agents, with lawyers, and lawyers, and more lawyers and more negotiation, and it's constant.

And the productorial thing of points in back of the scene: "Fifty percent of this and print costs and two percent of the gross and a half a point later on and what happens in this case and what happens in that case. What about stars, what percent are the stars going to get, and the producer doesn't want this and he doesn't want that." This is the stuff that's been occupying the last year of my life, waiting for this thing to happen, waiting for that thing to happen. The creative time spent has been one tenth of that.

It's incredibly fascinating. It's a whole entity unto itself, a whole scenario of intrigue. And they're into it. They are so completely into it that it's all they talk about. You make the deal, you shoot the deal, you edit the deal, and you release the deal. And you hope that the deal pays off. That's what it's about. It's a pizza pie going into the oven. You know, you take it out and you sell it. It's amazing: each component has its constituency, its legal representation, its agents, its own legal staff. It goes ad infinitum. And an entire city in the United States is devoted to that—Los Angeles. So, to me, it's a miracle when a movie ever gets to the screen, and if it's any good on top of that, it's pretty remarkable.

BARBARA KOPPLE

I scraped for the four years I was making *Harlan County*. At the end I was sixty thousand dollars in debt. I would go down there for six months, race home to New York, try to do a whole fund-raising thing, write desperate letters to people. We did the very best we could whether we had a lot of money or not. Being sixty thousand dollars in debt means I didn't scrimp on anything. We got as much footage as we needed, the very best people that we could get to work with us, who cared about it, which is so important to me. It's hard to work with people who are just doing a job. We did the very best we could and money had nothing to do with it. A little thing like money wasn't going to stop me from doing the film.

Some people may have their own money but they would never put it into their own film; but anything I could get my hands on—I used to look around this loft and say, "What can I sell?" I would just throw anything I had into it because that's what I wanted to do. I wouldn't wait until somebody came and said to me, "Here's some money." Anything I could scavenge together I would. Right now I do speaking tours and all that just goes into Cabin Creek Productions to pay people's salaries, to keep going forward, to do more research, whatever it is. I live from hand-to-mouth anyway.

And I don't think distribution is the problem. I think that if the film has quality, people will show it. I never worry about distribution. What I worry about is how to get the money just to do the film, because *Harlan County* showed in theaters throughout the country. In Boston it was the second top-grossing film, and wherever the area did really good publicity, the film did really well. Cinema Five was distributing it, but that didn't happen until after the film was made.

The film had showed at the New York Film Festival, and Rugoff [the owner of Cinema Five] who's a little crazy, fell asleep during the show—naturally—and the applause woke him up. So he didn't believe that the applause was for the movie. He believed that it was applause for Hazel Dickens. We did a whole number at the festival. Usually, they have this spotlight box, and you're supposed to stand up and they shine a spotlight on you and you take a bow. I just couldn't handle that. I just didn't want to do it. So I told the head of the festival, Richard Roud, "We have Hazel Dickens in the group and she's a coal miner's daughter. She's written most of the songs in *Harlan,* and we want to sing the last song of the film as the credits are going and fading out. And she'll be there singing when the house lights come on." He said, "We can't do that. It's not the tradition. You must stand in the spotlight box." I said, "None of us will be there." And he said, "Well, we're going to shine it." And I said, "Don't because we're going to be on the stage. Save the electricity." And so he just threw up his hands. He didn't want to do it, but we did it and it was incredible. I also Xeroxed one thousand song sheets, paid the ushers some money to put them in the programs, and the whole audience sang and danced, and all the miners and their wives and the lead people came out and sort of danced behind Hazel. It was really great.

So Rugoff had fallen asleep and figured that the clapping was for the music, so he offered me this ridiculous deal. I was trying to figure out at the time how I was going to distribute this film because I just deal with one step at a time. I was going to do self-distribution, and a group of people had helped me raise money so I could do that. Then I thought that I really didn't want to do that. I want to keep making films and keep moving forward and let this have a life of its own. So I went in and negotiated a somewhat better deal with Rugoff and let him do it.

I would work with a major studio if they were willing to let me do the kind of films I want to do. It's much easier in fund raising to be able to get the money you need and concentrate all the energy on the content of the film. Now my head is split in two. Half of it deals with continuing with the film, continuing with the content. The other half deals with how I raise money to keep going, since nobody has ever given me money and said, "Okay, go ahead and do it." If somebody did, I don't know what I'd do with this side of my head. It would take a while for me to say, "You mean I don't have to think about this anymore? I don't have to do foundation proposals? I don't have to think about who might want to invest, or donate, or give a grant, or whatever?" Most people think if they don't get money, they can't do their project, but I know there's another way. Maybe it's going to take longer and involve a lot of scrambling, but you can do it and that's what keeps me going. So if somebody who has money says no to me, it doesn't bother me; I just say, "Okay, that's a no. How do I proceed, how do I keep going?"

MARK RAPPAPORT

My first film was done out of pocket. I was earning a living while I was making the film. The budget was seven thousand dollars. But I had made several shots before that. Every time I would run out of film, I would have to go back to work, so that's why it took a year and a half to make. Then I've gotten grants and sales from previous films that have helped pay for subsequent films. My last film was made for German television, and I'm beginning to realize that my future is probably more with European financing, partly because they don't have that much money and so they are interested in backing a really low-budget film. I also know how to make a really low-budget film, but you can't have horses or simulated war in a really low-budget film. So what does low budget mean? It means an intimate little melodrama. How fortunate for me that that's what I'm interested in anyway. On the other hand, that may be why I'm attracted to this kind of low-budget filmmaking, because that's where my interests are and if I wanted to make a spectacle that required six million extras dressed in Roman gladiator costumes, I'd have to learn to play Hollywood better.

Beauty is expensive to make, especially with escalating costs, and it's the first thing to fall by the wayside. You figure you can't afford a tracking shot in this scene, so forget it. You can't build a whole set for one scene, it's too expensive, so forget that. This is the financing of beauty and the politics of low-budget filmmaking. Nobody really talks a whole lot about the politics of low-budget filmmaking and the ways in which financial restrictions determine aesthetics.

HENRY JAGLOM

Bert Schneider produced my first movie. I had cut *Easy Rider* from five and a half hours: Jack Nicholson and I really cut it down into its present shape under Bert Schneider's supervision. I had gone to Israel during the Six Day War and bought a little 8mm Instamatic camera. Because I didn't know anything about cutting—I was scared of the technology, which I'm still very bad at—I cut *in* the picture while shooting. In other words, I ran up to a soldier and did a close-up and then ran back to get a long shot. Then I did a panning shot of the tanks and then I ran up to get a close-up of it. I didn't know that you could do them at different times and later cut them and put them together. I believed in movies. I grew up on them. I thought that one shot came after another shot as it did in completed films. I had had access, because of my relations with many people in Israel, to a lot of things, restricted locations, army camps, and so on, so I had made an extraordinary little 8mm home movie on the war. I can't believe how I bored my friends with it, made them sit through it endlessly, but one of those friends was Bert Schneider.

Two years later, he was having trouble with the first movie he produced; Dennis Hopper had made *Easy Rider* and it was five hours long, and Dennis had decided it was in perfect shape at that length and didn't want to cut it anymore. So Bert remembered my Israeli home movie, and I spent eight weeks with Jack, Dennis, Bert, and Bob Rafelson cutting it down to its present shape. It was an incredible experience. Bert was really the man responsible, but everybody connected with that film got a chance later to direct his own movie. That would have been unheard of in the past. An editor would have been an editor for the rest of his life. That's how I got to do *A Safe Place*. *Tracks* was financed by a tax shelter group.

Now that's finished, but when you're using the corruption of a system, they're only interested in their corruption. They want to make money. They don't care about final cut. *Sitting Ducks*, my third film, is independently financed, and what has happened now is that my films have done very well in Europe. They don't do much business here so far. Maybe *Sitting Ducks* will; it looks like it might be the first commercial one here in America, but I really don't know. The others don't do much here except on college campuses. They're cult films; they have very nice, bright audiences. They respond strongly but the films can't make money that way. But German television has just paid me a fortune for *Sitting Ducks* and for my first two movies and for my next movie without knowing what it is. The contract calls for "Jaglom number four." And the Italians and the French and the Scandinavians, the Spanish and the Japanese are lining up to pay me money for future films, so I can essentially make as many films as I want now and have complete control and freedom as long as I keep the economics reasonable, which is really quite easy to do.

Now that kind of financing was impossible when Orson Welles was making films, when he started, for instance. And it's a shame, it's a crime. Imagine what things we're not going to see from Orson Welles. Still, with all the pain, he's managed to make some extraordinarily good films, one after another, but not nearly enough.

So I could get the money for any film. It's always distribution. Columbia, for example, did *A Safe Place*, but Bert Schneider was there to protect me. They didn't release it right, so I made a deal with them. I said, "You don't want this. You

don't know what to do with this. It's going to cost you money.
I'll make a deal. I'll take it away from you and I'll release it
myself and make all the arrangements and we'll split fifty-fifty."
As a result of that I've made a lot of money. If it had been a big
success on the original deal, I wouldn't have made a penny.
Ironic. I took it to Cannes. I found these French people who
loved it, they showed it, and it made a lot of money in France,
and, as a result, in Italy, England, Germany, and so on. And I
get fifty percent of all the money that it makes because Columbia is no longer involved. Here it's being distributed by a small
company. They can't do more than they can do, so the chances
are it's always going to be a sort of cult film here.

What I like is that I think of films very much as paintings in a
sense: once you're through with them *they exist*. Forget the economics. Forget how much it costs. That's not really what's important, finally. You made it work. It's got this shape to it. It
exists in these five cans and it will continue to exist, like a painting. It will show here and there. You know, Orson Welles said
to me early on when I was making my first movie and everybody was trying to pressure me to make it commercial, "You've
got to make a movie that you are happy to live with the rest of
your life. Because you're going to keep seeing it forever, and
you might as well make it for you. Nobody knows what's commercial anyway. Don't worry about that." And I did that and
I've been doing that with each of my movies and I love it, because every week I get invited to go to a festival in this city or
that country. You know, it's a cottage industry. I can make
quite a living traveling around the world, showing my films. I
love it. The films have their own life.

There's a different reason for television than for movies.
Television has to sell stuff. But I think television has done a
wonderful thing for films: it has taken over the functions of B
movies. There has always been a need on the part of the majority of people for mass entertainment, and they used to get it
from movies. That's why I'm very hopeful. When they were
getting it from movies, it was much harder to make films cre-
atively.

Television is entertainment; it will in the future leave film two kinds of things. There's going to be the big *Earthquake,* *King Kong, Star Wars* kinds of films—event films, where people go and get shaken up and scared and go through all kinds of occurrences, just some huge false entertainment, but it's something bigger than they can get at home on television. And then there's going to be serious work that there's no room for on television as it's economically constructed now. Under the economics of television the function is to get the biggest audience. If you don't have thirty million people watching, you've failed. In a system where you have to get thirty million people watching it means you have to get the lowest common denominator and you've got to sell and that's what you have to concern yourself with. So that's good in a way, because it takes the pressure off the filmmaker. And I think film is going to become like books are with hard and soft covers. Those of us who are trying to make serious films are making the hard cover edition, and the soft cover is going to be the records that they're going to make out of our films to put into the players to watch at home. And that way they'll be able to have the numbers of people and make the money the way books do. If you publish one hundred, one hundred and fifty thousand copies of a book, you've got a huge success. But if one hundred, one hundred and fifty thousand people see a film, it's a failure. That's insane. So the way to support that economic theory is simple: all you need is one hundred, one hundred and fifty thousand people seeing it in the theaters and then millions watching it when they buy the records, the cassettes, for home. That's where we're going.

JOAN MICKLIN SILVER AND RAPHAEL D. SILVER

J.S. That whole studio system is very seductive. It's very exciting to be kind of a part of it, but it's awfully hard on American filmmakers to emerge the way, say, Wim Wenders did.

R.S. That kind of filmmaker would find it really impossible to work in that style in the U.S. because in Germany, where you have a state-supported film world, you can make a succession of films with small budgets and develop skills. In the U.S. you can make one film and you've about exhausted all your contacts, your energy, your effort, your finances, and your mental health in the process. And unless that one launches you into something larger, that is to say, working for a studio, it's hard to do another one.

There are lots and lots of wonderful films that would never be seen in America if it were not for the fact that a number of independent distributors exist who are willing to work with smaller movies that will not amalgamate national audiences necessarily, but will have the ability to be seen and enjoyed by lots of people. I would suspect that in the absence of those distributors we would just basically get big, big films, one after another. See, the problem is that there is no such thing from the point of view of the studios as small films. The small films are very expensive to make and expensive to promote, and there's no longer a desire on the part of the studios to have a large number of films that do fairly well and one or two films that do exceptionally well. There are exceptions, but, generally, they go in for the big films. They've learned that what they're doing is right. They're making more money than they ever made, and they're producing bigger films than they ever produced before, so what they're learning is that the use of the media and the use of big stars and big important stories tends to bring larger audiences than ever to see a movie. And the small films, which have limited but real success, they view as a positive aspect of the film business. They're not against them, but they view them as something somebody else should be doing and somebody else should be distributing. What the studios have concluded is that the closest they can come to a sure-fire thing is to buy a popular book, put big stars in it, and promote it that way. The main thing the studios are doing that is helping them is they're learning how to promote films very skillfully, principally through television, and they are spending as much money promoting the films as they spend making them. Independent filmmakers, on the other hand, have to be very particular and their distributors have to be very careful, move much more slowly. Independent distributors do not have as wide an access to theaters, and they have to pick their spots very carefully.

J.S. They haven't the funds for a media blitz. No distributors that we know wanted to distribute *Hester Street*. They felt that it would not have too much of an audience, and they were determined that they were right.

But there are certain filmmakers in America who work in a style I would call independent, such as Robert Altman. Altman doesn't choose materials because he thinks they are commercial, or select stars because they're in the top ten at the box office. He has the support of the studios and he certainly deserves it, and apparently gets to make just about everything he's ready to make. So that's an example of a kind of independent filmmaker who works with the support of the studios. I would put Scorsese, I think, in the same vein, although not entirely. I think he's wonderful.

·11·

CONCLUSION

"I don't have any theory. For me, it's what I need."

—Chantal Akerman

Anything can be done in any way if that is how the filmmaker wants it done. Finally, one's vision is all that matters. For this reason the best filmmakers are reluctant to theorize, to constrict the possibilities of exploring and realizing this chameleon-like art that so fascinates them. Their answers to my questions usually refer to their individual purposes and styles and are not meant to be overgeneralized. Their negative judgments are usually based on a condemnation of techniques, effects, and, above all, intentions that are dishonest and false.

Keeping in mind once more that contraries are not necessarily contradictions, the following capsulizes the differences and similarities in points of view and methods for each section of this book.

In "Cinematography," most of the filmmakers stressed the importance of what is left out of the camera frame. Framing implies choice on the part of the filmmaker, that is, a revelation of intention. Framing also provokes the viewer to wonder and imagine what was framed out, creating tension through the expectation that what was left out will eventually come in. Dušan Makavejev, who consistently stresses the subliminal Jungian effect of movies, speaks of framing as a provocation for the viewer to "complete" the movie:

"What is important to understand is that in movies there is nothing else—whatever is in the frame is all there is. There is nothing else. Everything else is fantasy, and what is outside the frame does not really depend on what was outside the frame during the shooting."

On the subject of preferences for different types of shots, André Tech-ine and Lina Wertmuller enjoy bringing the camera in close to an expressive actor's face, whereas many others exercise restraint over the use of close-ups, considering them to be a facile way of eliciting viewer reaction. Robert Altman likes to use zoom or long lenses at times so actors can be shot from a distance undistracted by equipment and the knowledge of when the camera is focused on them. Techine also uses fairly long lenses, and for precisely the same reason that most others do not: to avoid the natural effect of normal lenses.

Techine frankly manipulates the viewer's vision, as does Wertmuller, "tying up" the spectator who, in effect, has paid in order to have his vision captured for a few hours. This is in direct contrast to others like Ermanno Olmi, whose ambition "is to look at the world with others, not so much as an aristocratic intellectual, an elite, but mixing as much as possible with others."

Another issue concerns where the film "happens," in the shoot or in the editing. The film really begins for George Romero when he gets to work on his editing table, and Wertmuller's ideal is to "shoot everything and afterwards to decide. . . . That way you are left with richer pos-sibilities of telling the story. . . . We always try not to make a choice before the editing, but often we do because we have to." For her, "fifty percent of the film is created in the editing." In contrast, Nestor Al-mendros frowns on "bombarding the scene from different angles, what they call 'coverage' in Hollywood," calling this method a kind of "fly now, pay later" approach: "Ideally, a director should know where the camera should be at any moment in any kind of situation. . . . The form of the film comes from the concept. If there's no concept to begin with, there's no style."

He's right, of course, and so are Olmi and Jean Rouch, directors who wouldn't turn over their cameras to anyone, not even to Nestor Almendros, because the visual element of their films comes from deep inside, spontaneously, provoked by the moment. But Wertmuller is "right," as well, as are all the filmmakers who "break" rules that apply only to the unexceptional.

As the film form has developed, sound has become much more than an adjunct to the image. Sound engages more than the ears; together with the image it elicits what Benoît Jacquot calls the regard, "some-thing that comes from the body as a whole. . . . In French, 'regarder' means to engage a desire in what you are looking at. But 'to see' is just

to put your eyes on an object." *Yves Yersin expands: "Sound works
enormously, deeply, and it doesn't always travel through the intellect.
It's a poetic way to speak to someone." For Rouch, "sound makes the
reality," and Werner Schroeter adds that it completes the emotion in the
actor's face. But Techine disturbs the illusion of reality conventionally
created through sound by contrasting the messages of sound and of the
actor's face. Makavejev also rejects the "additional illusion that 'this is
a piece of reality'" brought by direct sound, "so it's very important if
you do direct sound to undermine it with all kinds of commentaries."*

*Interestingly enough, Robert Altman and Jean-Luc Godard often
have actors speaking inaudibly, thereby avoiding the illusion of perfect
sound, but they do so by opposite methods. Altman borrows the methods
of multiple miking and tracks from the music field, achieving total freedom of choice in the mix, whereas Godard simply crams all the sounds
onto one or two tracks, achieving an "imperfect" soundtrack without
controlling for that effect in the mix.*

*Henry Jaglom, Milos Forman, and Perry Henzel all spoke of allow-
ing music to dictate the image content by using the words and melody of
the musician to carry the emotional message of the scene. For many
filmmakers, conscious use of sound as more than an assist to the image
solicits active participation of the viewer as a collaborator in making
the movie. As Bertolucci puts it, "Sound will start when the spectator
becomes conscious of it," as conscious as they are of the object of their
projections—the actor.*

*According to Altman, actors are the "living, moving presence" of his
films, expressing a "combination of what I want and what they want."
Praising their "sense of space and charisma," Makavejev refers to the
actors as his assistants. For Elio Petri, it is the actor who brings the
viewer into the film, their relationship being a "confluence of solitudes."
Godard, however, speaks of the difficulty in working with professionals:
as stars they're afraid to take chances. On the other hand, if they are
inexperienced amateurs, they are too raw. George Romero prefers to use
"real-looking" people, but complains that unless one signs a recognized
star, backing is hard to get—a practical and sobering note amidst a
discussion revolving mainly on aesthetic considerations.*

*Olmi uses only non-professionals for the same reason he prefers real
landscapes: to "continue my relationship with reality. . . . [real people]
bring to the film a weight, really a constitution of truth." Unlike many*

others, he, Al Maysles, and Jean Rouch enjoy the fact that non-profes-
sionals cannot repeat the same action take after take. Milos Forman
seeks those "small, unrepeatable moments" frequent with non-profes-
sionals, but he does so by skillfully employing on professionals "psycho-
logical tricks" that he learned in his early work. Like Jaglom, he mixes
"real" people with professionals, aiming for the benefits of both.

Like sound, rhythm and structure—the more abstract elements—in-
trigue most filmmakers, many of them comparing movies more to the
cutting into space exercised by architecture than to the novel or play or
photography. Film should be more architectural, says Makavejev, full
of the "contradictions and discontinuities" we don't acknowledge in our
lives. Most films are "reduced" rather than "multi-leveled" and, as
Scorsese notes, audiences must learn to accept the lack of resolution in
good films because they reflect the true complexity of life.

While some filmmakers such as Chabrol and Techine respect a "cin-
ema that tells stories," others such as Godard chafe against that restric-
tion: "I think one should follow the line of a story . . . but the line can
come from the line of a landscape or . . . the shape of a tree."

Despite its architectural elements, film is nevertheless grounded in its
surpassingly close resemblance to physical reality. In fact, Nestor Al-
mendros notes that film even "transforms" and improves reality:

"There's magic in movies, a camera enhances everything. I notice
sometimes I even like movies made by people I don't like person-
ally. Movies are often superior to the people who make them,
which proves that they are helped by something—the medium."

For Godard, films clarify reality: "Making pictures is to clean, like a
window you clean to be able to see." Most would agree that the best
films do this, but how to clean the window and what it reveals is a
different matter. Olmi's "critically penetrated" documentaries "re-
propose" rather than reproduce life. Bertolucci specifies that film shows
"reality in progress." Jacquot acknowledges that the "fascination" of
film comes in its "connection to reality," but like Jaglom, Makavejev,
Techine, and others, he rejects the notion that truth is found in docu-
mentary. Makavejev deals with "images," not with reality, and Jaglom
circumvents the external, which obscures focus on the subjective vision.
This discussion makes clear that film is a generous form, for as Techine

notes, "It lets us carve reality according to our own desires." But what are those desires? Perhaps the last word is had by Jean-Marie Straub, whose films evidence integrity of vision and a complete disregard for the commercial aspects of filmmaking: "Above all, the filmmaker must know how he confronts reality."

And reality encompasses more than aesthetic issues. The filmmaker is a kind of juggler, managing technical, logistical, and financial elements and dealing with large groups of diversely qualified people. He must be conscious of what he is doing and, even more important, why. He must maintain integrity of vision throughout the three major phases of making the film: writing, shooting, and editing. As may be expected, making a film is often seen as a matter of overcoming one problem after another.

Godard and Jaglom, who are unconcerned about technical perfection, find difficulty in the crew's overinvolvement with the limits of their technology—the "rules"—and must exert themselves to trick the crew to do "the impossible." Scorsese, whose great success has put him in the mega-budget league, complains of the unwieldiness of big camera equipment and the difficulties of dealing with large union crews.

Most of the discussion concerns the issue of control over the film during its major phases, with some filmmakers such as the Maysles, Olmi, and Rouch characteristically giving up that control, following the film, waiting for the edit to, as Olmi terms it, "add up the bill." Makavejev also works from "no idea [at the beginning] of what I will do." His editing is also intuitive, more a matter of watching how the film "breathes." Lumet and Fassbinder, seemingly very different filmmakers, both stress the individuality of each film, some lending themselves more readily to improvisation, others to strict planning. Most would agree that there are elements of control and of improvisation within every film. The filmmaker may be trying to hold to his original concept, while the film is always threatening to escape.

What is the role of the viewer in making these moving pictures? Must he be seduced and manipulated, forced to go further than a "superficial reading," as Wertmuller suggests, or should "films be made so that people can leave the room," as Straub advocates? When a viewer goes into a moviehouse, Chabrol maintains, "the problem isn't for him to understand the world. . . . He deserves to be entertained." Others want the viewer to work, taking him in and out of the illusion, insuring *that the film will do more than entertain, helping him, in fact, to understand the world. For Makavejev, good movies create a "kind of glue" between them and the viewer: "Since movies are based on seeing what isn't allowed, since they are always working basically with a taboo field, since the structure of movies is always a system of alibis to get on the screen some things that are not allowed to be shown, since this dirty little game is part of watching movies, why not be aware of it?"*

And what of the masses of viewers? What effects can film have on society at large? Can film end war, as Albert Maysles suggests could have happened if the right film had been made during the Vietnam War? Is film "the avant garde of politics," allowing us to stretch our imaginations and tolerance by viewing the Other, as Rouch and Zanussi maintain? For Chabrol, however, film is a way to do nothing, either playing to an audience already convinced or offering what Olmi describes as a "false comfort" analogous to the fairy tales heard on our grandmother's knee. It is unlikely that film by itself, without the support of other elements in the society, can create effective political action, but it is certain, even unavoidable, that film preserves culture. As soon as the camera begins to run, bits and pieces of the culture are recorded, sparking a desire, conscious or unconscious, on the viewer's part to complete the picture.

This book ends with the discussion on the business of making movies because financing and distribution are indeed the bottom line. As Bertolucci notes, "The filmmaker is the one who gets the money." No filmmaker has been so successful that he has escaped the pain and frustration of fighting for and losing money, either to make the film or for the means to have it shown. Many here saw hope in the booming home video market, which may provide access for a more low-budget product, as well as a release from the obligation to provide viewers with formula entertainment. If television and video take over from film as the "nickelodeon," film may be released to deal with more innovative content and form. In this section alone, the filmmakers seemed sadly in accord. As Robert Altman so aptly puts it: "It all comes down to the filthy lucre. . . . It's like gambling: if you win the first race, you get to bet more in the second."